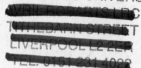
SOCIAL POLICY
AND THE
ENVIRONMENT

SOCIAL POLICY AND THE ENVIRONMENT

MEG HUBY

Open University Press
Buckingham • Philadelphia

Open University Press
Celtic Court
22 Ballmoor
Buckingham
MK18 1XW

email: enquiries@openup.co.uk
world wide web: http://www.openup.co.uk

and

325 Chestnut Street
Philadelphia, PA 19106, USA

First Published 1998

A catalogue record of this book is available from the British Library

ISBN 0 335 19829 5 (pb)   0 335 19830 9 (hb)

Library of Congress Cataloging-in-Publication Data
Huby, Meg.
    Social policy and the environment / Meg Huby.
        p.   cm.
    Includes bibliographical references (p.   ) and index.
    ISBN 0–335–19830–9 (hb). ISBN 0–335–19829–5 (pb)
    1. Social policy—Environmental aspects.   2. Environmental
responsibility.   3. Sustainable development.   4. Human ecology.
5. Great Britain—Social policy—Environmental aspects.   I. Title.
HN17.5.H83 1998
304.2—dc21   97–43056
                                                        CIP

Printed on 100% recycled paper
Typeset by Graphicraft Typesetters Limited, Hong Kong
Printed in Great Britain by Biddles Limited, Guildford and Kings Lynn

CONTENTS

FIGURES

TABLES

BOXES

PREFACE

The idea for this book was born on a late summer evening when, over a fine scotch whisky, I was complaining about the dearth of textbooks for a new undergraduate course I was teaching in social policy. The immediate response of my friends and colleagues, Jonathan Bradshaw and Eithne McLaughlin, was that I should write one.

The course I teach at York reflects the growing awareness of the close links between social policy and the environment and the need to bridge the divide between the natural and the social sciences in studies of human welfare and well-being. In Western industrialized societies a split has developed between fields of knowledge, the social sciences being those dealing with people in social organization, while the natural sciences deal with 'nature'. These divisions are now being challenged and the boundaries between natural and social sciences relaxed. As the environment attains a higher profile in tertiary education there is a growing need for textbooks which make scientific and technical debates accessible to students from non-science backgrounds.

Reassuringly, the literature crossing the boundaries of social and environmental sciences is growing. Little material is produced at undergraduate level, however, to encourage students to approach issues from a holistic point of view, understanding the social dimensions of environmental change as well as the environmental dimensions of social change. It is difficult to find introductory texts which cover environmental issues in a way that makes them accessible to students from a background in the social sciences.

In a core social policy text (*Understanding Social Policy*) Michael Hill (1993) recognizes that public policies should be seen as a whole, since most are inextricably linked with one another. Policies not conventionally identified as 'social' can have important impacts on welfare. In his latest book (*Social Policy: a Comparative Analysis*), the same author notes that:

> It is not an exaggeration to say that some of the more specific kinds of social welfare policy which are trying to compensate people who are the casualties of modern societies may be seen to be beside the point in an unsafe environment. In these circumstances they will be merely offering 'sticking plasters' to deal with injuries which need not have occurred.

(Hill 1996: 232)

While Hill's chapter on environmental policy is a welcome broadening in approaches to social policy, it is largely concerned with environmental regulation and control as a public policy issue. In contrast, this book leaves to one side actual policies for environmental protection. Instead it considers the environment as an integral element in the study of social welfare. It is not the aim of this book to discuss possible solutions to environmental problems or to examine environmental policy issues, but rather to illustrate how social and environmental processes work together, making environmental issues a legitimate area of concern for social scientists.

The book is designed for undergraduate students in the social sciences, but it is not intended to give a comprehensive coverage of social policy or environmental studies. Its aim is to provide information and explanations to give students the confidence to argue across traditional disciplinary boundaries, to get them to think beyond single policy areas and to demonstrate how it is possible to find linkages between the social and natural sciences which can enhance understanding of the natural and social world.

In 1995, the Economic and Social Research Council developed nine themes to indicate its priorities for research funding. The theme of Environment and Sustainability sits alongside more traditional social themes such as Lifespan, Lifestyles and Health and Social Integration and Exclusion. 'The recognition that human behaviour can affect what happens to the environment presents social science with a distinctive and substantial research agenda' (ESRC 1995: 2). Unless students are exposed to the underlying ideas of both the social and natural sciences, there is a danger that the future generation of researchers will preserve and perhaps exacerbate the current trend, studying either social science or natural science, with only a superficial recognition of the links between the two. This will preclude realization of the enormous potential for addressing social and environmental problems as a part of an integrated whole. It is no longer sufficient to study social policy without considering its potential impacts on the environment – and consequently its effects on social development.

ACKNOWLEDGEMENTS

This book could not have been written without the support of colleagues in the Department of Social Policy and Social Work at the University of York. I am grateful for the period of research leave which gave me space and time for writing and thank all those in the department who took on extra administrative and teaching work during my absence. My friends and family all helped me to enjoy the writing period enormously, keeping me sane and happy but also ensuring that I kept working hard! My daughter Clare Huby and friends Carol Bingley, Tom Cannon and Sarah MacPherson gave me constant encouragement and read draft chapters, offering invaluable comments and suggestions. Academic experts likewise provided helpful criticism and advice and I am particularly grateful to Jonathan Bradshaw, Roger Burrows, Anne Corden, John Forrester and Sandra Hutton of York University, Adrian Davis of the Open University and Tim Lang of Thames Valley University.

ACRONYMS AND ABBREVIATIONS

AIDS	acquired immune deficiency syndrome
BMA	British Medical Association
BSE	bovine spongiform encephalopathy
CJD	Creutzfeldt-Jakob disease
DSS	Department of Social Security
DWI	Drinking Water Inspectorate
EPA	Environment Protection Agency
EU	European Union
GDP	gross domestic product
GNP	gross national product
HIV	human immuno-deficiency virus
IBRD	International Bank for Reconstruction and Development (World Bank)
IUCN	International Union for the Conservation of Nature and Natural Resources (now World Conservation Union)
MAFF	Ministry of Agriculture, Fisheries and Food
NRA	National Rivers Authority
OECD	Organization for Economic Co-operation and Development
OFWAT	Office of Water Services
PUAF	Public Utilities Access Forum
RSPB	Royal Society for the Protection of Birds
UNEP	United Nations Environment Programme
UNESCO	United Nations Educational, Scientific and Cultural Organization
WCED	World Commission on Environment and Development
WHO	World Health Organization
WWF	World Wildlife Fund (now Worldwide Fund for Nature)

Chapter
one
INTRODUCTION

The things that people do in their lives to meet their everyday needs inevitably have effects on the environment. These effects can be damaging to the natural world, but they also carry social costs which are borne to differing extents by different sectors of society, affecting their further activity. The circularity of this situation has been described in terms of a 'pressure–state–response' relationship. 'Human activities exert *pressures* on the environment, and change its *state* in terms of its quality and its stocks of natural resources. Society *responds* to these changes through general environmental, economic and sectoral policies, and through changes in behaviour, thus affecting the *pressures* caused by human activities' (Department of the Environment 1996c: 9).

A growing awareness of these changes and effects has led to increasing public concern but there is still, as yet, little consensus about how the environment can best be protected while allowing for further social and economic development at national and global levels. One problem is that the burdens of environmental degradation do not always fall directly upon those parts of society which are responsible for causing them, and often the people who suffer most from poor environmental quality are different from those who reap the benefits of the activities in question. Second, the isolated actions of a particular individual, firm or nation may not always be perceived by the actors as having any substantially damaging effects. A third difficulty lies in the fact that social structures and organization place some people in positions where they are unable to take actions which might limit environmental damage, even though they would like to do so.

Nevertheless, it is increasingly apparent that a continuation of the present levels of resource use and waste generation is likely to lead to environmental deterioration on a growing scale and, since human beings are so critically dependent on the natural environment for meeting their most basic needs, this will inevitably lead to social crises and even societal breakdown (Dobson 1991; Martell 1994). There is consequently much deliberation about the need to pursue policies for development which are sustainable not only economically but also socially and environmentally. The capacity for sustainable development in its broadest sense depends, however, on achieving a consensus about the nature and severity of various risks to the environment and about whether continuing economic growth is a necessary prerequisite or an obstacle which must be pushed aside and discarded before such development is possible. It also depends on how far people's needs can be defined or identified and the extent to which those needs can be met in ways that are fair and equitable without causing further harm to the environment.

The discipline of social policy has a key role to play in contributing to a wider understanding of human need. Its emphasis on the ways in which structured social divisions and inequalities pervade the outcomes of policies designed to improve social well-being can help to identify how these influence the potential for sustainable social development. But it is also important to recognize how specific social policies indirectly influence people's relationships to and interactions with the environment, and to acknowledge the role of the environment in contributing to well-being and the quality of human lives.

Traditionally, the study of social policy encompasses the 'big five' areas of social security, housing, education, health and social services, and is occupied with the extent to which government policies in these areas enable people to achieve particular levels of welfare. It examines how such policies are developed and implemented and how they are shaped by dominant political values and ideas about social responsibility and accountability. The environment has not traditionally been considered as a subject of concern for social policy. This book, however, attempts to show that since people's lives are crucially shaped by the environments in which they live, environmental issues have a valid place on the social policy agenda.

This is particularly the case when we consider the notion of social well-being as opposed to more restricted, conventional ideas of welfare. Spicker (1995) argues that improving the provision of welfare services is not the same as improving well-being. The latter is instead seen as a possible end result of the former. It encompasses more than simply material satisfaction of needs, taking account of less tangible aspects of people's lives, such as the quality of their neighbourhoods, work and leisure environments and their abilities to participate fully in the society in which they live. Despite current debates surrounding the various definitions of need in the subject areas of social policy, few would argue that the survival of human societies is dependent on access to water and food. Fuel providing energy for warmth and housing to provide shelter might also be added to these in defining basic physical needs. Yet it has long been recognized that social well-being requires more than provision of these basic necessities and is also a function of transport, mobility and access to amenities and services. It is only in the context of all these factors that it becomes possible to make rational sense of concepts such as participation, equity and choice in discussing social well-being, living standards and the quality of life.

However, the very processes of accessing and utilizing water, food, energy, housing, transport and amenities entail consumption of resources and production of waste. This can lead to environmental change, which itself can alter the nature of goods and services that are available in the longer term and the extent to which they can be attained, consequently influencing the potential and limitations for continuing social well-being and social development. Access to these elements of well-being is governed then not only by social but also by environmental factors. The aim of this book is to identify and illustrate some of the complex interdependencies of social and environmental factors and the way that they shape living standards and the quality of life. If social policy is concerned with the provision of services not for their own sake but because of how that provision influences well-being, it is essential to consider the interactive relationship between social welfare and the environmental context in which it is provided.

Social policy is now not only studied at a national level, but also incorporates many comparative studies, mainly of industrialized states with established systems for social welfare provision. At a global level the transfer of the means to meet the needs of the poor is studied as 'development'. Development studies have much in common with studies of social policy, and although this book does not purport to tackle all issues of development, its main themes are explored at national, supranational and global levels. It thus seeks to add an international dimension to the debate about social policy and the environment. Social and environmental problems in different countries are essentially similar in nature although they vary enormously in scale. 'Famines in Africa are as real to most people as unemployment in Scunthorpe: both are evidence of breakdown in the capacity of human societies to deal with complex socio-economic and environmental problems' (Morse and Stocking 1995: v).

Just as social policy has not traditionally included the environment as part of its sphere of interest, so there are aspects of environmental science which are presented as devoid of any social considerations. Nevertheless, the study of social policy and studies of the environment have a number of features in common. Both draw on theoretical frameworks developed in other disciplines, the so-called 'social sciences' and 'natural sciences' respectively, within which to analyse and interpret empirical material. Just as there is no specifically taught 'theory of social policy', so neither is there a particular 'theory of environmental study'. The two areas of study also have in common a concern with practical problems. Spicker (1995: 10) observes that 'many people in social policy have no interest at all in being dispassionate about the subject; they are in it for a reason, and that reason is to bring about change.' The same could certainly be said of many people involved in environmental studies. But similarities run deeper than this, and it is possible to identify themes which are common to both social policy and studies of the environment. These include inequality, sustainability and responsibility, and these form unifying threads which run through the main chapters of this book.

Inequality

Spicker (1995: 26) defines critical social policy as 'a view of social policy which emphasises the importance of all structured inequality, and seeks to interpret problems and policy primarily in terms of patterned relationships of social division.' Structured inequalities are those which arise as a result of the way in which societies and social relations are organized, rather than inequalities stemming from people's intrinsic characteristics. This book illustrates how structured inequalities can be reinforced by and in turn can influence the environmental context in which they occur. Within social divisions between rich and poor and between men and women lie further distinctions between people who are disabled or ill and those who are not, between people from different ethnic groups and between the elderly and younger members of society. These distinctions come to the fore in later chapters in relation to differing experiences of environmental change, as, for example, in influencing the extent to which people are exposed to varying levels of pollution or are limited in their use of leisure time. They all constitute social divisions which Spicker (1995: 48) refers to as 'the "fault lines" of a society'.

Resources

One, although not the only, objective of social welfare provision is to ensure that people living in a society enjoy acceptable material standards of living, are able to participate in social and political life and experience feelings of general well-being. A prerequisite for this state of affairs is that they should have access to the means to meet their material needs. In many industrialized countries such means include cash income from paid work, social security, private investment or rent or some combination of these. For some people in developing countries, the means to meet material needs may, to a greater or lesser extent, include ownership of or rights of access to land or water resources. Inequalities in resources to meet basic needs occur at local, national and global levels. Table 1.1 shows that the share of post-tax income of the poorest 20 per cent of households in the UK dropped from 9 per cent in 1977 to 6 per cent in 1995, while the share of the richest 20 per cent increased from 37 per cent to 42 per cent over the same period.

Within industrialized countries, the poorest 40 per cent of households receive only 18 per cent of total income (United Nations Development Programme 1995), and comparative data show that income inequalities increased in 11 out of 18 industrialized countries during the 1970s and 1980s (Hills 1995). Although the average per capita income in OECD countries is

Table 1.1 Percentage distribution of post-tax income of households in the United Kingdom, adjusted for family size and composition and broken down into quintile groups

Quintile group	1977 (%)	1993 (%)	1995 (%)
Bottom 20 per cent	9	7	6
Second 20 per cent	14	11	11
Third 20 per cent	17	16	17
Fourth 20 per cent	23	22	24
Top 20 per cent	37	44	42

Source: Central Statistical Office (1994, 1996).

US$20,000, more than 100 million people live below national poverty lines and more than five million are homeless (United Nations Development Programme 1996).

At a global level, the traditional measure of gross national product (GNP) is only a rough indicator of national economic development. GNP currently measures national real consumption of goods and services and takes no account of less tangible, and consequently more difficult to measure, aspects of well-being, such as environmental quality, health or educational provision. Nor does it give any indication of the inequalities in resource distribution within countries. Nevertheless, GNP comparisons do give some idea of inequalities between different kinds of countries at a global level. The average GNP per capita for countries with low income economies in 1990 was US$350, compared to US$2220 for middle income economies and US$19,590 for high income economies (International Bank for Reconstruction and Development 1992). In the early 1990s, the richest 20 per cent of the world's population received 150 times the income of the poorest 20 per cent (United Nations Development Programme 1993).

The redistributive effects of national social security and fiscal systems and international aid may be to reduce or enhance inequalities, and a major concern of social policy is to examine and analyse these effects. But in an imperfect world the fact remains that some people remain poorer than others in terms of being able to meet their basic needs. In addition, the impacts of environmental pollution and degradation are experienced unequally in most societies, and material inequalities are often mirrored at an environmental level. The spatial segregation of the poorer sectors of society can mean that these people tend to live in areas where pollution or other environmental degradation is more pronounced. The siting of polluting or degrading industries and facilities, such as chemical plants, radioactive waste repositories and toxic waste incinerators, is often chosen according to whether or not there is likely to be resistance from local communities. Economically depressed areas where local people are least likely to be able to exert power by mobilizing opposition effectively are therefore often chosen for such developments.

One reason for this is that material poverty is associated with powerlessness, stemming from the limitations imposed on the ability to participate in the kind of social and political activity enjoyed by wealthier people. The marginalization of the poor, their exclusion from the normal services and benefits of society and from political decision-making, means that they are more likely than the rich to bear the brunt of environmental problems.

> Poor families often lack the resources to avoid degrading their environment. The very poor, struggling at the edge of subsistence, are preoccupied with day-to-day survival. It is not that the poor have inherently short horizons; poor communities often have a strong ethic of stewardship in managing their traditional lands. But their fragile and limited resources, their often poorly defined property rights and their limited access to credit and insurance markets prevent them from investing as much as they should in environmental protection.
>
> (International Bank for Reconstruction and Development 1992: 30)

This quotation refers to poor communities in developing countries with low income economies, but in principle it could refer equally well to poor sectors of the population in richer industrialized countries.

Not only do the poor lack the means and resources to avoid immediate negative environmental impacts of, for example, heavy air pollution, proximity of toxic waste disposal sites or simply a degraded and unpleasant local environment, but their immediate concerns must necessarily be with the short-term day-to-day requirements of living. People who are better off in material terms have at their disposal more options for dealing with local environmental problems. They are usually better educated and are more likely to be able to use existing bureaucratic frameworks to register complaints or to militate politically against future environmental damage. But they are also better able to deal with existing environmental problems. They often have more choice about where they live or can afford to take ameliorative actions such as insulating their homes against noise, installing air conditioning, buying bottled water and investing in efficient household devices to conserve energy and water. There is little opportunity or leisure for the poor to consider less tangible, less local environmental concerns which may, after all, not have any physical impact until the future. Feelings of cynicism and disempowerment enhance the tendency to leave such concerns to others. It is hard to be poor and green.

We shall see in later chapters how the links between inequalities in material well-being and inequalities in the kinds of environment in which people spend most of their lives can be reinforced by positive feedback loops. In the case of transport, as we shall see in Chapter 6, poorer people tend to make less use than the more affluent of private cars. They make a smaller contribution to the air pollution created by vehicle exhausts but are more likely to suffer from the adverse effects of pollution on health. If, however, fuel prices are increased in attempts to reduce car use and exhaust emissions, it is the poor who find their transport options more restricted, while the better off can afford to pay the required amounts and travel as usual. Poorer people not only suffer the worst effects of environmental damage, but all too often they pay a disproportionate price for environmental protection. The associated costs, whether tangible or intangible, are rarely equally distributed.

Gender

Gender inequalities are now firmly ensconced on the social policy agenda, and the assumption that women can be treated merely as dependants on male earners rather than as individuals with their own citizenship rights has been widely challenged. The implications for social policy of the unequal treatment of men and women with regard to employment, job security and promotion, social security benefit systems and retirement and pension rights form a major subject for discussion in many core social policy texts (Williams 1989; Glendinning and Millar 1992; Hill 1996).

Increasing numbers of women in the United Kingdom are in some kind of paid work, but in 1995 the average gross weekly pay of women in full-time work was only 72 per cent that of men (Department of Employment 1995). This is partly because proportionately more women than men are employed to do less skilled work or are in poorly paid industries. Low waged domestic work, housework and childcare, for example, are almost always carried out by women (Cahill 1994). As well as receiving lower rates of pay, women tend to work fewer hours than men do and they do less overtime. They are still seen as carrying most responsibility for the bulk of domestic work in the home, even when in full-time paid employment. This domestic responsibility, however, is not usually reflected in women's greater access to household resources or in their role in financial decision making (Walker and Parker 1988).

Traditional roles of men as earners and of women as nurturers and carers have implications for other aspects of women's lifestyles. Their home management responsibilities leave them with less free time than men for leisure pursuits. Not only do they participate less than men in most leisure activities, but the activities they do pursue cover a narrower range (Clarke and Critcher 1985). Gender differences are also manifested in the modes of transport most frequently used, women being more likely than men to use public transport and to use the household car less frequently (Cahill 1994). Differences in education patterns for girls and boys in Great Britain are gradually being eroded but education indicators based on UNESCO sources show the extent to which gender differences occur in access to schooling in different countries across the world. The figures suggest that in 1989 in countries classed as low-income economies, only 64 females for every 100 males continued their education at secondary school for at least four years. This compares with a ratio of 100 females to every 100 males in countries with high-income economies (International Bank for Reconstruction and Development 1992). 'Women still constitute 70% of the world's poor and two thirds of the world's illiterates' (United Nations Development Report 1995: iii).

Bearing children exposes women to health risks and vulnerability to death in childbirth, especially in poorer developing countries where childbearing is still the commonest cause of death for women of reproductive age. In 1980, maternal mortality per 100,000 live births was 2000 in Ethiopia and 1680 in Benin, compared to only two in Canada and seven in the United Kingdom (International Bank for Reconstruction and Development 1992).

Gender differences such as these are not solely related to poverty and lack of resources. Even in richer industrialized countries the reproductive role of women makes them more susceptible to environmental health risks. In 1983, the extent of pollution of rivers, streams and lakes in the state of New York led the Department of Health to recommend that residents should eat no more than one meal a month of freshwater fish caught in the state and that 'pregnant women, women of child-bearing age, nursing mothers and children under 15 should eat no fish at all from the state' (Seitz 1995: 148).

Jackson (1995) has illustrated how gender analysis can highlight differences in the ways in which men and women in the developing countries relate to their environments, and emphasizes the gendered nature of human and environmental interactions. 'Since men and women occupy different positions in processes of production and reproduction, they will experience changes in the environment differently' (Jackson 1995: 116). She relates these differing experiences of both environmental degradation and environmental conservation to gender divisions of labour, responsibility, income and access to and control of resources. Chavangi (1993) vividly describes this phenomenon in rural households in Kakamega in Western Kenya. Women deal with the routine tasks of childrearing, tending food crops, fetching water, collecting fuelwood and preparing food. Only rarely do men participate in these activities, but it is they who have overall control over household resources; women are expected to seek their husbands' opinions and consent before doing anything that may affect the allocation of those resources. With increases in the local population leading to more pressure on land, women are left to make do with a declining environmental resource base to meet basic food and fuel needs. They cannot use wood from the trees the men cultivate for cash income, but must gather firewood from hedges and crop residues (Bradley 1991).

The use of brushwood, straw and dung as fuel for cooking and heating in many developing countries produces air pollution in enclosed kitchens which routinely exceeds the safe levels recommended by the World Health Organization (WHO) by several orders of magnitude. Of the 400–700 million people exposed to this kind of health risk, the majority are women and children (International Bank for Reconstruction and Development 1992). The deforestation and environmental degradation which lead women to rely on woody biomass for fuel and the poverty which prohibits them from access to other methods of cooking and heating are compounded by the gendered division of household labour, providing a clear illustration of the impacts of both environmental and social factors in influencing well-being.

Sustainable development

A second theme linking social policy and the environment is sustainability. Despite widespread disagreement about the definition of sustainable development, the phrase has recently become common currency in the fields of social and economic development as well as among environmentalists. In 1987, the Report of the Brundtland Commission stressed that the idea of sustainable development must include consideration of economic and social factors, being 'development that meets the needs of the present without compromising the ability of future generations to meet their own needs' (Brundtland 1987: 43). This definition is probably the one most often quoted today. It was used at the 1992 United Nations Earth Summit in Rio de Janeiro in Agenda 21, which pointed out that the ability of a country to follow sustainable development paths is determined to a large extent by the capacity of its people and its institutions as well as by its ecological and geographical conditions (United Nations 1993). These ideas were picked up in the report on sustainable development by the Department of the Environment in the UK in 1994. 'Most societies want to achieve economic development to secure higher standards of living, now and for future generations. They also seek to protect and enhance their environment, now and for their children' (HMSO 1994a: 6).

Although on the one hand sustainable development can be seen as a statement of idealistic philosophy, on the other it can appear to be a confused and contradictory concept reflecting ambivalent social goals. It has been criticized for its implicit suggestion that it is possible to deal with environmental problems without undermining the lifestyles prevalent in the wealthier nations of the world. 'Our willingness to authenticate sustainability by reference to societies which possess no such concept . . . carries serious implications for "global" strategies of development which ensure the continued economic hegemony of northern industrialised countries' (Redclift 1993: 5). The subject is already extensively covered in the literature (Carley and Christie 1992; Pearce 1993; Morse and Stocking 1995; Reid 1995), but some of the reasons for difficulties in formulating sustainable development policies are worth discussing here, since they raise issues related to the conceptual themes of this book. These take us back to the idea of needs and equity and also include uncertainty, risk and views about economic growth.

Needs and equity

According to the Brundtland report, 'sustainable development requires meeting the basic needs of all and extending to all the opportunity to satisfy their aspirations for a better life' (Brundtland 1987: 44). There is a vast social policy literature on the subject of need, preoccupied with how needs can be measured, whether they are subjective and relative and whether common basic needs can even be identified (Doyal and Gough 1991; Wetherly 1996). Most people would agree that water, food, warmth and shelter are basic biological needs which must be met if societies are to survive and reproduce. But questions and conflicts arise when we consider the addition of education and healthcare to this list, let alone the wide range of other items and services which would allow people to live according to the prevailing norms of their society. Definitions of need depend on who is doing the defining, and there is a tendency to ignore issues of equity between different societies. Instead, 'attention has focused on the future costs of development to our own societies, as if the satisfaction of our future needs is the principle bone of contention, rather than the way we currently satisfy our needs at other people's expense' (Redclift 1993: 8). Yet the difficulties in defining basic needs pale into insignificance compared to those in defining aspirations for a better life. Similarly difficulties arise in attempting to predict the needs and preferences of future generations whose claims become easier to ignore the further away from the present they become.

Policies for sustainable development must be founded on principles of equity and the concept of need is integral to these. 'The right to development must be fulfilled so as to equitably meet developmental and environmental needs of present and future generations' (United Nations Development Programme 1993: 9). Whereas equality implies equal slices of cake for everyone, equity allows more to be given to those in greater need. It might be regarded as inequitable for people living at social assistance level in the UK to pay the same tax on carbon fuels as the rich, who could be said to have less need of the money involved. Similarly, demands on Indonesia to conserve its rain forests can be construed as inequitable because Indonesia has a greater need than other industrialized countries for the cash income which it must forgo by doing so. 'Development that perpetuates today's inequalities is neither sustainable nor worth sustaining' (United Nations Development Programme 1996: 4).

Uncertainty and risk

The scientific knowledge that plays a vital role in identifying environmental problems is based on theory which is contestable and on evidence which is often a matter of interpretation or even conjecture. The phenomenon of global warming provides a good example (Box 1.1). While changing atmospheric composition is indubitably linked to changes in the earth's mean surface temperature, the exact extent to which anthropogenic or man-made emissions of greenhouse gases such as carbon dioxide are likely to enhance the natural greenhouse effect and result in climate change is far from certain.

Although the Intergovernmental Panel on Climate Change (IPCC) has produced policy scenarios under which future emissions of greenhouse gases can be forecast, their predictions are not exact because of a number of inherent scientific uncertainties. First, calculations are based on models of the atmosphere which have limited spatial resolution and which fail to incorporate adequately the effects of the oceans and living organisms in influencing carbon

Box 1.1   The greenhouse effect and global warming

The greenhouse effect

The mean temperature of the earth is around 15 °C, compared to the −18 °C it would be if the earth had no atmosphere. The effect of the atmosphere producing earth temperatures able to sustain life constitutes the natural greenhouse effect. Incoming short-wave radiation from the sun passes through the atmosphere to the earth's surface from which it is radiated back at longer wavelengths. Certain 'greenhouse gases' in the atmosphere selectively absorb radiation at these longer wavelengths, effectively 'trapping' it. The radiation is repeatedly absorbed and re-emitted by gas molecules until some is ultimately lost to space and some reaches the earth, where its energy warms the surface.

Greenhouse gases

Although nitrogen and oxygen make up 99 per cent of the atmosphere, it is other gases, present in trace amounts, which act as greenhouse gases. These include water vapour, carbon dioxide, methane and nitrous oxide, all of which are produced both naturally and as a result of human activity. Increasing use of fossil fuels and the burning and decay which follow the destruction of tropical forests release extra carbon dioxide to the atmosphere, while methane emissions are increased by the agricultural production of wetland rice. Methane is also released during gas, oil and coal production and from burning and decay of biomass. Other greenhouse gases do not occur in nature but are solely the products of human manufacture. These include the CFCs used in aerosol sprays and as refrigerants, and carbon tetrachloride, used as a dry cleaning agent.

Global warming

Ice core data show that levels of naturally occurring greenhouse gases remained relatively stable in the 800 years preceding the industrial revolution, suggesting that the increases observed since then may be linked to increasing anthropogenic emissions. As concentrations of greenhouse gases increase in the atmosphere, the natural greenhouse effect is enhanced, accelerating the warming of the earth's surface. If trends in current patterns of human activity continue, the mean global surface temperature is predicted to rise by 1 to 3.5 °C over the next century. Projected changes averaged over the earth's surface, however, mask significant regional variation both in the scale and rate of climatic change and in the impacts it is likely to have on both the environment and society.

dioxide dynamics. Second, the chemical models used to predict concentrations of other greenhouse gases do not allow for complex interactions between them in the atmosphere. Third, predicting temperature change from changing atmospheric composition includes the use of some figures for which there are no reliable empirical estimates. Finally, predictions cannot incorporate unpredictable changes in solar or volcanic activity or the possible feedback effects of cloud, water vapour or snow cover, or the effects of changing climate itself on the natural sources and sinks of greenhouse gases.

In addition to these scientific uncertainties, greenhouse gas emissions predicted under different policy scenarios use assumptions about projected population growth and economic development. Since carbon dioxide emissions, for example, are an intrinsic by-product of basic activities in contemporary human society, social, technological and political factors will all influence changing emission rates. In discussing the scientific uncertainties characterizing predictions of climate change, Liberatore (1995: 64) remarks that 'uncertainties also characterise the assessment of the various policy options in terms of their economic costs, social acceptability and political implications at the global, national and local levels. In other words, social science uncertainties, as well as natural ones, must be dealt with.'

Notions of scientific and social uncertainty are brought together by Beck (1992). He argues that changes in the social and economic positions of, for example, women, workers and minority ethnic groups have been accompanied by changes in patterns of social integration through structures such as families, health and care relationships and trades unions. Together, these changes have led to reduced levels of social certainty and increased pressures on individuals to deal with their own resultant anxieties and insecurities. In contemporary society they must cope with uncertainties surrounding a wide range of social and economic processes, including the stability of marital relationships, fertility, risks from HIV and AIDS, job security and income maintenance.

The acceptability of possibilities for dealing with uncertainties depends on the perceptions of risk which they introduce. Definitions of risk are a subject of continuing debate, but it is generally accepted that perceptions of risk are socially conditioned. Such perceptions depend on the position of an individual in society and the way in which possible consequences of accepting a risk affect particular individuals or groups; they depend on whether a risk is taken voluntarily and whether it is controllable; they depend on whether the possible consequences of risk are immediate or delayed and whether they are reversible or irreversible; and finally they depend on whether exposure to the risk is seen as a necessity or a luxury (Liberatore 1995).

Adams (1995) illustrates how differing views about both nature and human nature combine to produce cultural constructions of risk. He uses the environmental example of motor vehicle exhaust emissions to discuss disagreements about what constitutes an appropriate policy response to the health risk they pose. Participants in the debate may each argue rationally but, because they start from different premises, they can hold logical but opposing points of view. For example, those who perceive or experience greater benefits from the use of cars tend to perceive the risks from air pollution as lower. They require more evidence to justify any sacrifice of those benefits in order to reduce emissions. On the other hand, for people who consider the benefits of car use to be small or non-existent, even an inkling of environmental risk may be sufficient to justify policies to curb emissions.

In general, policies to curtail vehicle exhaust emissions challenge not only personal lifestyles but also established practices in industry, commerce and agriculture. Stakeholders in the vehicle and fuel industries wield power and influence at an economic and political level. Emission reduction policies challenge their interests as well as raising potential conflicts of interest between richer industrialized and poorer developing countries. All these factors can operate to lower perceptions of environmental risk for the groups most involved in formulating any policy response. Even though the perception of risk can be seen as a social construct, scientists and economists nevertheless continue to assess risk as a measured and calculated probability. However, probabilistic risk assessment is invariably dogged by the kinds of uncertainty discussed above, and rarely produces the kind of precise answers which society demands. A divide persists between those who seek to quantify environmental risk and those who seek to understand it in a social context.

Pearce (1993: 82) argues that in the case, for example, of the siting of waste disposal facilities, 'deeper and wider social concerns may also underlie local opposition, including invasion of home life and territory, loss of personal control, stress and lifestyle infringement, loss of trust in public agencies and lack of accountability of the "system".' He summarizes his argument by saying, 'the waste site is merely the catalyst for unlocking concerns about trends in society in general', but this surely misses the point. It fails to recognize that 'society in general' and the wider environment are part of the same whole. Thus 'trends in society' both contribute to waste and influence attitudes to methods for its disposal. Similarly, risks associated with the siting of waste disposal plants relate to both environmental and social impacts and have implications not only for the environment but also for social life and well-being.

Economic growth

One school of thought in social policy holds that economic growth is needed to produce the necessary resources to improve social well-being, whether through processes of redistribution, alleviating poverty or providing welfare services. Wealthier countries can better afford to be more generous in these respects. There is, however, a great deal of disagreement along the political spectrum about whether social policy should be seen as the 'handmaiden of economic growth' (for example, by ensuring a healthier, better educated workforce in a stable civil society), or whether economic growth should be seen as having as its prime objective the promotion of social well-being. When we extend the idea of social welfare to social well-being and consider relationships between societies and the environment, the issue of economic growth becomes even more contentious. People who all agree that social, environmental and economic sustainability is a worthy policy goal may be totally opposed in their views about whether growth is a solution to or a cause of environmental problems. The International Bank for Reconstruction and Development, or World Bank, has taken a middle stance. 'Economic growth is essential for sustained poverty reduction. But growth has often caused serious environmental damage. Fortunately, such adverse effects can be sharply reduced, and with effective policies and institutions, income growth will provide the resources for improved environmental management' (International Bank for Reconstruction and Development 1992: 25). It argues that many industrialized countries have achieved substantial improvements in environmental quality alongside continued economic growth. Where carbon dioxide emissions and municipal waste production do still appear to rise with income, this is explained simply by a lack of incentives, such as taxation and regulation, to promote environmental protection. The position of the United Kingdom government is equally clear.

> Economic growth is not an end in itself. It provides us with the means to live better and fuller lives. We should naturally avoid policies which secure growth in the short term at the expense of blighting our broader, longer term ambitions. But we should not be misled. Growth is a necessary though not a sufficient condition for achieving the higher quality of life that the world wants. In countries already beyond the dreams of a generation ago, growth is still needed to provide the resources to clean up the pollution of old industries and to produce the technology to accommodate tomorrow's industrial processes to cleaner surroundings.
>
> (HMSO 1990: 8)

Although recognizing that unrestrained economic growth does lead to environmental damage, Pearce (1993: 4) argues that there is extensive scope for decoupling economic activity from environmental impact so that 'it is possible to have economic growth *and* to use up fewer resources.'

One critique of the 'growth' position is based on the idea that under market capitalism, economic growth is achieved through competition and comparative advantage. This means that countries or regions unable to compete successfully become impoverished and their environments deteriorate, while those which are successful over-exploit the natural environment, with resulting pollution and resource depletion (Blowers and Glasbergen 1995). Proponents of 'green' ideology go further in their objections to dominant views about the need for growth, arguing that sustainable development requires not growth but new patterns of social organization and institutions with cooperative development at local levels (George and Wilding 1994).

Much of the debate about economic growth and sustainability centres upon the potential role of markets. Arguments are polarized around, on the one hand, the idea that the market is essential for economic growth, which in turn is necessary for sustainable development, and, on the other, the view that the market is intrinsically incapable of producing sustainable development. Discussions of the role of the market and the role of the state in promoting sustainable development are well covered in the literature (Pearce 1993; Spicker 1995; Blowers and Glasbergen 1996; Hill 1996). The point here is that conflicting views about economic growth and sustainable development are to be found in both social policy and environmental literature.

They are, in both cases, coloured by personal values and ideas about individual and social responsibility.

Responsibility

Underlying beliefs about what constitutes natural justice shape opinions about the relationship between individual and social responsibility. On the one hand is the belief that people are responsible only for themselves and that individuals have a right to property which they have acquired through their own endeavours. Further along the spectrum lies the belief that people all have responsibilities to one another and that those with access to more resources should provide for people who have less.

The very existence of social policy as an area of study reflects a belief held by society that some if not all members of society may at some point in their lives be dependent on the social provision of welfare services. Deep-seated beliefs about personal and public responsibility underlie attitudes to social welfare and consequently inform views about how, if at all, it should be provided by the state.

'Welfare' may be taken to include cash social security benefits, education, health and social services, as well as state assistance in the form of government subsidies or tax relief: for example, personal income tax allowances or mortgage tax relief. Under this wide definition of state welfare, virtually all members of society in the UK are benefit recipients as well as being taxpayers. Traditional definitions cover only health, education and social welfare benefits, but state spending on these is still largely supported by all income groups in the UK. 'The foundations of public support for the welfare state have never been more solid' (Taylor-Gooby 1995: 16).

Attitudes to the role of the state in providing for individual welfare are shaped by views about how far individuals should be reliant on themselves and their families for dealing with their own needs. Similarly, ideas about responsibility also influence attitudes to the environment. These range from the view that every little helps and that individuals have a crucial role to play in environmental protection, to the view that nothing any individual does can have any effect in the face of the huge contribution made by companies, industries and governments to environmental change. However, even those who are convinced that individual action to protect the environment (for example, by buying 'green' products and by conserving energy and water) is a necessary element of success usually recognize that it is not sufficient. State intervention is necessary at some level to regulate, legislate or otherwise exert control to ensure effective action.

Both social welfare and environmental protection rely on individuals taking responsibility and appropriate actions in their lives. But both also rely on the state to provide a legitimizing and enabling framework and to take responsibility where, for whatever reason, it is impossible for individuals acting alone to achieve effective results.

Summary and the rest of the book

This introductory chapter has sought to identify some of the key themes linking social policy and the environment. It has provided a brief illustration of how concepts of inequality, sustainability and responsibility are relevant to both areas of study and can provide a framework within which to explore the interdependency between the two.

Each of the following six chapters focuses on a particular element of social well-being. Taking water, food, housing, warmth and domestic energy, transport and leisure in turn, we can examine how access to these is influenced by social factors. At the same time, the way in which people use each of these elements has particular implications for the environment. The environmental effects of human activities result in changes which can alter the extent to which others can meet their needs for assuring their future well-being.

Each chapter addresses how the nature of access to an element of well-being can vary across different groups of people and how different kinds of access affect the environment. These effects in turn have the capacity to influence social well-being and development in ways which raise questions about inequality, sustainability and responsibility. We return to these three themes in the final chapter, which examines how tensions can arise between social and environmental interests, emphasizing the necessity of setting any analysis of social policy firmly in an environmental context.

Chapter two

WATER

Water plays a vital role in sustaining life in all organisms, from microbes to human beings. Supplies of fresh clean drinking water are essential to physical human survival, but water also influences many other aspects of social well-being. It is essential for plant growth, and field crops are often irrigated artificially when there is not enough rain. Its use in farming also includes livestock watering and the cleaning of dairies and farm buildings, as well as direct irrigation of crops. In addition to its domestic and agricultural value, water represents a vital economic resource for industry, where large amounts are used in production processes, as a coolant or as a medium for washing or conveying materials, as well as for waste disposal. In electricity generation, large volumes of water are used for cooling purposes and, in the case of hydroelectricity, as a source of energy to drive the generators themselves. Table 2.1 shows how water abstracted from surface water and groundwater in England and Wales in 1990 was used.

There are continuing debates in social policy about the extent to which there is collective responsibility for meeting the need for domestic water supplies. In addition to being essential and non-substitutable, in economic terms water is also a merit good. That is, it is one of the goods 'the provision of which, society (as distinct from the preferences of the individual consumer) wishes to encourage' (Musgrave and Musgrave 1984: 78). In addition, merit goods 'are goods that, on basically ethical grounds, society believes should be supplied to – and where appropriate actually consumed by – everybody, perhaps only to certain minimum levels, whether they like it or not and whether they can pay for it or not' (Beckerman 1986: 17). The provision of water services carries positive externalities in the form of benefits to public health and well-being of piped water supplies, sewage treatment

Table 2.1 Water abstracted for various uses in England and Wales, 1994

Use	Megalitres per day	%
Electricity supply industry	27,732	51.7
Public water supply (piped mains water)	16,735	31.2
Other industry	4292	8.0
Fish farming, cress growing, amenity ponds	3983	7.4
Spray irrigation	285	0.5
Mineral washing	223	0.4
Agriculture (excluding spray irrigation)	119	0.2
Private water supply	85	0.2
Other	196	0.4
Total	53,640	100.00

Source: Department of the Environment (1996b).

Table 2.2 Relative proportions of average household water use in England and Wales, 1991

Use	Litres per person per day	%
Water closet flushing	44.8	32
Bathing and showering	23.8	17
Washing machine	16.8	12
Outside use (gardening, car washing, swimming pools)	4.2	3
Dish washing	1.4	1
Miscellaneous (drinking, cooking and leakage)	49.0	35
Total	140.0	100

Source: Water Services Association (1991).

and environmental protection. Taken together, all these factors provide an argument for the intervention of governments both to secure equity of access to water and to protect the environment.

Domestic uses of water include not only drinking and cooking but also washing, bathing and the disposal of domestic wastes. In the UK, about 80 per cent of public water supplied ends up as waste water in sewers. The Water Services Association estimated that in 1991 the average person in England or Wales used 140 litres of water a day for the variety of purposes shown in Table 2.2.

Water plays a crucial role in shaping the natural environment. Many landscapes owe their characteristic features to the weathering action of water in rainfall and rivers over thousands of years. Water levels and flows in particular areas help to determine patterns of natural vegetation growth and hence the diversity of wildlife habitats. People living in or visiting the countryside often derive aesthetic, spiritual or scientific pleasure, and streams, rivers and lakes are used directly in many parts of the world for leisure and recreational purposes, an aspect of water use which is covered in detail in Chapter 7.

This chapter concentrates first of all on the nature of global water resources and the variations in their accessibility to different sectors of society. It then moves on to examine how the kind of use which is made of water by societies has environmental effects which not only influence the quantity and quality of water available for further use but also have wider reaching impacts on standards of living and social well-being.

Hydrology and the availability of fresh water

Water occurs not only in liquid form but also as water vapour and ice. The volume present on the planet is constant and water can be seen as a renewable resource in the sense that its molecules move on a global scale through a cycle of transformations between these different states. Figure 2.1 provides a simplified picture of the hydrological cycle, showing how water which evaporates into the atmosphere is returned to the surface of the earth as precipitation – rainfall, hail and snow.

The rate of water loss to the atmosphere through evaporation is increased by transpiration, the process through which plants take up water from the soil and return it to the air from pores in their leaf surfaces. Once in the atmosphere, water vapour is circulated by winds and air currents until it cools and condenses, falling back to earth as precipitation. Much of this fresh water returns to the saline oceans. Some infiltrates into the soil and percolates through underlying layers of rock, eventually seeping to the sea. Only a small amount remains on the earth's surface, slowly feeding and replenishing streams, lakes and rivers.

This cycle is continually in motion, but at any one time the amount of fresh water available for human use is extremely limited. Ninety-eight per cent of water is held in the seas and oceans which cover 70 per cent of the earth's surface, and much of the remaining 2 per cent is locked up in ice-sheets and glaciers. Only a tiny fraction is present at one time as fresh water in lakes, rivers and the underground layers of porous water-bearing rocks known as aquifers. Most of the water used by people comes from these sources, although a small amount is obtained by the desalination of salt water.

Water scarcity is commonly seen to be a severe constraint on social development where renewable water resources fall below 1000 cubic metres per capita but, as a global average, 7000 cubic metres per capita each year enter rivers, lakes and aquifers (International Bank for Reconstruction and Development 1992). However, the global average masks a wide range of regional variation and twenty-two countries already have annual renewable water resources of less than 1000 cubic metres per capita. The World Bank has predicted that by the end of the 1990s, six East African countries and all North African countries will have annual supplies below the level at which societies

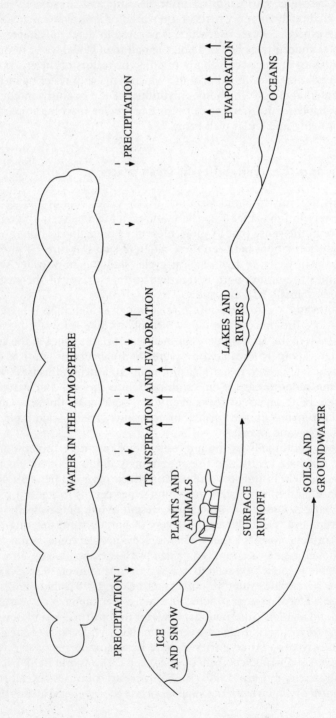

Figure 2.1 The hydrological cycle, showing water reservoirs and water flows.

generally experience water shortage. Demand regularly exceeds supply in the Middle East, Northern China, East Java and parts of India. Problems arise partly because of huge regional climatic differences; fresh water is not always replenished when and where it is needed by people. But they also occur as a result of human activity: for example, in Mexico City groundwater is pumped out at rates which are 40 per cent higher than the rate of natural recharge (International Bank for Reconstruction and Development 1992).

Accessibility and domestic use of water

Households' access to domestic water supplies depends first on environmental conditions and the natural availability of fresh water in a particular area. But it is also dependent on social organization and responsibilities. In some societies, water is carried physically by individuals, usually women, from its source to the places where it is needed for domestic use. In others, central or local governments may take responsibility and provide the infrastructure to pipe water to standpipes or domestic dwellings. Water may also be privately provided, either piped directly to homes or sold in bottles or other containers. The extent to which different households are able to obtain the water they need is influenced, then, not only by natural conditions but also by their ability to pay for its delivery and, in some cases, its treatment and purification.

Variations in levels of natural supply

Patterns in global hydrology and climatic conditions lead to wide variation in annual renewable water resources in different parts of the world (Table 2.3).

Demands on water resources vary with levels of domestic consumption, related to income and household use of water-intensive appliances such as washing machines and dishwashers, with levels of industrial and agricultural activity and with rates of loss from mains supply systems. However, the main influence on demand is population size, and Table 2.3 shows that the regions with the scarcest water resources are often those with the highest rates of population growth. The rapidly increasing population in the Middle East, for example, puts immense pressure on limited supplies of water. Both Syria and Jordan are currently close to their limits on natural supplies, yet by the year 2025 their populations are expected to treble and quadruple respectively (Cairncross 1993). In the Persian Gulf, which experiences similar pressures, fresh water has been described as 'more valuable than oil' (Hinrichsen 1990: 42).

Even where water is naturally available, human activity can lead to scarcity. Nearly all the rivers in the western United States have been diverted for human use, and communities are now drawing on underground supplies which cannot be quickly replenished. In some areas water is being pumped out at rates that exceed rates of refilling by 130 to 160 per cent (Yearley 1996). In the UK, 70 per cent of the public water supply is drawn from surface

Table 2.3   Water availability and population growth

Region	Annual internal renewable water resources (thousand cubic metres per capita)	% of population in countries with less than 1000 cubic metres per capita	Average annual rate of population growth 1980–90
Sub-Saharan Africa	7.1	8	3.1
East Asia and the Pacific	5.3	<1	1.6
South Asia	4.2	0	2.2
Eastern Europe and former USSR	11.4	3	n.a.
Other Europe	4.6	6	0.8
Middle East and North Africa	1.0	53	3.1
Latin America and Caribbean	23.9	<1	2.1
Canada and United States	19.4	0	0.9
World	7.7	4	1.7

Source: International Bank for Reconstruction and Development (1992).

waters and 30 per cent from groundwater and, although the overall supply of water exceeds demand, withdrawal rates have been increasing steadily since 1980 (HMSO 1994a). Furthermore, on a regional scale, geographical variations in rainfall do not always match with the variation in demand caused by differing levels of population, urbanization and industrialization.

Varying costs of provision

The fact that water is not always available where it is needed means that it must be transported, a process which has costs in terms of both time and money. WHO estimates suggest that worldwide more than 170 million people lack a source of potable water near their homes, and more than 855 million live in rural areas where there is no reliable supply of safe water (International Bank for Reconstruction and Development 1992). Those facing the greatest difficulties in obtaining water often have to rely on surface sources or shallow wells, and tend to have low consumption levels per capita. They are more likely to wash less and to drink polluted supplies than people with access to abundant supplies of water, with obvious effects on health and cleanliness.

Fetching water for household use can take up considerable amounts of time, particularly for women. In one neighbourhood in Ibadan, Nigeria, it was found that women in a third of all households spent over one and a half hours each day carrying water (Sarre 1991). During periods of water scarcity, demands on women's time are particularly onerous. 'When water supply is under stress, gender divisions of labour put women at the sharp end of water shortage' (Jackson 1995: 118). Research in Zimbabwe showed that the problem was exacerbated by the relative priorities given to the time of men and women. During drought, domestic users of borehole water, mainly women who daily walk for four to eight kilometres to collect water, had to give precedence to cattle watering, mainly the task of men (Elson and Cleaver 1994).

In regions of the world where water is generally in abundant supply, it is often taken for granted as a resource to which everyone has a right. But the financial costs associated with providing supplies where they are needed and, in many cases, the costs of water purification and of waste disposal lead to marked inequalities in the ways that different social groups are able to obtain and utilize water. The relationship between inequalities of access and income exist both within and between countries. 'A family in the top fifth income group in Peru, the Dominican Republic or Ghana is, respectively, three, six and twelve times more likely to have a house connection than a family in the bottom fifth income group in these countries' (International Bank for Reconstruction and Development 1992: 47).

Lack of a piped water supply characterizes poorer households in urban areas as well as rural households. In the 1970s, 45 per cent of urban households in Thailand had no piped domestic supply, 46 per cent in Mexico, 60 per cent in Jamaica and 62 per cent in Pakistan. Although some local authorities provide water which can be bought cheaply from tanker trucks, many households must buy from private vendors at high prices. Research in Port-au-Prince, Haiti, found that for a family of five people, water costs could be as much as 15 per cent of monthly household income (Sarre 1991). A very different situation exists in richer industrialized countries such as the UK, where piped supplies of clean domestic water are available to almost all.

Widespread access to piped water in the UK originated in the nineteenth century, when the growth of new industrial towns was accompanied by Acts of Parliament granting permission to both public authorities and private companies to provide supplies. Since the industry was privatized in England and Wales in 1989, responsibility for supply lies with ten water service companies and a number of water-only companies. Individual households are charged for the water supplies and sewerage services they receive. Together the companies are known as water undertakers, and their activities are monitored and regulated by government bodies: the Office of Water Services (OFWAT), the Drinking Water Inspectorate (DWI) and the Environment Agency. UK water regulations set detailed quality standards for public water supplies and companies must also meet certain European standards.

OFWAT has responsibility for 'securing that companies are able (in particular, by securing reasonable returns on their capital) to finance the proper carrying out of their functions' (Water Bill 1988: Clause 6(2)(b)), 'and subject to this (and only subject thereto) of ensuring protection of consumer interests' (Water Bill 1988: Clause 6(3)). Although there is a clear sequence of priority given first to the companies and second to consumers, the Director General of OFWAT has often reiterated that his 'duties to ensure that companies can finance their functions and to protect the interests of customers are complementary' (Byatt 1990). Revenue must be raised from customers not only to pay for maintaining, renewing, extending and improving water provision and sewerage services, but also to pay out 'reasonable interest and dividends' to shareholders who are funding companies' capital expenditure programmes (OFWAT 1993).

The need for increased capital investment for infrastructural improvements, the rising costs of transporting water and of treating it to meet increasingly stringent European Union (EU) water quality standards and the need to pay dividends to shareholders since privatization have all contributed to large price rises for water in England and Wales since 1989. Between 1989–90 and 1994–5, average household water and sewerage bills rose by 67 per cent (National Consumer Council 1994). Ernst (1994) has argued that, because water is absolutely necessary for physical and social well-being and because there are no alternative means for people to meet their water-related needs, domestic consumers are likely to maintain a relatively constant demand for water regardless of its price and irrespective of household income.

Increased prices affect rich and poor alike, and in England and Wales complaints about levels and increases in charges and billing queries accounted for half of all the complaints received by customer service committees in 1995 (OFWAT 1995). Some high-income households have the capacity to absorb additional costs of water services by simply paying more. Indeed, there is evidence of an increasing trend in non-essential household use of water, such as garden watering, in the UK. Sales of hosepipes and sprinklers more than doubled between 1992 and 1995, with up to 60 per cent estimated as being new, not replacement, sales (OFWAT 1996a). Those on high incomes and who pay for water by volume used are also able to economize by installing water efficient appliances or by reducing discretionary use such as car washing, garden watering and use of private swimming pools.

However, if low-income consumers are faced with increasing water charges they cannot reduce their consumption below certain levels without incurring hardship. Problems associated with the inability to pay for water include debt, disconnection and underconsumption in cases where water is paid for by the volume used. These problems do not arise uniformly but vary according to income group and circumstances such as family size and medical conditions. They also vary with region, since the setting of water charges and the methods of payment offered are different for different companies.

Water debt and disconnection in England and Wales

For some customers on low incomes in England and Wales, water charges can represent up to 10 per cent of household income, compared to a national average of only 1 per cent (OFWAT 1996b). Herbert and Kempson (1995) carried out a detailed study of water debt and disconnection and found that in 1994 almost two million households defaulted on their water bills, 9 per cent of all households in Britain. More than a quarter of these said they had been threatened with court action. Water debt was found to be significantly more likely to occur in low-income households, especially if income levels had fallen over the previous year. It was also more likely where families had two or more dependent children or were living in social housing. Nearly a third of households in debt had children under the age of five.

Those having a high risk of water debt included people in groups identified by the British Medical Association (BMA 1994) as 'vulnerable' with regard to water supplies. A quarter of all households headed by a sick or disabled person had defaulted on their water bills during the previous year, and customers who said they had to use extra water because some member of the household had a longstanding illness or disability were more likely than other households to have been in arrears with their bills (Herbert and Kempson 1995).

Although domestic water disconnections fell by 42 per cent to 5826 between 1994–5 and 1995–6 (OFWAT news release 7 May 1996), most are concentrated in low-income households. Herbert and Kempson (1995) found that 0.6 per cent of households which fell into arrears with their water bills ended up being disconnected. Domestic supplies can only legally be disconnected following the issue of a summons and a court order, a process which in itself can cause much distress, particularly to elderly people.

The extent to which increasing charges lead to water debt and the threat of disconnection depends on the resources which people have to meet their bills and certain organizational arrangements which may include help with making payments. Some people have their water bills paid directly from social assistance by the Department of Social Security (DSS); some live in housing supplied by local authorities which include water charges in council rents; and some have access to social services, money advice agencies or other organizations which offer help with budgeting strategies. There is also a Department of Health scheme under which local health authorities pay the costs of extra water use for metered customers using renal dialysis machines in their own homes. However, there is no agreement for helping people with other medical conditions, such as incontinence or certain skin conditions, which increase demands for extra water for toilet use, bathing or laundering. Finally, the water companies themselves may have policies and payment options designed to help customers to pay their bills more easily. However, the differences in policy and practice between water companies lead to regional variations which enhance the inequalities produced by income and family circumstances.

Regional inequalities in England and Wales

Charges for water in England and Wales vary considerably, mainly because in different areas of the country environmental conditions, population size and the state of existing infrastructure impose different costs on the companies responsible for water treatment and supply. The fragmentation of the water industry into individual profit seeking businesses has led to different charges being passed on to domestic consumers – in some areas average water bills are twice as high as in others.

The Association of Charity Officers has expressed concern about the extent to which charities are approached to help low-income households in areas where water charges are disproportionately high, and three water companies have set up their own charitable trusts to assist customers who have difficulties in paying their bills. OFWAT recognizes this phenomenon as a sign that companies 'are not ordinary commercial businesses but are monopolies with social responsibilities' (OFWAT 1996b: 15). The question of who should be responsible for ensuring that people living on low incomes have access to adequate water supplies remains, however, a matter of debate in Britain. The DSS provides social assistance benefits at rates which are set nationally and take no account of regional variation in water bills. Claimants get the same rate of payment, which includes a nominal but unspecified amount to meet water bills, regardless of where they live. Certain benefit claimants receive help with maintaining payments for water through the direct payment scheme. The scheme acts as a budgeting device through which payments for water bills are made directly from the DSS to the creditors and deducted at source from benefit payments. It aims to ensure continuity of supply to benefit recipients and regular payments to the water companies. It was never designed to solve the fundamental problem of rapid increases in water bills, and certain aspects of the scheme have long been subject to criticism (PUAF 1990). Over the period 1989 to 1994 there was a six-fold increase in the number of claimants using the direct payment scheme for water, and in 1995, 4 per cent of all income support recipients paid for their water in this way (DSS press release 30 November 1995). However, the percentage of claimants using direct payments varies with locality, ranging from less than 1 to more than 10 per cent (Anthony 1996). Although 16 per cent of this regional variation can be shown to be attributable to variations in the size of water bills, there are other sources of variation related to the types of payment options offered by different water companies.

One of the most recent payment options offered by some companies is the use of budget payment units which allow customers to pay for their water in instalments at agreed intervals. A unit is a control box fitted inside the home which is 'fed' or recharged using an electronic card. If the unit is not recharged, then, after an emergency credit period of usually seven days, the water supply is stopped. 'OFWAT does not believe that the customer's operation of the unit in this way amounts to action by the water company to cut off the customer's supply' (OFWAT information note no. 34, April 1996). However, in a household where no money is available to recharge the unit, there is clearly a possibility of self disconnection, which may go unrecorded in the water companies' figures. Even in a relatively rich country such as the UK, where clean water is in theory readily available at the turn of a tap, some people still experience water shortage because of their inability to pay for it.

Domestic waste water

The amount of water used for domestic purposes is closely correlated with the amount discharged as waste, which often goes directly back into the water supply. Where sewage treatment systems are inadequate or non-existent, problems of water pollution are exacerbated when rivers pass through large cities or industrial centres. In the late 1980s, only 40 per cent of waste water in Czechoslovakia was adequately treated, and the waste in half the cities in Poland and in many large cities in the Soviet Union received no treatment at all (French 1991). The Soviet Union was one of the first countries to formulate environmental quality standards and, by 1990, 77 per cent of sewage and industrial waste water in the country was purified, but still only 30 per cent was treated to the standards set by government at that time (Tellegen 1996).

Modern sewage collection and treatment systems are usually confined to developed industrialized countries and high-income areas in poorer countries. In the UK, some waste water is disposed of in septic tanks or as direct outfall to streams, rivers or the sea. However, sewers receive the majority of domestic wastes emanating from lavatories, bathing, clothes washing, food preparation and household cleaning. Together with certain industrial or trade discharges and water from surface run-off and infiltrating groundwater, sewage is usually conveyed to treatment plants for cleaning before it is discharged into rivers or other bodies of water. Levels of sewage treatment in the UK vary with region. Primary treatment is physical and chemical and involves the settlement and removal of suspended solids, while secondary treatment is biological and removes organic material. In some cases sewage undergoes tertiary treatment, further purification to produce particularly high-quality effluent. Because many sources of domestic water are also used as waste disposal channels, discharges by sewage treatment works, and also by industry and by farms, must be authorized by the relevant authority.

The use of water in industry and agriculture

So far our discussion has focused mainly on uses of water in the home. Yet water can be seen as an essential precursor to both social and industrial development. Pearce (1993) suggests that uses of water which might appear to be luxuries at low income levels become necessities at higher levels of income and industrialization. In more affluent industrialized countries the economic and social world has become so reliant on electricity that lack of water used for cooling in generating stations might cause social hardship. The processing of oil shale to produce synthetic oil and gas uses vast amounts of water, and the increase in this process is currently causing problems in the western United States, where water is already scarce (Seitz 1995). Table 2.4 demonstrates how water is essential for the production of items and materials usually taken for granted in British society.

Table 2.4   Some industrial uses of water

	Litres of water used in production
An average car	30,000
1 ton of steel	4546
1 ton of ready mixed concrete	454
1 pint of beer	4.5

Source: Department of the Environment (1992a).

Worldwide, since the 1960s, there has been a steady increase in the use of fresh water for irrigation, especially in the developing countries. Globally, one-fifth of all cropland is under irrigation, a trebling of area since 1950, and irrigated agriculture accounts for 70 per cent of the world's use of fresh water (Cairncross 1993). About two-thirds of this is wasted through overuse or leakage, possibly because its economic value often goes unrecognized. The undervaluing of water supplies and services is in danger of jeopardizing future supplies. Recent trends in England and Wales, however, show a decline in demand for water for industry and general industrial purposes, although demands for spray irrigation, fish farming and hydroelectric power are increasing.

Environmental effects of water use

Societies' abstraction of water from its natural sources and its return after use affect both the quantity and quality of water in the environment. In reality, of course, water quantity and water quality are interlinked, since declines in the flow rates of rivers slow down the dispersal and dilution of polluting effluents. The quality of piped water supplies can also be affected, as was demonstrated in 1995 when the prolonged drought in England and Wales was associated with a high demand for water. The changes in patterns of flow in water mains disturbed sediments containing iron, manganese and aluminium, causing problems of reduced water quality and increased turbidity (Environmental Data Services Report 258, July 1996).

Fresh water quantity

Human activities moving water from one place to another affect the amount of available water in two ways. On the one hand, over-abstraction of fresh water, together with the diversion of watercourses and leakage from water transportation systems, can lead to shortage of supply; on the other hand, excessive irrigation and dam building can result in flooding.

Fresh water fisheries can be affected by the abstraction of water for domestic and other uses and this can lead to the loss of a valuable source of food and sometimes livelihood. In Tamil Nadu in southern India, ten years of tubewell extraction to provide villages with drinking water have resulted in a drop of more than 25 metres in the water table. Where water is drawn from underground aquifers, over-abstraction can cause land subsidence in overlying areas, and in coastal regions there is an increased risk of saline intrusion. In Bangladesh, groundwater extraction is thought to have doubled the rate of natural land subsidence.

In the UK, new or increased groundwater abstractions lower water table levels and can cause problems of low flow in rivers, affecting their flora and fauna and reducing their aesthetic and amenity value. Domestic demands for water in England and Wales are projected to grow by around 25 per cent over the next 25 years, so abstraction rates are likely to increase, especially if current leakage problems are not reduced. Since a quarter of all water taken from natural systems by water companies is estimated to be wasted, leaking out of pipes before it reaches end users, much more water than is actually needed is abstracted, with concomitant effects on the environment. 'Over-abstraction, often for public water supplies, has led to unacceptably low flows in some rivers in England and Wales, thereby damaging wildlife habitats and having an adverse impact on water quality and recreational and amenity value' (HMSO 1994a: 57). Recently, English Nature found 56 wildlife sites which had been significantly affected by abstraction of water in 1995–6 (All-Party Parliamentary Water Group 1996). Wetland nature reserves are particularly vulnerable, and birds such as kingfishers, yellow wagtails and snipe, which depend on streams, rivers and damp meadows for feeding and breeding sites, have declined in numbers in the UK over the past 20 years as many wetland habitats have started to dry out.

On the other hand, too much water can also present environmental problems, such as when excessive irrigation and the building of dams leads to flooding and affects coastal stability and fisheries. Land which becomes waterlogged or saline as a result of irrigation is lost to agriculture, and urban problems occur when increasing groundwater levels lead to the flooding of tunnels and basements and sewage overflow. Risks of flooding are exacerbated by the climatic changes induced by global warming, and sea level rises threaten populations living in low-lying coastal areas such as the Nile and Ganges deltas. These are fertile agricultural regions supporting over 46 million people, but under the worst case scenario for global warming, a two metre rise in sea level would result in the loss of 18 per cent of all habitable land, displace 15 per cent of the population and reduce gross national product (GNP) by 13 per cent (Kelly and Granich 1995). Areas of India designated as prone to flooding increased from 20 million hectares in 1970 to 40 million hectares in 1980.

Fresh water quality

Human causes of fresh water pollution include not only disposal of domestic waste but also activities involved in urbanization, farming and agriculture, industry and mining. Some pollutants enter water systems in direct discharges of waste water, some in surface run-off and some, originally emanating from incinerators and fossil fuel burning, are deposited from the air. Leaching of pollutants from agricultural land, contaminated land, disused mines and landfill sites also causes problems. Groundwater is particularly vulnerable to this kind of pollution. The aquifers increasingly used as sources of water for human use have little or no capacity for self cleaning, because water only moves through them very slowly. Although the aquatic environment can be adversely affected by a whole range of forms of pollution, including heat, radioactivity and inert materials causing turbidity, we focus here on pollution by organic material from human sewage and farm effluents and on chemical pollution.

In many parts of the world, inadequate water supply and sewerage systems mean that people must drink from and wash in pond and river water, making them highly susceptible to disease from human wastes and excreta. World Bank estimates suggest that around 30 per cent of the global disease burden is owing to inadequate infrastructure, including poor water supplies and lack of sanitation (Kinnersley 1994).

Many diseases and disabling conditions are associated with water use. Certain pathogenic or disease-causing organisms are carried by water. These include various diarrhoeal pathogens, the bacteria which cause cholera and typhoid and the polio virus, all of which are found in the excreta and faeces of infected individuals. Infection is spread when contaminated water is used for drinking or in the preparation of food. Conditions such as scabies and trachoma which affect the skin or the eyes are more likely to be contracted where lack of water leads to infrequent washing and bathing. Other diseases are spread when the infecting agent enters the human skin during washing or swimming. An example is schistosomiasis or bilharzia, which affects 200 million people globally at any one time. It is caused by a flatworm whose larvae penetrate intact human skin and enter the body, where they develop to adulthood. They lay eggs which leave the human body in excreta and faeces and are released into sewage receiving waters once again. Finally, some diseases, such as malaria, are carried by insects which live in water at some stage of their life cycle.

Agricultural effluents can also pose risks to human health. Cryptosporidiosis is caused by a protozoan which is carried by livestock and enters fresh water in farm run-off and sewage. In 1989 it affected over 9000 people in Britain and, although public supplies of drinking water are generally of high quality, it remains a source of concern (HMSO 1994a).

Organic material from undiluted farm animal waste products (slurry) and grass which has been fermented without air to produce animal feed (silage) often enters rivers and lakes as a result of accidents or carelessness, causing serious pollution. Slurry is 100 times and silage 200 times more polluting than sewage (Department of the Environment 1992a). When organic wastes from human sewage and farm effluents enter aquatic ecosystems they are broken down by bacteria and other organisms. During the decomposition process, the organisms use up oxygen from the water, and as they thrive and

Box 2.1   Algal blooms and eutrophication

Algal blooms

The algae are a group of non-flowering plants which grow in damp or aquatic habitats. Many species are filamentous or microscopic and float on the surfaces of ponds and lakes, forming dense layers. Like other plants, they need water, oxygen, carbon dioxide, sunlight, mineral nutrients and suitable temperatures for successful growth, and during the winter their growth rates are low. In the summer months when the water is warmer and hours of daylight longer they can proliferate and form dense blankets of vegetation on the water surface. This phenomenon is known as an algal bloom. The algae are eaten by aquatic animals, including microscopic zooplankton which, in the presence of this rich source of food, themselves grow and reproduce at rapid rates. As the season progresses, the algae begin to exhaust supplies of nutrients such as nitrogen and phosphorus. Their growth can no longer keep pace with the rate at which they are eaten and the bloom subsides, leaving a clear water surface again until autumn winds mix the waters, disturbing bottom sediments and releasing more nutrients. A further autumn bloom may occur, but as winter sets in low temperatures and lack of sunlight again reduce growth to low levels.

Eutrophication

Eutrophication is the increase in the productivity of a body of water resulting from nutrient enrichment. The natural cycle of algal blooms is disturbed where water becomes eutrophic or enriched with additional nutrients, such as those entering the water from agricultural run-off or sewage effluent. Continuous supplies of nutrients allow the algae to thrive throughout the summer until eventually they block out the sunlight from the water below, inhibiting the growth of other plant species. At the same time their respiration uses up dissolved oxygen from the water, to the detriment of fish and other aquatic animals. Not only do the algae disturb the wildlife composition of the water body, but as they die off and decay they form an unpleasant smelling scum on the water surface, reducing amenity value for leisure and recreation. In addition, some species of blue-green algae produce toxic substances which can reach potentially dangerous concentrations in algal blooms and have been responsible recently in the UK for the banning of watersports in some lakes and reservoirs.

grow in numbers the dissolved oxygen in the water is used up, causing fish and plant life to suffer. The breakdown of organic material also releases large amounts of essential plant nutrients, which allow the rapid growth of tiny floating plants, algae, which may form dense blooms on the water surface. As the algae die and decompose, more oxygen is used up and the problem is exacerbated (Box 2.1).

Other pollutants from farm waste which pose risks to both human and environmental health are nitrates and pesticides, discussed in Chapter 3. These compounds enter water courses mainly through leaching and surface run-off. High nitrate levels in drinking water are thought to be responsible for methaemoglobinaemia or 'blue baby syndrome' and are the subject of an EU Directive. Some water sources in the UK which have high nitrate levels have been removed from public supply, and parts of the country have been designated as Nitrate Sensitive Areas (HMSO 1994a).

Pollution of water by potentially toxic chemicals and heavy metals, such as lead, cadmium and mercury, is attributable to domestic as well as industrial discharges to sewers. Lead from domestic plumbing systems is a particular cause for concern in the UK, and in richer countries at least, domestic waste water also contains detergents, fabric softeners, bleaches, perfumes and dyes from toiletries and household cleaners, disinfectants and oven and drain cleaners (Hirschhorn and Oldenburg 1991). It is this contamination which poses problems for the disposal of the sewage sludge which remains after treatment. Unless it can be rendered relatively non-toxic, the use of sludge as a fertilizer and soil conditioner is limited.

Where toxic chemicals and heavy metals from manufacturing, mining and the agro-chemical industry are permitted to enter aquatic ecosystems, they can accumulate in fish and shellfish, with concomitant health risks to humans as well as the environment. In Jakarta Bay, Indonesia, waters have been found to exceed WHO guidelines by 38 per cent for mercury, 44 per cent for lead and 76 per cent for cadmium (International Bank for Reconstruction and Development 1992). Pollution of water by pharmaceutical products is currently giving further cause for concern. Discarded or metabolized contraceptive drugs, for example, introduce complex compounds into sewage waste and have been implicated in recent debates about the causes of falling sperm counts in men.

Even where sophisticated waste disposal and water treatment programmes are in place, water quality is still an issue of concern. In the 1990s, half of all drinking water supplied in the Soviet Union was contaminated (L. R. Brown 1993). A survey by the Environment Protection Agency (EPA) in the United States found pesticide residues in around 10 per cent of all community water systems in 1990 and half of the underground water used to supply over 100 million Americans is threatened with contamination or is already contaminated by chemicals (Seitz 1995). In 1990, 95 per cent of fresh water rivers and canals in England and Wales were classified as being of fair or good quality, but nevertheless in July 1996 Thames Water was fined £80,000 for supplying water unfit for human consumption to thousands of customers in West London (Environmental Data Services Report 258, July 1996).

The problem is that no amount of control or regulation can prevent the occurrence of pollution incidents caused by accidental spillages, leakages from waste tips, fly tipping, vandalism or unlawful discharges. In 1991, 29,000 pollution incidents were reported in England and Wales, 22,000 of which were substantiated. By 1993, these figures had risen to 34,000 and 25,000 respectively. Table 2.5 shows the main sources of pollution.

The chemical industry is the source of many potentially toxic substances which find their way into water supplies either as wastes or as deliberate

Table 2.5 Substantiated water pollution incidents in England and Wales, 1994, by source of pollution

Source of pollution	Number of incidents	% of incidents
Oil	6908	27.2
Sewage	6278	24.7
Organic wastes	3175	12.5
Chemicals	1884	7.4
Other	7171	28.2
Total	25,416	100

Source: Department of the Environment (1996b).

additives. Fluorides, for example, are introduced into some UK supplies as a public health measure to prevent dental decay. Yet ironically the industry is also the supplier of the chemicals which are becoming increasingly necessary for the treatment of water in purification plants, creating what Beck (1992: 178) has called 'chains of problem solution and problem production'.

Social implications

The environmental impacts of human uses of fresh water have important implications for the quality of human and natural life, living standards and social development. Over-abstraction of water can destroy wildlife habitats, causing loss of amenity and recreational possibilities. Livelihoods and valuable food sources are threatened when fisheries are damaged or land is lost to agriculture because of subsidence, salinization or flooding.

Shortage of water can cause tensions at domestic, national and international levels. We have already seen how gender relations often mean that women bear the brunt of water scarcity, but shortages can also pose national problems. Predictions of water shortages in the Midwestern United States over the next 30 years are already leading to a decline in the rural population (Cairncross 1993). International problems stem from the fact that most of the world's rivers cross international boundaries, and more than 200 river systems which between them drain more than half of the land area of the earth are shared by two or more countries. Where rivers or aquifers extend across political boundaries countries downstream may receive less water or more polluted water than those upstream, raising the potential for international conflict over access to water. This situation is currently problematic in the Middle East where, although droughts have been common throughout history, increasing population density is exacerbating pressures on water supplies.

Impacts of water shortage, flooding and pollution are often felt most severely by the poor. Rivers suffering from a lack of dissolved oxygen as a result of pollution from human sewage, agro-industrial effluents and farm run-off have shown some improvement over the past decade in high-income countries. There has been little change in middle-income countries, while in low-income countries rivers have shown continuing deterioration.

Children and the elderly are most at risk of suffering health problems caused by faecal contamination of water. Diarrhoeal diseases kill around two million children and cause about 900 million episodes of illness every year. Water pollution from human wastes occurs in all countries, but it takes on a critical importance if treatment of water supplies cannot be afforded. Worldwide, 1.7 billion people have no access to sanitation services. In Latin America, for example, less than 2 per cent of sewage receives any treatment at all (International Bank for Reconstruction and Development 1992). The UK, on the other hand, has the highest percentage connection rate to sewers in the EU (96 per cent) and one of the highest levels of provision of sewage treatment (Department of the Environment 1996a).

The costs to most communities of indiscriminate use of fresh water are substantial. Its efficient use is in the long-term interests of everyone, since this means that the resource will be available for longer, the environment will be protected and, in the long term, prices will be kept comparatively low. However, it is people in the poorer sectors of society who suffer the most detrimental effects of water shortage and poor water quality.

Problems of water provision in China demonstrate the relationship between the environment, poverty and affluence. 'In late 1993, the Minister of Water Resources reported that more than 300 Chinese cities were short of water, with 100 in acute distress – at an estimated cost of US$14 billion in lost economic output each year' (Ryan and Flavin 1995: 118). Part of the shortfall in supplies is attributed to the increasing pollution of fresh water sources, particularly with the rise of new enterprises which contribute to the development of poor rural areas. Residential demands for water, however, are also rising rapidly and exacerbating the problem as more affluent sectors of the population make increasing use of showers, washing machines and flush lavatories. Poorer households are less able to act on environmental concerns by, for example, replacing their domestic plumbing systems to reduce lead pollution or by drinking bottled water. Consequences of a general neglect of natural water sources in the United States have led to a loss of confidence in public supplies in some areas, but the rich are able to buy bottled water or to purify their own tap water for drinking. American consumers annually consume on average 6.4 gallons of bottled water per capita, and during the 1980s sales of bottled water in some parts of the United States increased by 500 per cent, a faster growth than for any other beverage.

In the UK, the poor are also the people who are least able to cope with the rising costs of water provision associated with government attempts to protect the water environment. Moves to reduce the level of pesticides in drinking water to below the legal limits are costing the water industry around £1 billion but these costs will largely be passed on to domestic consumers in their water bills. 'The polluted, rather than the polluter, is paying for this

Table 2.6 British concern about selected environmental issues by social class

% *very concerned about*	Social class	
	Non-manual	*Manual*
Disposal of sewage	71	67
Insecticides, fertilizers and chemical sprays	59	56
Quality of drinking water	52	50

Source: Young (1991).

clean-up' (Taylor 1996: 6). Difficulties faced by the poor in paying the costs of maintaining supplies of clean water do not imply a lack of concern about the environment. The British Social Attitudes Survey shows a high level of concern in Britain, not related to social class, about a range of environmental issues (Table 2.6).

A 1992 consultation document produced by the UK Department of the Environment gives a comprehensive summary of the environmental case and suggests measures to increase efficiency of water use. These include recycling and reuse in industry, the remedying of loss by leakage, using metering to reduce consumer demand and encouraging the development of water efficient appliances. The paper gives clear support to the metering of domestic supplies, arguing that this would reduce water companies' costs (and by implication, prices) by facilitating leakage detection, improving demand forecasting and strategic planning and saving water by reducing waste. It notes, however, that 'there is a risk that a very small proportion of water company customers could suffer some form or degree of hardship if they have to pay for water by volume.' It recognizes the need to consider 'possible ways of alleviating the kind of difficulties experienced by some households' (Department of the Environment 1992b).

Only 8 per cent of households in England and Wales are currently metered, paying for their water in relation to the amount used. The environmental argument for metering is that it provides incentives to use water more efficiently and to install water efficient appliances. Table 2.7 shows the average water consumption of domestic appliances used in Britain.

Consumption levels could be substantially reduced by, for instance, installing dual flush lavatory cisterns which can deliver a five litre instead of a ten litre volume of water at each flush. Instantaneous hot water systems and improved types of installation can contribute to savings in both water and energy use. Similarly, the use of showers rather than baths could save large amounts of water and energy, but only 25 per cent of domestic properties in England and Wales are fitted with showers (Department of the Environment 1992b). The problem is that buying and fitting new efficient domestic appliances incurs capital costs which families living on low incomes are unlikely to be able to afford without subsidized support. In New York, the

Table 2.7   Average water consumption of domestic appliances

Appliance	Litres of water consumed by each use
Automatic washing machine	100
Dishwasher	50
Lavatory flush	10
Bath	80
Shower	30

Source: Department of the Environment (1992a: 83).

local authority began to address the problems of water affordability for low-income groups in the late 1980s, with schemes to subsidize the replacement of old lavatories and to install low-flow showers (Environmental Data Services Report 257, June 1996). No such schemes have yet been introduced in Britain, although the Environment Act 1995 created a new duty on water undertakers in England and Wales to promote the efficient use of water by customers, with compliance to be policed by OFWAT.

Low-income households are less likely than the better off to have cars, large gardens or swimming pools, and consequently are less able to economize on 'luxury' water use. A recent report on the impact of metering on low-income families found that although 70 per cent were taking measures to reduce their use of water, these measures were mainly limited to sharing baths or bathing less frequently, washing clothes less often, flushing the lavatory less often and preventing children from playing with water. In addition to worries about health and hygiene, parents' anxieties about their water bills were placing unique pressures on family life (Cuninghame *et al.* 1996).

The effects of metering on household budgets depend of course on the tariffs used for charging. The House of Commons Environment Committee's inquiry into water conservation and supply in 1996 received evidence from the new Environment Agency which included the suggestion that imaginative metering tariffs could be devised to allow households sufficient water for hygiene at a low cost, with usage beyond this level being charged at a higher rate (Environmental Data Services Report 257, June 1996). It was also suggested that the social security system should make allowances for the payment of water bills. This, of course, would not be an option in many countries. Even in the UK, privatization of the water industry has raised important questions about how responsibility for ensuring that all citizens have adequate water supplies should be allocated.

Summary points

- Water is essential to all forms of life and plays a crucial role in shaping the natural environment. The provision of clean water supplies and facilities for the treatment and disposal of sewage improve public health and benefit, both individual and social well-being.

- Access to fresh water depends largely on environmental conditions, but is also governed by social factors. The availability and quality of natural supplies vary widely on a global and regional scale. The costs associated with abstracting, treating and delivering water to where it is needed for human consumption are not evenly distributed, and can result in marked inequalities in the extent to which different groups in society are able to obtain and utilize water.

- Modern sewage collection and treatment facilities are usually confined to developed, industrialized countries and high-income groups in poorer countries.

- The quantity of water abstracted for use in human activities can lead to problems caused either by excessive drying out of the natural environment or by flooding.

- Used water returned to lakes and rivers is often polluted and, depending on the nature of the contaminants it carries, can pose risks to human and environmental health and can reduce the amenity value of the countryside.

- The costs of water shortage, flooding and pollution usually fall most heavily on the more vulnerable groups in society. Affluent people can afford to take action to avoid the immediate impacts of environmental damage and can pay the price for high-quality water services. Poorer sectors of society, however, have fewer options open to them either to pay for services or to adapt their lifestyles to conserve water and protect the environment.

Chapter three
FOOD

Food, like water, is essential for maintaining human life in the most basic biological sense. But unlike water, food can mean different things to different people. The plump pink prawns adorning cocktails on British dinner tables are regarded with disgust by some groups of people in western Kenya, while the staple food of tapioca or cassava in eastern Indonesia appears to Westerners to resemble (and taste like!) pieces of dried up bathroom sponge. Even within cultures with shared ideas about what constitutes 'normal' food, we find varying preferences in taste and different views about which foods are better and which worse for human health.

The food people eat varies considerably and depends on a complex of social, cultural, financial, attitudinal, behavioural and biophysical factors (Lang *et al.* 1996). Social factors play a role in determining food preferences. A birthday cake for a child in the UK, for example, has a value which goes beyond simply taste, health and nutrition. It confers a sense of self-esteem on the child or family, signifying 'belonging' and conforming to the norms of a particular social group. The choice of food we eat reflects a complex combination of perceptions about what tastes good, what is nutritionally valuable and free from attributes which could cause health risks and what is regarded as culturally acceptable in a wider sense. It also depends on what is available and affordable, so that patterns of food consumption are conditioned by a wide range of environmental factors which determine what foods *can* be produced, and economic factors which influence what *is* actually produced and how it is priced.

Social aspects of food

Resource inequalities

Clearly, people's use of food is limited by the choices which are available to them, and these depend on their resources, not only in terms of the cash they have to buy food but also the facilities they have to store and prepare it in acceptable ways. Access to a meal of, say, fresh meat and vegetables depends on whether the basic ingredients are available and can be afforded, whether they can be stored hygienically in a cool place before cooking and whether a cooker and appropriate utensils are available to prepare the meal. Inequalities in resource distribution therefore influence the kind of foods which are consumed by different income groups.

The purchase of food and non-alcoholic drinks represented the largest single item of regular expenditure for British households in 1995–6. But whereas this accounted for only 15 per cent of all spending in the richest tenth of households, over a quarter of the expenditure of the poorest tenth was on food (Office for National Statistics 1996). A study of people living on low incomes in 1991 found that people interviewed talked at length about the difficulties of staying within their budgets when shopping for food; the problem of simply providing enough food for each meal was mentioned before any concern about nutrition, taste or variety. While some people were clearly aware of the importance of a healthy diet, they did not always find it possible to afford fresh food, although spare cash left after basic shopping was sometimes used to buy extra fruit and vegetables. People frequently spoke about having to go without food they or their children liked, such as fresh meat and vegetables, cheese and butter (Huby and Dix 1992). The research showed that families with children face the least flexibility in their food budgeting but, nevertheless, food is one area of expenditure which can be reduced in order to meet unexpected and immediate demands for other payments. Parents putting their children's needs before their own appeared to be common practice, with some parents reporting that they regularly missed meals or lived on snacks.

In the UK, monthly shopping is common in better off households, but people living on low incomes are more likely to shop weekly. 'Changes in the food economy, particularly the arrival of supermarkets, [have] altered the shopping and dietary options of the poor' (Lang 1997b: 220). A monthly 'shop' requires either a large amount of money or access to credit, and possession of adequate freezing and refrigeration space for food storage. For families living on low weekly wages or benefits a weekly 'shop' makes budgeting easier to control, but lack of money still limits the choice of food purchased. 'The kids live on things like fish fingers and, you know, the convenience foods that are really cheap to buy in bulk and if I had more money I would feed them differently' (mother, in Kempson 1996: 32).

Joffe (1991) also points out that the flexibility of food as an item of household expenditure means that people in low-income households sometimes miss meals for economic reasons. He adds that 'they also tend to eat more fatty and sugary foods which provide inexpensive calories, and less fruit, vegetables and high fibre foods compared with those from high income households' (Joffe 1991: 52). The type of food bought is clearly dependent on income. It is often less expensive to buy meat frozen from supermarkets than fresh from the butcher, and although fresh vegetables may be preferred, frozen ones are cheaper and produce less waste in the kitchen. Fresh fruit is often regarded as a luxury, while snack foods such as biscuits and crisps may be seen as a necessity, especially for children at school. 'Parents would go without food to ensure that their children were not seen to be eating differently from their peers' (Dobson *et al.* 1994: 5). This last point highlights the cultural importance of different kinds of food, and Dobson *et al.* found that most families distinguished between high-status and low-status foods. Their study showed that fresh vegetables, salad, fruit and good cuts of meat were regarded as high status but, because of their cost, were not eaten very often. For children, high-status foods were those eaten by other children: crisps, chocolate and biscuits; 'for them acceptability meant conformity' (Dobson *et al.* 1994: 32).

High incomes also influence patterns of food consumption, and convenience foods are increasingly eaten by rich and poor alike. In 1993, more than one-third of average household food bills were for ready-made meals (Raven and Lang 1995). However, whereas for poorer families convenience foods are restricted to those which are cheaper, such as frozen pies, sausages, pizzas and fish fingers, richer households use convenience foods to save time and purchase luxury items such as prepared exotic dishes. The first cook-chilled convenience meals were introduced in the UK by Marks and Spencer in 1981 and were Chicken Kiev and Chicken Cordon Bleu. By 1987, chilled meals accounted for 75 per cent of the company's food sales (Raven and Lang 1995).

As well as eating different kinds of food, for their taste, quality and status, richer people may eat more food than they need to remain healthy. Increasing income and wealth have been shown to be associated with increases in food consumption. An average citizen in a Western industrialized country eats food providing far more calories and protein than is necessary for basic biological maintenance. In 1994, 17 per cent of women and 14 per cent of men in England were estimated to be 'obese', and diet-related illnesses have become major medical problems (HMSO 1996a).

Resource inequalities on a global scale throw differences within industrialized nations into sharp perspective. Agricultural development has meant that world food production has grown faster than population, and 'current and emerging food production and preservation capabilities are sufficient to ensure an adequate global supply of safe nutritious food' (WHO 1992: 60). Nevertheless, it is estimated that nearly 800 million people in the world do not get enough to eat, and about 500 million people are chronically malnourished (United Nations Development Programme 1995). The supply of calories per person per day has increased on average since the 1970s, but the global average masks major regional differences. In parts of Sub-Saharan

Africa, for example, calorie supply per person has actually fallen over the period. 'Food production has kept up with population growth, but has not been equitably distributed either within households, within countries or between countries' (Lang 1996: 46).

Gender

Changing family structures and the growth of lone parenthood, together with increasing pressures on women to enter the labour market, have major implications for patterns of food consumption. Over half of the low-income households in Britain today are families with children, many of these headed by a lone parent, usually the mother. Within families, the provision of meals in the home is still generally regarded as part of the nurturing and caring role of women. Women therefore tend to take responsibility for choosing and buying food within the constraints of the household purse, but also within the time available to them. Changing roles of women in the labour market are important here, since shopping and cooking may have to be fitted in to periods between paid work and other household tasks. Ironically, the growth in food processing and other related industries in the UK has meant that many women are now employed in low-paid jobs preparing food for consumption in the homes of others (Tilly and Scott 1987).

Figure 3.1 Fast food cartons and soft drinks cans cause problems of litter on the banks of the River Ouse.

There is often little time available for lengthy food preparation in their own homes.

Women in rural areas in developing countries are less likely to be employed in the labour market but have additional demands on their time, since they are usually responsible for the collection of fuel and water for the household. In Nepal, for example, women spend around three hours a day preparing and cooking food but in addition may spend four or five hours collecting fuel, water and fodder for the animals on the farm (Jackson 1995). A study in Western Kenya showed that increasing scarcity of firewood meant that women had to spend more of their time finding fuel for cooking in the kitchen. They had less time to spare for their many other household and childcare tasks, and it was common to find stresses and tensions developing between members of the family as a result (Huby 1990).

The responsibility taken by women for feeding their families can be a severe burden when time or resources are in short supply. The choice between providing cheaper, poorer quality foods or simply eating less is a difficult one, especially when feeding growing children. 'They seem healthy enough, but my conscience is pricked all the time because I feel I'm not doing the best for them' (mother, in Kempson 1996: 32).

Changing patterns of food production

Pressures to increase world food production have arisen partly from the need to feed an expanding population but also from changing patterns in economic and trade relationships. Although per capita food production in developing countries rose by more than 20 per cent over the past decade, trends have been geographically uneven (United Nations Development Programme 1995). Increasingly, food produced locally is consumed elsewhere, reflecting the impact of world markets and consumer demand. We have seen above how both poverty and affluence can act to increase demands for different kinds of food. The poor need food which is cheap, while the rich are becoming accustomed to access to food from a wide range of different countries, giving them more choice and variation in their diets.

Changing demands for both cheaper and more varied food have led to intensification of food production techniques in agriculture, livestock rearing and fisheries. But in addition, they have led to increased temporal and spatial separation between the point of food production and the point of consumption, which entails more than simply changing the amount of food produced. In the 1990s, much of the food consumed in industrialized countries is pre-processed, packaged convenience food which has been transported some way from its original point of production and which often requires refrigeration or other special storage conditions. Intensification of food production methods means that more food can be produced more cheaply, but apparently cheap food production carries a number of hidden costs to the environment.

Intensification of agriculture

Cropland covers about one-sixth of the world's biologically productive land area (Middleton 1995). Since the 1950s, nearly 77 per cent of the land area in the UK has been used for farming, but agriculture now employs only 2 per cent of the total workforce. This represents a two-thirds reduction over 40 years, indicating the increased productivity of agricultural land (HMSO 1994a). In the 1980s, an average hectare of land in England produced three times the amount of wheat harvested in the 1930s (Middleton 1995). Improvements in productivity have been achieved through changes in farm practices, including the use of fertilizers and pesticides, irrigation and mechanized cultivation and harvesting. Fertilizers and pesticides in addition help to ensure the uniform growing conditions needed to produce food products of certain size and uniformity which are increasingly demanded by consumers.

Fertilizers. Under natural conditions, plants use energy from sunlight to convert atmospheric carbon dioxide and water into sugars for new plant growth. They also require certain essential mineral nutrients (for example, nitrogen, potassium and sodium), which they obtain from the soil. If soil nutrients are depleted plant growth is limited, but in natural cycles minerals are replenished as plant residues and animal waste products are returned to the soil and broken down by micro-organisms into their basic constituents. This process takes time, and when the same land is planted with crops season after season the soil has little time to recover. Old rotation methods of farming allowed for fallow periods and seasons in which leguminous crops such as beans or clover were planted. Legumes bear nodules on their roots within which bacteria convert atmospheric nitrogen to a form in which plants can use it. Traditionally, nutrient-rich animal manure was also spread on the land to fertilize it, but as farming has intensified and become more specialized, manure is not always available exactly where and when it is needed, and it is often cheaper and less labour-intensive for farmers to use manufactured chemical fertilizers instead.

The fertilizer industry is now big business. Over the past 25 years fertilizer use in the United States has trebled; in Denmark it has doubled and in the Netherlands it has increased by 150 per cent (OECD 1989). Worldwide, the production of chemical fertilizers increased from 0.77 million tonnes in 1913 to 85 million tonnes in 1990 (Middleton 1995). Manufactured fertilizers are relatively compact and are produced in dry form, so that they are cheap to transport and simple to apply, thus reducing costs to the farmer. However, their production and use incurs environmental costs which are borne elsewhere.

The mining of minerals used in fertilizer production results in land degradation in the mining areas. When they are actually used, rates of application often exceed the rates at which nutrients are taken up by plant roots, so that excess amounts are left in the soil. In wet conditions excess nitrogen and phosphorus are leached out of the soil and run off into streams and bodies of water where they may cause problems of eutrophication (Box 2.1). Some

Box 3.1 The ozone layer

Ozone is a gas made up of oxygen atoms. But whereas normal oxygen in the air consists of molecules each containing two oxygen atoms (O_2), each molecule of ozone contains three atoms (O_3). About 10 per cent of the earth's ozone is in the lower atmosphere, the *troposphere*, near to ground level where it can cause pollution problems. The remaining 90 per cent or so is present at 15 to 50 kilometres above the ground, in the part of the atmosphere called the *stratosphere*. Here it forms what is commonly known as the *ozone layer*, which substantially reduces the amount of ultraviolet (UV) radiation from the sun reaching the surface of the earth.

The total amount of ozone in the ozone layer at any one time is normally fairly constant, but individual molecules are continually being formed and destroyed. However, certain chemical substances speed up the rate of ozone destruction and, if this rate exceeds the rate at which new molecules are being formed, the amount of ozone present falls. The ozone layer becomes depleted and allows more harmful UVB radiation to reach the earth.

UVB radiation can cause some types of skin cancer and can suppress the immune system, making it easier for tumours to take hold and spread, as well as making people more vulnerable to infectious diseases. UVB exposure is also associated with eye disorders such as cataracts, and has adverse effects on plant growth, harming agricultural crops and trees and affecting marine life.

Ozone depletion and human activity

There is now evidence that the ozone layer is thinning all over the world. The main culprits are man-made chemicals which are so stable that they do not break down when released into the lower atmosphere. They are carried up into the stratosphere, where their eventual breakdown releases the substances which speed up ozone destruction.

The most well known of these chemicals are chlorofluorocarbons (CFCs), which are used in plastic foam packaging and insulation material, refrigerants, air conditioning, aerosols, solvents and dry cleaning products. CFCs are wholly man-made, but other powerful ozone depleters, such as the halons used in fire extinguishers, also have natural sources.

In 1987, the Montreal Protocol, an international agreement limiting the production and consumption of ozone depleting chemicals, was signed by over 100 countries. Later revisions and reviews set targets for the phasing out of production and use of the most damaging substances, but their long lifetimes mean that, even if future emissions could be eliminated immediately, present concentrations will persist in the atmosphere for much of the next century.

excess nitrogen may be released into the air in the form of nitrous oxide, a greenhouse gas (Box 1.1) which is also implicated in depletion of the ozone layer (Box 3.1). Finally, the presence of excess soil nutrients from artificial fertilizers actually inhibits the production of natural fertilizer by bacteria on the root nodules of legumes, so that ever increasing amounts of chemicals are needed to maintain plant growth.

Pesticides. Cultivating land for food production changes the natural environment and alters habitats, so that the original plant and animal species living there can no longer survive. A new, usually less stable, wildlife community develops alongside the growing crop. The crop is most often a monoculture, a single species of plant covering a large area, so it provides a rich nutrient source for any insect or fungus which can feed on it. Such species can therefore grow and reproduce at a rapid rate. Monocultures also provide a relatively homogeneous physical environment which is susceptible to invasion by any other species of plant that is able to coexist with the crop. Both insects and fungi feeding on the crop and other plants competing with the crop for water, nutrients and sunlight reduce the quality or yield of the crop for human consumption, and thus become 'pests'. The use of pesticides to kill or control these other species means that crop yields and quality can be improved. More high-quality food can be produced at lower prices.

Pesticides are, by definition, capable of biological damage. In particular concentrations and conditions they are toxic to living organisms. Problems arise when this toxicity affects organisms other than the pests which are the intended targets, and the extent to which this occurs depends on the amounts of the pesticide used, the method of application and its chemical nature. The chances of a pesticide causing unintended harm to other species, including human beings, depends on a number of factors: first, its persistence, or how long it stays in the pest organism or the environment before it is broken down to less toxic components; second, whether it accumulates in the food chain (Box 3.2), so that it harms not only the pest but anything which feeds on the pest and anything else which feeds on that; third, the concentrations which are needed to produce a toxic effect and the type of biochemical mechanism through which toxicity occurs; and finally, how far it is dispersed, whether it remains within the body of the pest or whether it is eventually transported into the water, soil or air environment.

Further problems arise when the action of pesticides disrupts the ecological balance: for example, when they destroy the natural enemies of pests so that the original pest problem is exacerbated, or when they destroy the natural predators of previously harmless species. These can then multiply at a faster rate and become pests themselves.

Irrigation.. Intensive food production often involves the growth of more than one crop a year on a particular area of land, or the use of greenhouses to provide controllable growing conditions. This divorce of crop production from natural seasonal cycles may require the building and operation of large-scale irrigation systems which themselves have negative impacts on the environment. On the one hand, excessive irrigation can lead to a rise in the water table, causing waterlogging and salinization, both detrimental to plant growth. When irrigation water runs off into streams and water bodies it carries with it leached fertilizer and pesticides causing pollution. On the other hand, the abstraction of water for irrigation can lead to ground water depletion in the areas from which it is taken.

Box 3.2   Food chains

All living organisms need to obtain food in some form to provide energy for growth, reproduction and cell maintenance. Plants manufacture their own energy source through *photosynthesis*, using energy from sunlight to convert carbon dioxide and water directly into carbohydrates, releasing oxygen in the process. Plants also need certain mineral nutrients for growth, but they do not depend on existing organic material from other living organisms and are consequently known as *primary producers*.

The herbivores which feed on plants and the carnivores which feed on other animals are collectively known as *consumers*. Energy flows from the sun to primary producers and then, in the form of food, to consumers.

Dead producers and consumers and their waste and excretory products in turn form food for other organisms, known as *detritivores* and *decomposers*. In breaking down organic matter to obtain energy, these organisms release inorganic mineral nutrients into the environment, where they are again taken up by plants. This whole cycle of interdependency is called a *food chain*.

A simple example of a food chain

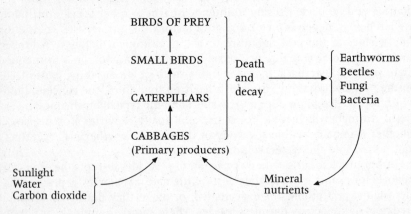

Of course, the real world is never this simple. Cabbages are eaten by many other species as well as caterpillars, and these are in turn eaten by a wide range of carnivores. A food 'chain' is really a complex web through which energy flows between living organisms.

Mechanization.   As agriculture becomes more intensive, human and horse power is replaced by farm machinery, speeding up tasks such as ploughing, planting and harvesting. However, the building and operation of machines requires the use of fossil fuels, producing carbon dioxide and other exhaust emissions which pollute the air and contribute to the greenhouse effect (Box 1.1). Large machinery can operate most effectively on well drained, large areas of land and its increased use has been accompanied by the drainage of wetlands, the ploughing up of old grassland and the removal of trees and hedgerows. In England alone, 85,000 kilometres of hedgerows are estimated to have been lost between 1984 and 1990. This loss of natural habitats leads to changes in wildlife communities and many species are declining in numbers in the UK in intensively farmed agricultural areas. Linnets, for example, are small birds which rely for their food on the seeds of weeds growing in arable areas. In recent years their clutch size, the number of eggs laid by each female, has been declining, and there are fears that the viability of the species is at risk. 'Farming that becomes so efficient, squeaky-clean with weed-free landscapes, ultimately leads to a bird-free countryside, empty of wildflowers, butterflies, grasshoppers and birdsong' (Royal Society for the Protection of Birds 1996: 20). The RSPB estimates that over half the populations of skylarks and song thrushes in the UK have been lost in the past 25 years, and the organization is pressing for reforms to achieve environmental goals and reduce agricultural intensification.

Intensification of livestock production

Changing demands for food have also had their impact on livestock farming. In the industrialized world, livestock products constitute 30 per cent of human calorie intake, compared to less than 10 per cent in developing countries (Middleton 1995). As incomes rise, demand for meat and meat products also tends to increase, and livestock farming is intensified.

Intensification of livestock production raises some complex ethical issues and considerations about animal welfare and factory farming, but it also causes its own environmental problems, which are reaching acute levels, for example, in the densely populated south and east Netherlands. In these relatively infertile sandy soil areas, rural families have traditionally farmed pigs. Over the generations children have inherited equal shares in family farms, so that individual farm sizes have gradually decreased and farming methods have become more intensive. Animals are kept in heated buildings and are fed mechanically, using energy from fossil fuels, with concomitant emissions of greenhouse gases to the atmosphere. The drainage of land and building of roads to transport materials into and out of the farms also uses energy, destroys natural habitats and reduces biodiversity (Box 3.3).

Manure produced by farm animals must be disposed of, but its high proportion of mineral and nutrient content increases risks of pollution of watercourses, affecting river and coastal fisheries and posing a threat to supplies of clean drinking water. The smells emanating from manure affect the living and working environment of the local population and have had adverse effects on recreation and tourism in the area (Bolsius and Frouws 1996). The rearing of animals in artificial conditions also creates the need to produce feed, usually in the form of cereals and fish meal concentrates, putting more pressure not only on agricultural production but also on the fishing industry, as described in the following section. In confined spaces animals become susceptible to the spread of disease, and feed is often supplemented

---

Box 3.3   Biodiversity

The number of different species of organisms living in a particular area or ecosystem is known as its *species richness*. Individuals of these species may be present in similar numbers, or it might be that a few species are present in large numbers, while others are represented by only one or two individuals. Technically, *biodiversity* is a combined measure of both the species richness and the evenness of an ecological community. As a popular term, however, it is often used to mean simply global species richness or 'the variety of life on earth or any given part of it' (HMSO 1994a: 237).

At the 1992 Earth Summit in Rio de Janeiro, the UN Biodiversity Convention, signed by 160 countries, recognized the importance of biodiversity, in the context of sustainable development, by seeking to ensure the protection of species and habitats for future generations.

Loss of species resulting in a decline in biodiversity is a cause for concern, not only among those people who believe that all living things have an intrinsic value in themselves or among those who take pleasure in the rich complexity and variety of the natural world. High levels of biodiversity also bring more concrete benefits because of the dependence of human beings on other species for a range of basic necessities, including food. 'Overall the economic benefits from wild species to pharmaceuticals, agriculture, forestry, fisheries, and the chemical industry adds up to more than $87 billion annually – more than 4 per cent of the US gross domestic product' (French 1995: 175).

The cost of species extinction and reduction of biodiversity can be calculated as an actual loss of the world's resources, but it also represents a loss of potential resources: for example, in the development of medicines or new strains of food crops from wild plants.

Finally, loss of biodiversity can have indirect effects on human well-being. Complex interrelationships between living organisms are still imperfectly understood, but it is possible that a reduction in numbers of certain species may impact on ecological processes, disturbing the balance of nature and leading to unforeseeable environmental change.

---

by medicines which persist in manure wastes and add to the problems of waste disposal.

Intensification of fisheries

Fish represent a potentially renewable and valuable human food source but, as with land-based food production, pressures to increase productivity have led to rapid changes in the way fish are harvested. Industrial fisheries now take over 50 per cent of all fish landed from the North Sea, and although 599,000 tonnes of fish were landed in the UK by UK vessels in 1992, a further 731,600 tonnes were imported. The capacity of industrial ships to increase catches has led to the over-fishing of many species, depleting stocks to unsustainable levels. Indiscriminate methods of fishing tend to kill many immature fish, and populations are unable to reproduce at a fast enough rate to replenish the stocks removed. In the 1960s and 1970s, for example, the North Sea herring and mackerel fisheries collapsed completely. The mackerel have never recovered and even though herring stocks recovered briefly following a ban on fishing, they still remain at dangerously low levels in the 1990s.

Industrial methods of fishing do not only affect fish destined for direct human consumption. Sandeels, for example, are tiny fish which swim in vast shoals in the bottom waters of the sea. Their concentrated distribution makes them easy prey for industrial fishing vessels which use ultra-fine nets and operate like giant 'hoovers' to catch the fish in vast numbers. The sandeels are processed into industrial fish oils, used in a wide range of human food products, including cheap soft margarines. The solids are processed to make the meal concentrates increasingly demanded by the intensive livestock industry to feed pigs, chickens and cows. However, sandeels provide a major source of food for other fish, such as whiting, cod and haddock, and also for dolphins, seals and whales and many species of wild birds. In the breeding season puffins rely on sandeels for 90 per cent of their diet. Large-scale removal by industrial fishing is likely to have dramatic effects on other marine and maritime animals.

Detrimental effects on wildlife are also caused by the incidental capture of birds and marine mammals in fishing nets, and the heavy beam trawls and dredges used by some industrial vessels can have damaging long-term effects on life on the sea bed.

Fish farming is not a new technique but, like other methods of food production, it has intensified in recent years, especially in developing countries. In 1995, aquaculture was responsible for 13 per cent of global fish production, with China producing about half of the global total. Fish are reared in a series of ponds or cages and are provided with food and protection from predators and disease. In some cases fish farms can be environmentally beneficial in providing a sink for waste disposal. Sewage and farm wastes can be used to encourage the growth of algae, which are then eaten by the fish. However, in more intensive systems, fish farms themselves produce wastes which cause problems of effluent discharge into surrounding waters, and such wastes are often polluted with chemical compounds, introduced to the system to control pests and disease. The abstraction of water from surrounding areas to supply the ponds can have negative environmental impacts, and the siting of the farms can lead to loss of local amenity because of their appearance.

Processing and packaging

Food which is grown at any distance from its point of consumption often needs to be processed to prevent deterioration. At the same time, rises in the extent of food processing are attributable to market forces. Where the food industry is unable to increase its share of the market by increasing the amount of food supplied, it focuses on diversifying its products by processing food in a variety of ways (Joffe 1991). A visit to even a small supermarket in the UK reveals an enormous range of, for example, frozen foods, meat products, snacks and breakfast cereals, which differ from one another not so much in their nutritional content as in the way they are processed and packaged. The food processing industry has environmental impacts largely because of the massive amounts of organic waste it generates, but it is also a major user of energy. Only 45 per cent of the energy used to produce an average loaf of bread is consumed on the farm, and the figure for a tin of sweetcorn is even lower at 15 per cent.

Processed food must be packaged appropriately for storage and distribution. Big supermarkets rely on large-scale industrial production of food products, long-haul freight transport and extended shelf-lives for food, all of which entail the use of vast quantities of packaging material. Packaging may increase sales by making food look more attractive to consumers, and supermarkets also benefit from improved efficiency at the point of sale, where packaged food does not need to be weighed and priced at the till. For consumers, packaging offers an assurance of hygiene, odour containment and the protection of perishable fresh foods. They may benefit from the provision of information on packaging, describing not only the contents of the product but also how and for how long it should be stored. Recipes and ideas for serving the product also often appear on packaging.

Ironically, one often quoted benefit to consumers of packaged food is that it saves waste. True, there is little organic waste present in packaged and processed food, but this is usually because any natural packaging such as skin or peel has been discarded at processing plants which generate large volumes of effluent containing carbohydrates, proteins and fats. Substitute wrappings are inert and odour free, and become invisible to the consumer once they have been thrown in the rubbish bin for municipal collection. In the United States, packaging is estimated to constitute 43 per cent by weight of all municipal solid waste (Cairncross 1993) and over two-thirds of packaging is now used to protect food and drink (Raven and Lang 1995). 'In Britain an estimated 90 per cent of food packaging bought by an average family each week is thrown away after a single use' (Lang 1995: 5).

It is the very qualities which make materials suitable for packaging that pose problems for waste disposal. The huge diversity of plastics provides a wide potential for their use, preserving food products and often extending their shelf-life from a few days to several weeks or more. They are manufactured as flexible thin film packaging, as thicker, high barrier films for vacuum packing, as tough bottles for drinks or cooking oils and as foam food trays, cups or hamburger boxes. They are relatively unbreakable, may be clear or opaque, smooth or textured, white or coloured; they are shapeable, moisture resistant, lightweight and long-lasting. Importantly, they are cheap to produce, with the result that they can be thrown away at little immediate cost to the consumer. The high bulk of plastic wastes is becoming increasingly problematic as pressures grow to limit and regulate the extent and content of landfill sites in the UK. But the environmental problems stemming from methods of disposal, as well as those resulting from production processes, vary with the chemical composition of the form of plastic concerned. Many plastics are selected for use in packaging because they do not biodegrade or break down readily, so that they remain unaltered in landfill for many years. On the other hand, incineration of plastic waste threatens air quality, especially in the case of certain polystyrene foams which release gases that can damage the ozone layer (Box 3.1) and PVCs which can release highly toxic compounds such as dioxins.

Aluminium is a popular form of packaging, ideal for making trays for frozen foods or bakery products and for caps, liners and lids for both dry and moist foods. Its suitability stems not only from its malleability but also from the fact that it is impermeable, greaseproof, non-absorptive and inert, the very properties which make it slow to oxidize and degrade and render its disposal a problem. Recycling is potentially possible but usually limited to cans, since foils are difficult to separate out at household level. Paper waste is likewise all potentially recyclable but, apart from newspaper, most paper waste goes to landfill sites, where its light weight makes it the source of extensive litter problems (Stilwell *et al.* 1991).

Environmental problems posed by packaging occur at the stage of production as well as at the stage of disposal. Mining wastes are generated during excavations for the aluminium, iron and tin used in the manufacture of cans and during the extraction of oil for making plastics. Forests are harvested to provide much of the wood fibre used in making paper and cardboard, while the chemical processes of pulping and bleaching pollute both air and water environments. The packaging industry as a whole is energy intensive and currently accounts for 5 per cent of energy consumption in the UK (Raven and Lang 1995).

Transport and storage

The effects of changing patterns of food production and consumption on energy use are also reflected through the impacts they have on transport. In industrialized countries even the most perishable goods are transported for hundreds of miles from producer to consumer. 'The average European weekend shopping trolley contains goods that have already travelled 4,000 km before we take them home' (Lang 1995: 14). In addition to this, more people than ever are travelling to shops by private car. More than three-quarters of the total mileage for shopping is by car, compared to only one in 14 miles on foot (Raven and Lang 1995).

This is at least partly attributable to the growth of out-of-town supermarkets. The convenience and price advantages they offer are, however, often beyond the reach of people living on low incomes, especially lone parents, people with disabilities and pensioners. In the UK, there is a strong correlation between social class and distances travelled for shopping. In the professional and managerial social groups, fewer than 25 per cent of shoppers travel less than one mile, compared to more than 40 per cent of those in the unskilled manual social class (Raven and Lang 1995).

Storage of food, during its transport from producer to retailer, during its life in the shop and during its time in the home, increasingly requires the use of freezing or refrigeration. This once again has environmental implications because of the use of energy, but also because most of the stable, non-flammable, non-toxic compounds used as coolants in refrigerators are capable of damaging the ozone layer when appliances are disposed of at the end of their lives.

Sustainability of food production systems

The need to produce more food to feed a growing world population and demands for different kinds of food have resulted in changing techniques of food production in agriculture, livestock farming and fisheries. Together with the associated growth in food processing, packaging and distribution industries, these are affecting the environment in ways which raise questions about the long-term sustainability of food production.

Land becomes unavailable for agricultural use when it is physically degraded by mining to obtain raw materials for the manufacture of fertilizers and other agro-chemicals. Its productivity declines when soil erosion occurs as a result of the clearance of trees and hedgerows to allow easier access for heavy farm machinery, or as a result of large-scale deforestation to provide wood pulp for the paper packaging industry. Extensive irrigation in some areas produces soil compaction, waterlogging and salinization, while abstraction of water either for irrigation or to supply fish farms can lead to disturbance of the water table, loss of water and even desertification in surrounding districts. Toxic pollution of land by pesticides can cause severe problems both for future land use and for food contamination. Pesticide use in Romania increased from 5900 tonnes in 1950 to 1.2 million tonnes in 1985, leaving more than 900,000 hectares chemically polluted, 200,000 hectares of which were excessively affected by pesticide toxicity (Turnock 1993). Pesticide pollution also causes problems for livestock production. The Ministry of Agriculture, Food and Fisheries (MAFF) in the UK is currently investigating the occurrence of the pesticide lindane, which has been found to be present at levels above recommended limits in milk and milk products (The Food Commission 1996).

Pressures on land arise from increased demands for landfill sites for waste disposal and road-building to provide the transport infrastructure for servicing the food industry. As these pressures grow, the land left available for agricultural production will necessarily be more marginal and further away from centres of population. It will be increasingly costly to develop and increased costs of food production will ultimately have to be met by consumers.

Food production systems contribute to anthropogenic or man-made emissions of greenhouse gases (Box 1.1), including methane produced by farm animals, landfill gases and nitrous oxide from chemical fertilizers. The major contributor, however, is the carbon dioxide emitted during the burning of fossil fuels to supply energy to run farm machinery, heat intensive livestock buildings, process food, produce packaging materials, run refrigeration equipment and transport food products, not only within the food and retail industry but also from retailer to kitchen. 'The large reduction in health risks from food contamination in the developed world owes much to improved food handling, storing, packaging and cooking, all of which are dependent on fossil fuels or electricity' (WHO 1992: 147).

Although current predictions of climate change resulting from increasing emissions of greenhouse gases to the atmosphere suggest that conditions for agricultural productivity will be improved in some parts of the world, they will be worse in others. Geographical patchiness is likely to result in differential effects on both the amounts and type of food which can be produced, depending on exact patterns of temperature, rainfall and length of growing season. However, it is developing countries in the South which are likely to experience the greatest reduction in plant productivity, 'and this loss of production, combined with rising agricultural prices, is predicted to increase the number of people at risk from hunger in the order of 5 to 50 per cent depending on the climatic scenario' (Middleton 1995: 107). Plant growth will also be affected by increased levels of solar ultraviolet radiation reaching the earth's surface as a result of the loss of stratospheric ozone. CFCs, chemicals known to be implicated in the depletion of the ozone layer, have for many years been used in the food industry to produce polystyrene foam containers and as coolants for freezers and refrigerators.

The environmental impacts of food production are not limited to the land. Both marine and freshwater fisheries are susceptible to toxic pollution of the aquatic environment by pesticides, fish farm effluents and the chemicals and bleaches used in the paper packaging industry. Less directly, fish populations may be affected by lack of oxygen where waters have become eutrophic (Box 2.1) as a result of excess nutrient inputs from agricultural run-off, waste from intensive livestock farming, fish farm effluents and organic wastes from food processing plants. Where over-fishing reduces stocks to unsustainable levels, fisheries may collapse completely. Environmental disturbances in both terrestrial and aquatic ecosystems can alter the balance of natural food chains, often with unforeseen consequences for human food production. As species diversity is reduced, the capacity to develop new food species declines, placing limits on the potential of science and technology to resolve problems of food supply.

Social implications

The previous section has painted a gloomy picture of the potential impacts of current methods of food production on the environment and consequently on the possibilities for sustainability. Socially, the costs of environmental constraints on food production will be distributed unevenly, with the poor bearing a disproportionate burden. Lower incomes allow less choice in buying food, partly because of prices and partly because of the barriers they place on travelling to cheaper shops. So, if food prices rise as a result of increased production and energy costs, the poorest will suffer first. They will have to consume less food or food of poorer quality.

This is already the case in some parts of the world. In Nigeria and the Ivory Coast, for example, intensification of land use initially led to increased productivity, but over time soils became degraded and the removal of vegetation, and erosion by water and wind, ultimately resulted in desertification and loss of land available for growing food (Dixon *et al.* 1989). Further losses occur when land use is diverted to produce grain for livestock feed. Although this meets the demands for meat and meat products in high-income countries and among the more affluent sectors in developing countries, it also means that less land is available to grow the vegetable and cereal products which form the major part of the diets of poorer households. 'Chronic hunger is due less to food shortage than to lack of purchasing power or of land on which food can be produced, or disruption of food distribution systems by civil unrest or violence' (WHO 1992: 60). Similarly, acute food shortages or famines rarely occur simply because of harvest failure, but result from the interplay of complex social, economic and political forces influencing the distribution of food. The poor lack the resources to buy in food from alternative sources (Thomas and Middleton 1994; Sen 1995).

The poor suffer the effects of changing patterns of food production not only as consumers but also when they are producers themselves. During the 1960s, for example, attempts were made to solve the problem of inadequate food supplies in developing Asian countries by introducing more intensive farming methods and new technologies – the Green Revolution. New genetic varieties of cereal seeds were produced, capable of very high yields when grown under the right conditions. High levels of fertilizer and irrigation were required and pest control essential, since the new seeds were less resistant to disease than traditional varieties. The results were impressive, with India, for example, doubling its wheat production over a six-year period. It soon became apparent, however, that the benefits of the Green Revolution were distributed anything but evenly. Only richer farmers with money or access to credit were able to take advantage of the new seeds, since only they could afford the necessary investments in fertilizers, irrigation systems and pesticides. Consequently, while these larger farmers reaped the benefits of intensification and increased yields, poorer, smaller farmers actually became worse off.

More recent examples can be found in Western industrialized countries, where new intensive methods of farming also require increasing financial investment. Larger farms have increased in number, out-competing smaller family-owned farms. In the United States in 1940 there were 6,400,000 farms with an average size of 170 acres. By 1990 the number of farms had decreased to 2,100,000, but the average farm size was 460 acres (Seitz 1995).

The effects of environmental protection policies on employment are the subject of much debate (Barde and Potier 1996; Tindale 1996). It has been estimated, for example, that the alleviation of the severe environmental problems caused by intensive pig-farming in the Netherlands would require a decrease of production of five million pigs a year and would mean the loss of 28,000 jobs locally in the agricultural, industrial and service sectors. On the other hand, environmental protection is often required to sustain levels of employment. The fishing industry in the UK employs 24,200 fishermen as well as 32,600 people working in ancillary industries (HMSO 1994a). We have seen how large-scale fishing of sandeels in the North Sea is having adverse effects on marine life, but the livelihoods of people are also threatened. 'If you haven't got sandeels you haven't got fish. If you haven't got fish you haven't got seabirds and mammals. But more importantly, if you haven't got fish the fishermen go hungry. It's as simple as that' (*East Lothian Courier* 3 May 1996). If there are no fish there are also implications for the food processing industry. Unilever, which controls 25 per cent of the frozen fish business in Europe, stopped using the industrial fish oil derived from sandeels in its products in April 1996, aware that if stocks of cod and haddock collapsed, its £600 million business would be placed in jeopardy (Greenpeace 1996).

Changes in food production have had their impacts even within households. When Lang *et al.* (1996) explored attitudes and behaviour with regard to cooking by analysing the UK Health Education Authority's 1993 Health and Lifestyles Survey, they found major differences based on income, gender and social class. Increasing dependence on pre-processed food is leading to 'deskilling' at household level. Lang (1995) discusses the social and economic background to the transfer of the cooking process from home to factory, and points out that 'now in western societies, generations are being produced where there are few or even no cooking skills' (Lang 1995: 10).

Another impact on cooking practices, this time in response to shortage of fuel for cooking, was apparent in a study of poor rural households in western Kenya. Women in these households, solely responsible for the time-consuming task of collecting firewood, had a sophisticated knowledge regarding the qualities of different kinds of wood. Their preferences were related to their needs for cooking different kinds of food; some types of wood gave more intense heat while some burned slowly and were better for fires used for simmering food. The increasing scarcity of supplies, however, meant that often little choice of firewood was available. Women collected what they could from bushes and hedgerows and bought from local markets when the price was low enough. Sometimes they could find nothing but agricultural residues, dried maize cobs or sugar cane stalks, which made poor cooking fires and also reduced the amount of organic material returned to the land. Where shortages were most acute women were even beginning to change their cooking practices. They cooked fewer hot meals, chose more foodstuffs with shorter cooking times or cooked in bulk on the morning fire so that meals only required briefly heating up later in the day (Huby 1990).

Food is produced locally, regionally and globally in different parts of the world and for different markets. But in general there is increasing geographical and temporal separation of the point of production from the point of consumption. Consumers are less aware of how the food they eat is actually produced, and are thus more susceptible to fears and uncertainty about food value and safety. Direct sensory information used in choosing fresh food (for example, feeling fruit to test its ripeness) has been replaced by information supplied, not always in a comprehensible or comprehensive form, on the outside of packaging. The increased use of synthetic additives and preservatives and the attractiveness of the packaging makes it harder to judge food quality from its appearance. Responsibility for ensuring particular levels of food quality is increasingly delegated to the supplier.

People rely largely on the media for information about health and diet, but this means they are also exposed to the power of advertisers whose allegiance is to the food industry rather than the consumer. The disempowerment of consumers is reflected in the confusion surrounding recent food scares in the UK, the most recent being the fear that bovine spongiform encephalopathy (BSE) or 'mad cow disease' in cattle can be transmitted in beef to humans in the form of Creutzfeldt-Jakob disease (CJD). BSE has provided 'a timely reminder of what can happen when public health measures break down in any state' (Lang 1996: 48). Current scientific uncertainty means that 'experts' are unable to give any categorical assessment of the risks from eating beef, and politicians are able to interpret the evidence which does exist to suit their own political ends. This all compounds the confusion of consumers who lack the direct information and evidence with which to make their own rational decisions. All too often, in poor households, these decisions are based not on well informed judgements about health risks but on the cost of beef on the supermarket shelf.

The growing separation between consumers of food and food production is a result of social and economic processes and relations. Food security is not simply a matter of growing sufficient food, but depends on how it is distributed. This in turn is affected by balances of power and trade in the modern political economy of food. As markets have expanded globally, food policy has moved up the political agenda, but at the same time 'a new baronial food class is emerging' (Lang 1997a: 16). A single company currently controls 60 per cent of the world cereal market, and the top ten agro-chemical companies account for 94 per cent of the world market. Lang (1997a) outlines the need for the development of food policy, which not only incorporates food production, processing and retailing, but takes on board concerns about advertising and education with regard to food, environmental and public health, and considers the roles states should play at international, regional and local levels.

. Many current methods of food production and supply raise issues which are both social and environmental. Not only do they threaten the natural productivity of ecosystems through pollution and resource depletion, but they pose risks to human health, exacerbate poverty and inequality and reduce for many the quality of life through their damaging effects on wildlife habitats. 'Even in the rich world, the possibility of feeding people well in a socially just and environmentally sustainable manner is fracturing before our eyes' (Lang 1997a: 224).

Summary points

- A wide range of social and cultural factors influence people's attitudes to food. Diets are influenced by the kinds of food and cooking facilities available, and income plays a large part in determining consumption patterns.
- Within families it is usually women who take responsibility for buying and preparing food, but their choices are often constrained by both money and time.
- Changing demands for different amounts and types of food have led to an intensification of agriculture, with increased use of agro-chemicals such as fertilizers and pesticides, as well as more abstraction of water for irrigation and increased reliance on mechanized farming methods. Pressures have also grown for more intensive livestock production and industrialized fishing techniques.
- Food is increasingly produced at greater distances from where it is consumed, and this means that more processing, packaging, storage and transport is necessary.
- These changes raise questions about the sustainability of modern food production methods which are resulting in environmental damage and bringing increasing risks to public health.
- At the same time the political economy of food, in which international trade plays a key role, places disproportionate amounts of power in the hands of the food industry. In the absence of any integrated food policies, citizens are treated merely as consumers for whom 'consumer choice' has little real meaning.

Chapter four

HOUSING

People's basic needs for housing vary according to the climate in which they live, but also according to personal and social factors such as age, health and the kinds of living conditions seen as 'normal' in the society in which they live. The very young and the very old are particularly vulnerable to the cold, and housing provides physical shelter from the elements and living space which can be heated during cold periods of the year. However, in the English language, a home means much more than simply a house. A home is a place which ideally provides less tangible elements of well-being, such as a sense of security, comfort and a pleasant environment – a sense of place and belonging. The types of dwellings available for people in which to make their homes are different in different societies, and within societies there are inequalities in the extent to which shelter, in the form of adequate housing, can be found.

> In virtually all countries, the needs of a proportion of the population for shelter and basic services are not met. Some 600 million urban dwellers and more than 1000 million rural inhabitants live in life-threatening and health-threatening houses and conditions characterized by over-crowding and lack of basic services such as piped water, sanitation, and health care.
>
> (WHO 1992: 198)

In this chapter we shall see how social divisions affect access to housing, how the construction and use of different kinds of housing have different impacts on the environment and how these impacts fall differentially on different social groups, reinforcing existing inequalities.

Inequalities in housing provision

Inequalities in housing across the world reflect inequalities in income and wealth. Although the contrasts between rich and poor are often more marked in developing countries, they are still in evidence in so-called developed countries, where access to affordable housing of adequate size and in a reasonable state of repair varies enormously with income levels. On average, the size of houses in industrialized countries has increased over the past 50 years, but the average number of people living in each household has fallen (Lenssen and Roodman 1995).

In the UK in 1994, the stock of permanent housing was estimated as 24.2 million dwellings (Wilcox 1996), but the number of households is expected to increase at a faster rate than the population over the next 20 years, putting pressure on housing provision. Between 1991 and 2011, the population of England is projected to grow by 5.3 per cent, compared to a projected growth in the number of households of over 18 per cent (Office for National Statistics 1997). The discrepancy between the projected growth rates for numbers of people and numbers of households comes about because the average number of people in a household is falling, owing to both demographic and social change. More people are living alone, partly because of increasing life expectancy and partly because of a shift towards the provision of care services for the elderly and people who are ill or disabled in their own homes rather than in institutions. At the same time, rising rates of relationship breakdown and divorce and reduced rates of remarriage mean that more small households are being formed.

While some dwellings are owned by their occupiers, others are rented either privately or from the social housing sector, owned by local authorities or housing associations and supported by some form of public subsidy. Table 4.1 shows that at the end of the 1980s the UK had a relatively high proportion of social rented housing compared with many other industrialized countries. Social housing still accounted for 23.5 per cent of dwellings in the UK in 1994, 19.6 per cent provided by local authorities and 3.9 per cent by housing associations. In the mid-1970s, social housing was occupied by a fairly broad mix of income groups. Only the top income quintile had fewer than 25 per cent of members in social housing, and no group had more than 50 per cent (Social Security Advisory Committee 1995). By 1994–5, however, 58 per cent of the lowest income decile were living in local authority or housing association accommodation (Wilcox 1996).

Increasing demand for affordable housing restricts access, and the poor have fewer choices than the rich about the types of dwelling and the kinds of housing environment in which they live. UK local authority housing is allocated according to various priority systems based on administrative judgements about need, and it is only those who can afford to wait until their preferred kind of accommodation becomes available who can exercise any choice. The result is that people who are least able to exercise a choice have to take properties that others are able to refuse, and so people who are

Table 4.1   Percentage distributions of the three main kinds of housing tenure in various societies

Country	Social rented	Private rented	Owner occupied	Year
Australia	5	25	70	1988
Belgium	6	30	62	1986
Denmark	21	21	58	1990
France	17	30	53	1990
Germany	25	38	37	1990
Ireland	14	9	78	1990
Italy	5	24	64	1990
Netherlands	43	13	44	1988
Spain	1	11	88	1989
United Kingdom	27	7	66	1990
United States	2	32	66	1980

Source: Hill (1996: 152).

Figure 4.1   Many people have little choice about their residential environments.
Photographer: © Robert Brook, 1993

Table 4.2 Changes in the conditions and amenities of dwellings in England, 1971–1991

	1971	1981	1991
% of dwellings lacking basic amenities	16.4	5.0	1.0
% of dwellings lacking central heating	69.9	43.0	16.0
% of dwellings classed as unfit by 1969 standards	7.5	6.2	4.1

Source: Department of the Environment (1993).

desperate and most in need are likely to receive the worst housing' (Spicker 1995: 162).

The increasing reliance of the poor on social housing therefore leads to concentrations of poorer households in the less desirable areas of towns and cities. This spatial segregation cuts many people off from work opportunities and leads to what Power (1994) describes as a 'spiral of decline'.

> It is generally recognised that such concentrations of people who may be predominantly poor, dependent and sometimes alienated can have undesirable results for society as a whole, exacerbating a cycle of poor health, unemployment, poverty, crime, drug dependence and other social ills which are not only unwelcome but create a need for even greater expenditure.
>
> (Social Security Advisory Committee 1995: 20)

The quality of existing housing in the UK has improved over the past 20 years (Table 4.2), but many of the poorest families still live in housing which is far from adequate. 'Living in damp, draughty homes, waiting for repairs, being overcrowded, are all ways in which poverty impinges on people's lives' (Oppenheim and Harker 1996: 82).

Not everyone has access to a permanent dwelling of any kind. The political encouragement of home ownership, the restriction of new building by local authorities and the deregulation of private rents in the 1980s all contributed to an overall decline in the availability of cheaper rented accommodation. 'Between 1991 and 1994 rents rose in cash terms by 43% for housing association new tenants, 41% for council tenants and 44% for private tenants' (Social Security Advisory Committee 1995: 19). High rents together with increasing numbers of mortgage repossessions have contributed to the growth in homelessness of many people on low incomes (Ford 1997). In 1995, 120,810 households in England were accepted as homeless by local authorities (Pleace *et al.* 1997). When people are accepted as homeless, priority is usually given to families with children, pregnant women and those who are vulnerable because of old age, ill health or disability. Consequently, the official count does not include many single people, couples without children or people sleeping rough or temporarily sharing accommodation with friends or relatives (Oppenheim and Harker 1996). Housing costs also pose growing problems in other parts of the world. In centrally planned economies such as those in Central and Eastern Europe, rents for public housing were in the past extremely low, 'and governments and enterprises bore most of the costs of construction, maintenance and utilities' (International Bank for Reconstruction and Development 1996: 61). With the transition to market economies, housing has been largely privatized. Rents are increasing and in remaining state housing most tenants are now charged for utilities and maintenance in addition to rent. Although some people are benefiting from transition, the countries of Central and Eastern Europe and the newly independent states are experiencing growing inequalities and a rise in levels of poverty.

In many developing countries, rural poverty has encouraged migration to cities, where the high cost of accommodation relative to incomes results in overcrowding and poor levels of services. 'Low income housing conditions in most parts of Africa, Asia and Latin America are horrifying to those of us living in developed countries' (Gilbert 1991: 259). The poorest sectors of the population are housed in tenement areas, often renting rooms shared with other families, or in shanty towns and self-help settlements with weak physical fabric and rudimentary infrastructure. Among the urban poor, home ownership can often be achieved only by self-building, the quality of which depends on access to land, services and building materials. Wood, bricks and corrugated iron must be purchased, usually at high prices, or scavenged from rubbish heaps. 'At least 600 million urban dwellers live in such poor quality housing with such inadequacies in the provision of water, sanitation, drains, garbage collection and other basic services that their life and health are continually under threat' (Satterthwaite 1994: 20). In the same cities, wealthy areas are characterized by luxurious homes with large gardens and swimming pools. Increasing social polarization in urban areas results in a startling 'juxtaposition between the new rich and the new poor' which has major implications for further social development (Burrows 1997).

Hong Kong, one of the most affluent economies in the world in terms of its GDP, has particularly marked housing problems. It has an exceptionally high population density, with 5308 people per square kilometre, compared to, for example, 234 people per square kilometre in Britain. Much of its physical geography is steep and mountainous, so that only a limited area of land is available for housing development and the main city is highly congested. Substantial income disparities among the population are reflected in very different forms of housing for different income groups. The shortage of land means that housing costs in the private sector are high, and even small flats are often prohibitively expensive. Those who cannot afford private housing must often wait for years before public housing becomes available, and in the meantime have to resort to alternative forms of accommodation, such as squatter huts or temporary housing. 'Squatters, in general, are among those with the lowest socio-economic status in Hong Kong, with the lowest household incomes and the lowest educational attainment' (Fai 1993: 104). At the end of 1990, it was estimated that around 307,000 people were living in makeshift squatter settlements in huts built wherever space was available.

'New structures could even be found under pedestrian bridges, next to gas storage tanks, and on the pavement' (Fai 1993: 104). In addition to squatters, a further 82,000 people were living in government provided Temporary Housing Areas in 1991, where living space is allocated at only 3.4 square metres per person (Choi 1993).

Urbanization and the environment

City housing has many potential advantages. The concentration of large numbers of people living in the same area minimizes the need for transportation of water, energy, materials, products and people, and economies of scale reduce the costs of the provision of basic utilities and services. Urban inhabitants have access to a variety of facilities and services such as shops, pubs, schools, doctors' surgeries and public transport, while the diversity of people and activities in the city offers exciting cultural and entertainment possibilities. The quality of urban life, however, depends not only on the goods and services available but also on the cleanliness and security of the city, on the extent of public green space and on the actual location and condition of homes and workplaces. The development of urban housing is limited by pressures on space. It is estimated that land in urban use in England will have increased from 10.2 per cent in 1981 to 11.0 per cent in the year 2001 (Department of the Environment 1992a). However, this increase only includes land transferred from agricultural use as city developments push outwards. Of land currently being developed for city housing in England, 36 per cent is estimated to have been developed previously. Much of the derelict land which could potentially be used for new housing is environmentally contaminated by the build up of waste gases from old landfill sites used for waste disposal or by toxic pollution from past industrial activities, such as gas works, metal extraction and mineral processing. Pressures on space for social housing are often greatest in areas where human activities have left behind a legacy of land which may be contaminated. 'All over Europe the past is tripping up the future. Wasteful, careless and dangerous industrial practices common when no-one cared or no-one was looking have created a swathe of derelict land' (*Innovations in Social Housing* no. 6, December 1993).

Even where derelict land can be used for housing development or where deteriorating buildings can be renovated, the benefits are not evenly distributed among the urban population. Slum clearance may improve the material standards of the wider society, but not necessarily improve the well-being of the hitherto slum dwellers. 'Where housing in previously depressed inner-city areas has become popular with owner-occupiers, prices are bid up, often forcing the existing population out of the market. Housing quality tends to improve, but the beneficiaries are not the original residents of the area and thus economic, social and environmental problems are not redressed but relocated' (Elkin and McLaren 1991: 206).

Table 4.3   Quality of housing environments by tenure in England, 1991

Problem experienced to a significant extent	Tenure type (%)				
	Owner occupied	Private rented	Local authority	Housing association	Vacant
Unkempt	1.1	3.6	7.5	5.4	9.1
Maintenance	3.4	5.1	3:4	4.0	5.0
Abandonment	1.0	2.1	1.7	3.0	3.8
Industry	0.4	0.4	0.6	0.1	0.4
Traffic	13.8	26.1	12.9	17.0	26.7
Noise	2.1	2.4	2.0	3.0	3.0
Dwellings in sample	12,994	1626	3859	606	640

Source: adapted from Department of the Environment (1993: 225–6).

Dobson *et al.* (1996) studied one UK city in detail and found that, like poverty, housing deprivation, largely due to overcrowding, was spatially clustered within the city, leading to what has been referred to as 'new social inequalities of place in contemporary society' (Cahill 1994: 185). The economic disadvantage of many city dwellers has led to their concentration in poor environments, characterized by areas of dereliction, property in need of repair, poor lighting, lack of public green space, intrusive traffic noise and air pollution and litter. In the UK, the English House Condition Survey (Department of the Environment 1993) classifies environmental problems of housing according to six criteria. First, housing may be in an *unkempt* area where there are problems with litter, rubbish dumping, scruffy gardens, vandalism or graffiti. The area may be in need of *maintenance* where roads, paths, pavements or street furniture are in poor condition. The third criterion relates to the degree of *abandonment* of the area and the extent of vacant sites and non-conforming uses of nearby shops or businesses. Where *industry* is based in or near to a residential area, industrial waste, pollution or noise may cause problems. Finally, *traffic* problems or nuisance caused by street parking may occur and further *noise* intrusion come from railways or aircraft. Table 4.3 shows that these problems are experienced to different degrees for dwellings with different types of tenure. Rented dwellings of any tenure type, for example, are more than three times as likely as owner occupied properties to be in unkempt areas while local authority housing is least likely to experience traffic problems, probably because of the relatively low levels of car ownership among the people living on social housing estates.

Urban growth is highest in lower income economy countries (Table 4.4), and even though poverty is unevenly distributed within countries, urban areas have a greater tendency to be more segregated in terms of poverty and wealth than do more rural regions (Green 1994).

The kinds of urban environmental problems confronting people living in other parts of the world are, in essence, the same as those described above

Table 4.4   Growth rates in urbanization, 1990–1994

	Average annual growth rate in urbanization (%)
Low-income economies	3.8
Middle-income economies	2.4
High-income economies	0.3
World	2.3

Source: International Bank for Reconstruction and Development (1996).

for city dwellers in the UK. However, these problems often become more severe in their effects where communities are living in greater poverty. In developing countries of the world, poor families often live in large clusters of dwellings built on land which is cheap because it is unsuitable for commercial development. Homes established on steep and often unstable hillsides or on flood plains or desert land are vulnerable to landslides, flooding and waterlogging, and occupants' lives and health are constantly at risk (WHO 1992). In Hong Kong, extreme overcrowding of residents in unsafe buildings means that the risk of fire must be added to these problems, and this has been the cause of some devastating tragedies in recent years.

Even where they are basically safe, housing environments can be perceived as poor because of the appearance of the houses themselves. In Albania, for example, 'in both urban and rural areas, such is the housing shortage that families are often moved into apartments and houses before the external decor is finished' (Hall 1993: 30). The shortage of building materials is compounded by problems of distribution, so that often buildings are never finished and present 'a very shoddy outward impression of such residential units.'

A survey in 1991 found that 22 per cent of households in England were unhappy about the amount of rubbish in the immediate areas around their homes (Department of the Environment 1993), but problems caused by the generation of litter and solid wastes are particularly marked in some cities in developing countries. Eighty per cent of solid wastes in Dar es Salaam, 66 per cent in Karachi and 30 per cent in Jakarta go uncollected, and even wastes which are collected go to open dumps or landfill sites (International Bank for Reconstruction and Development 1992). The lack of regulated waste disposal systems together with an absence of adequate sewerage facilities results in high levels of organic pollution, which can have serious effects on human health. Some '30–50% of solid waste generated in urban centres is left uncollected. It accumulates on streets and in open spaces between houses, causing or contributing to serious health problems. The poorer households suffer most since it is overwhelmingly in the poorer areas of cities that there are no services to collect garbage or the services are very inadequate' (WHO 1992: 211).

In some cities, however, the rich as well as the poor suffer from environmental pollution around their homes. A study in Houston, one of the richest cities in the United States, looked at the health of children living in two areas of the city in relation to levels of air pollution (Cerni 1993). The first residential area was situated close to a number of industrial plants where neighbourhoods were periodically affected by air pollutants and accidental spills of hazardous chemicals, and where atmospheric levels of ozone and sulphur dioxide were high. Households were also surveyed in a less polluted residential area about 20 miles from industrial and port facilities. Although children in both areas had a higher than expected incidence of ill health, a significantly higher number of families in the more polluted area reported ill health in children: 73 per cent, compared to 63 per cent in the less polluted area. This difference was not correlated with class, income or demographic variables, but appeared to be associated only with the locations of the two areas.

Rural housing

Rural areas in industrialized countries are often perceived as safer and healthier living environments than are towns and cities, and the nature of the countryside environment can improve the quality of life for some rural residents. A survey of lifestyles in rural England, for example, revealed that 'many respondents considered the pleasant aspects of their rural environment as a benefit of living in rural areas, and cultural assumptions about beauty were frequently embedded in descriptions of the area in which they lived' (Cloke *et al.* 1994: 154). Although some respondents expressed concern about ill health thought to be related to agricultural activities such as spraying crops with pesticides and fertilizers, the open rural environment was generally perceived as offering clean, fresh air as one of the benefits of country living.

Income inequalities, however, are just as much a feature of rural life as of life in towns and cities, and they result in large disparities in the types of housing and services available. Increasing numbers of rural dwellings are used as second homes by wealthier households. In 1995–6 there were 65,000 people in England with a holiday, weekend or retirement cottage (Office for National Statistics 1997). Because these people have permanent residences elsewhere, they have little need of local services, which consequently tend to decline. In the North York Moors, for example, 'some villages are now without any shops whatever, except perhaps a craft shop or cafe intended mainly for tourists. The larger villages may have a grocer and/or a Post Office but very few have a butcher, bakery or bank' (North York Moors National Park 1995).

On the other hand, many English villages have attracted incoming permanent residents from urban areas, particularly retired people seeking peace and quiet in their later years and more affluent younger working families. Keeble identified 'selective migration by managers, professionals and more highly qualified workers and their families from cities to smaller towns and villages, largely for quality of life and environmental reasons' (Keeble 1990:

240). This trend of 'gentrification' has pushed up the price of housing beyond the reach of many local people, and conflicts arise between the need to preserve the look and character of villages and the need to build more affordable housing (Statham 1991).

Substantial levels of unemployment and low average incomes combine to present particular problems for young people in rural areas who cannot afford to buy property and must compete for the limited supply of rented housing (Ford *et al.* 1996). Homelessness is less obvious in the country than in towns, but 'some 15,000 people per annum are being accepted as homeless in Britain's rural areas and there are grounds for believing that the real number of homeless was probably higher' (Cloke *et al.* 1994: 40). However, meeting demands for cheaper housing in the countryside has implications for the environment, as it often entails further encroachment of buildings on to hitherto undeveloped land. Attempts are being made to regenerate derelict land in cities, but it is recognized that 'some new housing will be needed on the edges of towns and villages, or in new self-contained settlements on green field sites' (HMSO 1994a: 159).

House construction and the environment

Housing development has effects on the environment in terms of land use, loss of amenity and waste production, and these effects are felt unevenly by different sectors of society. But the construction of housing, whether sophisticated homes for the affluent or the makeshift structures of wood, iron–zinc plates and asbestos roofing which are typical of shanty areas in many developing countries, in itself has environmental impacts. The building of homes and offices is estimated to consume between one-sixth and one-half of the world's physical resources: wood, minerals, energy and water (Lenssen and Roodman 1995).

Building purposes account for more than a quarter of wood used in the world, either directly as timber or to make plywood, chipboard or veneers. Its strength, light weight and easy transportability make wood ideal as a building material. Conifers, or softwood trees, grow relatively quickly even in harsh climates. The timber they produce is easier to work than hardwood, and is extensively used in house building, as well as for fencing, packing cases, railway sleepers and telegraph poles and for making paper and board. Hardwood, in contrast, comes from broadleaved trees, which take far longer to reach maturity, many species needing 80 to 150 years for full growth. This long 'production' time means that hardwood trees cannot be replaced quickly and this pushes up the price of hardwood timber. Although they are more durable than softwood, the higher price of hardwoods means that they are usually used for panelling and veneers and for furniture, rather than for basic structural purposes. Hardwoods are, however, used to produce long lasting doors and window frames, and these are often obtained at the expense of tropical forests. 'Over 2 million doors were imported into Britain from tropical countries in 1989' (Elkin and McLaren 1991: 34).

Some of the most valuable hardwoods used in furniture, such as ebony, mahogany, teak and rosewood, grow only in tropical rain forests. Their high prices partly reflect their scarcity, but this increases their value to commercial logging companies and is largely to blame for much forest destruction in tropical countries. Deforestation has both local and global impacts on the environment, affecting soil conditions, water relations, greenhouse gas production and biodiversity (Box 4.1). Some areas of forest are clear-felled to obtain timber, but even where selective logging of valuable trees is carried out, extensive damage to surrounding areas occurs in the process. It is estimated that only 1 or 2 per cent of the total forest area harvested reaches the export market. The remainder is used locally, burned or left to decompose.

The extraction of raw materials such as mineral ores, stone and cement for building necessitates quarrying and mining activities which, together with the heavy transport systems required for their distribution, can have negative effects on the wildlife and amenity value of the countryside. Damage caused to landscapes and wildlife habitats is often underestimated, however, since it is usually caused at some distance from the point at which the extracted materials are used, and even further from the homes where people enjoy their benefits.

Large amounts of energy and water are used in the manufacture of building materials such as brick, steel and glass, materials usually taken for granted in the industrialized world. But the manufacture of heavily processed materials for use in housing results in more obvious environmental damage. Copper, for example, is used extensively for pipes and electrical wiring. The United States alone uses 530,000 tons per year for these purposes, and this copper must be purified from low grade ores, producing massive amounts of waste ores or 'tailings'. In addition to the environmental problems posed by mining and waste production, the copper purification process releases toxic metals such as arsenic and cadmium, and sulphur dioxide, which contributes to acid deposition (Lenssen and Roodman 1995).

Some materials used in housing construction are wholly manufactured, often using material such as coal and coal products. Polyvinyl chloride (PVC), for example, is used in construction for window and door frames, pipes, panelling, gutters and cables, and is used inside housing in flooring, wallpaper, blinds and shower curtains. PVC creates environmental problems through the generation of numerous toxic pollutants which contaminate air and water both during production processes and when it is disposed of after use by incineration.

The manufacture, use and disposal of paints and chemicals for treating timber can also cause toxic pollution of land, water and air. Treatment processes can prolong the life of houses but, in Germany, for example, 'treated timber is defined as a toxic waste and has to be buried in a licensed tip. In Canada it has to be sealed for transport and disposal' (Elkin and McLaren 1991: 34). Some insulation and fire protection materials, air conditioning and refrigeration systems contain CFCs or other compounds capable of damaging

Box 4.1   Deforestation

Nearly one-fifth of the world's forests have been cut and cleared since 1950. Although, in the northern hemisphere, the deforestation which has occurred in the past has now largely been halted, in 1990 it was estimated that around one acre of tropical forest was being destroyed every second. Reasons for felling natural as opposed to managed forests can be attributed to both poverty and affluence. In some parts of the world where land resources are distributed unequally, small-scale farmers clear areas of forest for slash and burn style agriculture or shifting cultivation. On the other hand, the development of world trade in commodity goods has led to large-scale clearances of forests to make way for commercial crop plantations or ranch pastures for rearing beef cattle. Finally, international markets for timber encourage the activities of commercial logging companies, and rates of industrial logging have more than doubled since 1950.

Environmental effects

Mature natural forests form complex ecosystems in which many diverse species of plants and animals live in intricately interdependent relationships with each other and with the physical environment. The removal of trees from such areas consequently has wide ranging impacts.

The loss of tree cover exposes underlying soils to the action of rainfall, wind and sun. Soil is rapidly eroded, especially in tropical rain forests where topsoils are poor and thin and rainfall is heavy. Nutrients are leached away and this, together with soil compaction as the earth dries out in hot sunny periods, reduces the potential for further plant growth. Large quantities of water are stored in forest trees and returned to the atmosphere by evapotranspiration. The removal of trees therefore affects the hydrological cycle and, with accompanying changes in soil surfaces and drainage, can result in flooding or desertification depending on local conditions.

Trees also act as a reservoir for carbon, removed from the air as carbon dioxide in photosynthesis. The felling of trees not only depletes this reservoir but releases more of the greenhouse gas carbon dioxide when woody residues are burned or left to decompose. Deforestation therefore makes a twofold contribution to the greenhouse effect.

It is estimated that the deforestation of tropical moist forests leads to the extinction of 12,000 to 57,000 species each year. This reduction in biodiversity represents the loss of a rich source of genetic potential: for example, for the development of new pharmaceutical products or of new improved strains of food crops from forest species. Finally, but very importantly, the destruction of tropical forests can mean the loss of homes and livelihoods for indigenous forest people.

the ozone layer if they leak into the atmosphere during their lifetimes, or when goods containing them are disposed of after use (Box 3.1).

In addition to the environmental effects of resource use and materials processing for house construction, the demolition of houses which are no longer suitable or safe for habitation produces massive amounts of waste, including potentially toxic manufactured materials as well as more inert forms of waste or rubble. 'Erecting a typical 150-ton home in the United States sends some 7 tons of refuse to the local dump. At the same time, for every six houses or apartment buildings constructed in the country, one falls to the wrecking ball – about 150,000 each year' (Lenssen and Roodman 1995: 98).

Housing and energy efficiency

Energy is consumed in the production and in the use of housing, and significant amounts of energy are used in the manufacture and transport of building materials such as concrete, steel and plastics. Additionally, in northern countries such as the UK, Germany, Canada and Scandinavia, around a half of all energy consumed in the domestic sector is used to heat buildings (Blunden and Reddish 1991). Energy requirements for space heating in homes can be reduced by raising the thermal efficiency of existing buildings and ensuring that new ones are built to meet high thermal standards. Heat is lost from outer walls of buildings, so shared walls save energy and the energy use for each square metre of floor area in a flat is only two-thirds of that in a detached house (Elkin and McLaren 1991). Large areas of glazing on south facing walls help to provide passive solar heating during sunny periods, while insulation blinds and the use of suitable construction materials can minimize heat loss in the night and during cold weather.

In the USA and the UK, some builders have taken part in schemes which certify that new housing meets certain minimum standards for energy efficient construction. UK building regulations were strengthened in 1995 to incorporate higher standards for thermal insulation and ventilation, and new dwellings and conversions are now required to have a Standard Assessment Procedure (SAP) rating, which indicates the relative energy efficiency of the property. These measures may act to encourage the building and purchase of more energy efficient homes, but standards are still well below the 'superinsulation' of homes developed in parts of Sweden, Canada, Denmark and the northern USA. 'Superinsulation' incorporates exceptional insulation with draughtproof construction, triple glazing and controlled ventilation systems which, in winter, use 70 to 80 per cent of the heat in out-going stale air to pre-heat incoming fresh air (Oliver *et al.* 1991).

Social implications

We have discussed above the ways in which the poorest sectors of society in any country are those with the least choice about the housing environment in which they live. Council housing in the UK is concentrated in particular estates rather than scattered across towns and cities and, since it is now mainly occupied by low-income households, this means that poorer people are now also concentrated in the same neighbourhoods (Hills 1995). The phenomenon is also apparent in other countries, notably Hong Kong, where the very poorest people live in squatter settlements or temporary housing areas. People living on very little money have concerns in their lives which are much more immediate and pressing to them than wider environmental considerations. In Hong Kong, for example, 'people mainly care about when the huts in which they live will be cleared and where they will be rehoused; environmental matters therefore are often understated' (Fai 1993: 113).

The World Health Organization identifies groups of people who are especially at risk when their homes are situated in environmentally degraded areas. These include women, children, the elderly and people with disabilities or ill-health, the homeless and street children. Problems are not confined to physical risks but also include factors affecting social relations.

> Many of the physical characteristics of the housing and living environ-
> ment have a major influence on mental disorder and social pathology
> through such stressful factors as noise, air, soil or water pollution, over-
> crowding, inappropriate design, inadequate maintenance of the physical
> structure and services, poor sanitation, or a high concentration of specific
> toxic substances.
>
> (WHO 1992: 215)

The quality of life and the personal development of children, for example, are influenced by their housing and neighbourhood environments, which affect the range of their play areas and their scope for pursuing independent activities. Personal safety and dangers from traffic accidents and pollution are important elements in determining the extent to which children are free to use parks and other public space around their homes without parental supervision (Davis and Jones 1996a; 1996b). Similarly, experiences of living in rural environments may be characterized by loneliness and isolation stemming from the absence of means to visit and play with friends (Cloke *et al.* 1994).

The quality of people's lives inside their homes can also be influenced by environmental factors, especially the ability to keep warm. We have seen above how the structure of housing is critical in determining its efficiency with regard to energy use. Of course, the capital costs of improving energy efficiency in homes are high, and this is reflected in the finding that, in the UK, in terms of the thermal qualities of building fabrics, the energy efficiency of the homes of the richest 25 per cent of households is on average over four times as high as that of the homes of the poorest 25 per cent (Neighbourhood Energy Action 1996). Poorer families are prevented by cost from buying better constructed homes or from improving their existing accommodation. Some of those who live in social housing may, however, be at an advantage in this respect. The UK Home Energy Conservation Act 1995, for example, now requires local authorities to identify 'practicable, cost-effective measures likely to improve significantly the energy efficiency of residential accommodation' (Department of the Environment 1996a: 19), and in the Netherlands the government has liaised with the housing corporations which own a considerable proportion of housing in the social sector to obtain agreement to improve insulation in a specified number of houses (Bakker 1993). The impact of energy efficiency on both the environment and people's ability to keep warm and comfortable inside their homes is discussed in detail in Chapter 5.

Summary points

- The kinds of housing which people need vary in different parts of the world with differing climatic conditions. Within this, there are wide variations between rich and poor in the extent to which they are able to meet their housing needs.
- Pressures on housing are different in urban and rural areas. The concentration of large numbers of people living in cities brings some advantages, but space can be problematic and depressed urban areas are often characterized by overcrowding, dereliction, air pollution and litter.
- In the UK, more affluent city dwellers are increasingly relocating to permanent or second homes in the countryside. This pushes up the price of rural housing, often beyond the reach of local people, and demands for new cheaper housing place pressure on green field sites.
- Housing development has a direct environmental impact on land use and amenity, but can also have indirect effects. The production, processing and transport of wood, metals, plastics, paints and other materials used in construction and decoration can lead to detrimental effects on the environment at some distance from where the housing is actually built. Other indirect impacts relate to the implications of house design for domestic energy consumption (Chapter 5).
- People living in secure, good standard housing tend to be protected from the worst effects of development. It is those who must live in poorer areas or near the sites of mining and industry who bear the highest environmental costs, costs which lower their quality of life and contribute further to their disadvantaged situations.

Chapter five

WARMTH AND DOMESTIC ENERGY

We have seen in Chapter 4 how social inequalities within and between countries persist in the kind of housing environment which is available to different groups of people. These inequalities are reflected in the extent to which people are able to obtain energy for domestic purposes such as the heating of rooms and the cooking of food. Some people are unable to afford to pay for the energy they need; for others, the fuel to provide domestic energy is simply not available.

A concern for social policy is the question of how to ensure that everyone has access to sufficient energy for his or her basic well-being. However, as we shall see, increasing the provision and consumption of energy, especially from fossil fuels, carries high costs to the environment. A tension arises between the need to improve access to energy and the need for environmental protection. If energy consumption were to be reduced across the board, the poorest sectors of society would suffer a disproportionate decline in their well-being. On the other hand, if energy consumption continues to rise at current rates, the local and global environmental repercussions are likely to be felt most severely by the poor.

Access to domestic energy supplies

Disparities between the rich and poor in their access to domestic energy supplies occur throughout the world. In some cases, they arise as a result of fuel shortage, often coupled with high population densities and demand for fuel. In other cases, housing and heating systems are so energy inefficient that it is difficult for poorer households to pay for enough energy to meet their needs. Even when energy is in plentiful supply, its cost may prove prohibitive to families living on very low incomes.

In Kenya, where wood and wood products account for three-quarters of total energy use, expanding demand coupled with diminishing supplies is pushing more and more people into positions of hardship (Huby 1990). 'Firewood has traditionally been collected as a free good from the commons. It was provided by nature, just like the grass that sustained the livestock, and the rainfall that provided water for the household' (Bradley 1991: 220). Consumption rates, however, are now exceeding rates of production, and the shortfall predicted in wood supplies by the year 2000 is expected to represent 65 per cent of national demand. Once again it is the poorest members of society who will suffer the most, the better off being able to afford to substitute alternative fuels, such as kerosene or electricity, for woodfuel.

It is a rapidly growing population which places high demands on energy production in China, and shortages are most acute in rural areas.

The fuel comes from literally any burnable tree and forest biomass: not only branches and twigs, roots and stumps, but also bark off of the living trees, needles, leaves and grasses, and carved-out and dried pieces of sod. People carefully raking any organic debris accumulated on the floor of even small groves, peasants drastically pruning the summer growth of shrubs and trees, and children gathering tufts of grass into their back baskets are common sights in China's fuel-short countryside.

(Smil 1988: 51–2)

Prior to the transition to market-based economies, countries in Central and Eastern Europe enjoyed very low energy prices, but these have risen substantially in recent years, leaving many households suffering from fuel poverty. In Hungary, for example, 50 per cent of the population live below the official poverty line, and 40 per cent of the 3.6 million residential dwellings are apartments, mostly occupied by low-income families. A high percentage of apartments are connected to district heating systems or are centrally heated from within the buildings, but their style of construction from prefabricated panels is such that they lose heat rapidly and the type of heating system does not allow for thermostatic control. The consequence of this is a massively inefficient use of energy, with low-income households faced by high bills for heating. 'Because of the construction of the buildings, and the system of heat and hot water delivery, they are being forced to consume more energy than they either need or can afford to buy' (I. Brown 1993: 22). Low-income families in Budapest spend around 35 per cent of household income on energy to provide heat and hot water. Ironically, people in Central and Eastern Europe might face even greater difficulties in meeting their fuel bills were it not for the fact that they have far less living space and fewer electrical appliances at their disposal than people in OECD countries (Tellegen 1996).

In colder and temperate zone countries, when outside temperatures reach low levels, the home provides a space in which warmth can be provided not only for physical comfort but also for the maintenance of health. Hypothermia only accounts for a small proportion of winter deaths in the UK, but cold conditions can trigger other illnesses, such as strokes or heart attacks. Condensation and damp are often a problem in cold houses and encourage the growth of moulds and mites, which can exacerbate allergies such as asthma and other respiratory complaints. It is estimated that in the UK, over 30,000 deaths each winter are related to cold living conditions (Boardman 1993).

Although some winter morbidity and death might be attributable to behavioural factors, most is a consequence of low incomes, inefficient and uneconomic heating systems and cold, damp housing. A cold home environment can also reduce the quality of life of households by effectively reducing living space. In countries with seasonal climates, parts of a house which are fully used during the summer may be left unused during colder months if they cannot be heated to comfortable temperatures.

Space heating accounts for about 40 per cent of fuel expenditure in the average home (Boardman 1991). In addition to warmth, domestic energy is used to heat water, to provide lighting, run appliances and keep and cook food safely. Bradshaw and Hutton (1993: 250) suggest that most people would accept that 'fuel for cooking, light and perhaps heating water are basic needs and that in addition space heating is a basic need of the very old and sick and the very young and that space heating for the rest of us, if not a basic need, is at least recognised as part of normal living standards and to be without it is a severe deprivation'. Nevertheless, many households do have difficulties in obtaining sufficient fuel to meet domestic needs.

When any members of the family are elderly, ill or disabled or unemployed, or where there are babies or young children, more time is spent in the home and demands on fuel for domestic use tend to be high, particularly during periods of cold weather. Ironically, these are the kinds of families most likely to be living on low incomes and consequently finding it hardest to pay for fuel. Low-income households spend a disproportionately large part of their income on domestic energy. In 1995–6 in the UK, spending on fuel and power accounted for just over 10 per cent of all expenditure in the poorest 10 per cent of households. In contrast, in the richest 10 per cent of households fuel expenditure accounted for less than 3 per cent of the total.

A recent review of studies of people living on low incomes found:

> Most people were cautious about their use of heating, with interviewers often reporting that, in winter, homes were bitterly cold. Individual rooms were heated as needed – normally during the coldest part of the late evening. Central heating, even where it was available, was not used. For people who were at home all day, the costs of heating their homes was of particular concern – especially if they needed to stay warm either for health reasons or because they had young children.
>
> (Kempson 1996: 34)

Paying for electricity and gas was the second most common financial concern identified by respondents in a 1991 survey of people living at social assistance level. None of the local authority or housing association tenants interviewed had any choice about the type of heating or fuel supplied to their homes, and 'faulty thermostats and insufficient control over the radiator system were felt by some to be contributing to high consumption costs' (Huby and Dix 1992: 12). The UK Department of Social Security (DSS) does provide a Fuel Direct scheme which allows people in receipt of certain means-tested benefits to have their gas and electricity payments made directly from their regular social assistance benefits, and increasing difficulties in meeting fuel bills are evidenced by the growing numbers of claimants using this scheme. In 1994, 305,000 people used Fuel Direct, compared with 223,000 in 1990 (House of Commons *Hansard* 18 July 1994, Col. 1099).

Energy and the environment

Energy is notoriously difficult to define, but perhaps the easiest way to think of it is as an attribute which confers the ability to do something. Muscular energy, for example, allows us to move parts of our bodies, chemical energy enables substances to undergo chemical reactions and gravitational energy pulls falling objects towards the earth. Energy is present in many more forms but, according to the scientific 'principle of energy conservation', it is never created or destroyed. It can, however, be converted from one form to another. Heat is a form of energy and the production of heat for warming homes, heating water or cooking food involves the conversion of some other form of energy from a variety of sources into useful heat.

Primary energy sources are those which are converted to heat directly. Wood and other burnable organic material (biomass) and the fossil fuels (for example, coal, gas and oil formed underground over millions of years) contain chemical energy which is converted to heat energy by burning or combustion. Secondary energy sources are used to provide electricity, another form of energy which can in turn be converted to heat. Fossil fuels can act as secondary sources when they are used in electricity generation, but electrical energy can also be derived from other sources, such as nuclear energy or energy from the sun, wind or moving water.

The types of fuel used to produce energy for domestic use depend largely on a combination of availability and price, but these factors are themselves influenced by currently available technologies and economic, trade and political considerations at national and global levels. The UK, for example, is still largely dependent on fossil fuels. Use of coal in the domestic sector has declined since the 1970s as natural gas has become increasingly preferred as a relatively cheap and clean alternative. Coal production dropped from 200 million tonnes a year in the 1960s to 96 million tonnes in 1991. Of 1991 production, only 11 per cent was used directly for heating in the domestic and industrial sectors. One per cent was used in the production of smokeless fuels and 9 per cent as coke for blast furnaces, while 78 per cent was used for generating electricity. Natural gas now accounts for 65 per cent of domestic fuel use in the UK, with North Sea sources providing 80 per cent of total gas produced and the remainder coming from petroleum processing, blast furnaces, coke ovens and colliery methane. In addition, the UK processes around 90 million tonnes of crude oil a year, and more than 85 per cent of oil products are used for energy, 11 per cent of these in the generation of electricity (Department of the Environment 1992a).

In recent years, concerns about the world's supplies of fossil fuel resources and about the possible effects of fossil fuel combustion on the earth's atmosphere and climate have introduced environmental considerations into decisions regarding energy supplies. The impacts of different fuels as sources of energy emanate from both production processes and the use of fuels to produce heat or electricity. In the sections that follow we examine some of the main environmental impacts of different types of fuel.

Biomass

Wood, wood products such as charcoal and other forms of biomass from agricultural and forestry residues account for around 10 to 15 per cent of total world energy use each year. Over 80 per cent of this energy from biomass is used in the developing countries, where it represents 35 per cent of energy supplies. Nearly half of the world's population rely directly on wood for their domestic energy, more than for any other type of fuel, and many have no alternative source of energy, either because there are no local supplies or because of the prohibitive cost of alternatives such as kerosene, gas or electricity (Blunden and Reddish 1991; Bradley and Huby 1993).

The environmental effects of direct burning of biomass to produce domestic energy include serious levels of indoor air pollution where kitchens or other parts of the home are poorly ventilated (Chapter 1). In addition, the felling of trees for burning leads to deforestation (Box 4.1), which can culminate in soil erosion and degradation, affecting the capacity of the land to be used for further agricultural or forest production. Further depletion of soil productivity occurs when dung and crop residues are used as fuels rather than being returned to the land as fertilizers and soil conditioners. Crop, animal and human wastes are used on a large scale in villages in India and China for conversion to other forms of fuel, such as methane gas and alcohol, but in areas of rural China where fuel is scarce, most forms of biomass are burned directly. 'Environmental consequences of this often desperate search for fuel are predictably severe: rapid nutrient loss and erosion of slope sites stripped of trees or of the protective floor-debris cover not infrequently result in the total loss of the site for eventual regeneration' (Smil 1988: 52).

Landfill gas (Box 7.1) from waste disposal sites contains high volumes of methane. Methane is an important greenhouse gas (Box 1.1), but it can be converted to electricity, and landfill gas is increasingly being used in the UK and the USA for electricity generation. To some extent this solves a growing problem of disposal of municipal waste, and immediate deleterious environmental effects are confined to leakage during gas production and the foul odours emanating from production plants.

Table 5.1   Domestic sources of air pollution in the UK, 1994

Pollutant	Total emissions (tonnes)	% contribution from domestic energy use	% contribution from power stations	% contribution from road transport
Black smoke	426,000	22	4	58
Carbon dioxide	149,000,000	15	30	20
Nitrogen oxides	2,218,000	3	24	49
Sulphur dioxide	2,718,000	3	65	2

Source: Department of Trade and Industry (1996).

Fossil fuels

A major impact of fossil fuel production on the environment stems from the disturbance to natural and human habitats caused by mining and drilling operations. Mining activities release the greenhouse gas methane (Box 1.1), and coal mining is estimated to have produced 19 per cent of total methane emissions in the UK in 1990, a further 21 per cent coming from offshore gas production and 8 per cent from leakage of gas distribution systems (Department of the Environment 1992a). Mining and drilling can also affect land stability, and subsidence due to mining led to British Coal being faced with 8315 claims for damages in 1990–1. In 1988, coal mining activities left 4700 hectares of land derelict in England and 965 hectares in Scotland, while over five million tonnes of colliery waste are disposed of each year on beaches and at sea, lowering amenity values for leisure and recreation. Spoil tips are often unsightly but, more seriously perhaps, mining wastes are acidic and run-off from them can cause serious water pollution problems, affecting plant growth and wildlife habitats.

The oil industry also makes a significant contribution to water pollution and was responsible for 24 per cent of all reported pollution incidents in England and Wales in 1991 (Department of the Environment 1992a). Offshore production causes marine pollution from accidental spillages as well as from discharge of chemicals and oil contaminated drillings and washing waters. Oil pollution can have devastating effects on sea-bird populations and other wildlife, as well as affecting inshore fisheries and tourist amenities. The production, storage and distribution of oil and oil products is accompanied by some evaporation of polluting volatile organic compounds (VOCs, Box 6.2), and air pollution by partially burnt products and oily waste occurs during flaring processes.

When fossil fuels are burned to produce energy they release, among other combustion products, carbon dioxide, methane, black smoke, oxides of nitrogen and sulphur dioxide. Table 5.1 shows that domestic sources make a major contribution to air pollution in the UK, but the situation is even more serious in some other places, especially in cities in developing countries. In India, for example, it has been estimated that the burning of domestic fuel generates about half of all Delhi's air pollution (WHO 1992).

Fossil fuel burning releases soot, black smoke and tiny particles of s... material which are suspended in the air, lowering visibility, soiling buildings and causing respiratory irritation and damage. Although domestic fuel burning produces nearly a quarter of all UK black smoke emissions, the main contribution is made by road transport, a topic covered in detail in Chapter 6. A further major source of air pollution is the power generating industry. In converting fossil fuels to electricity, the industry accounts for nearly a third of the UK's emissions of carbon dioxide, 24 per cent of nitrogen oxides and 65 per cent of its sulphur dioxide.

Oxides of nitrogen, known collectively as NO_x, include a variety of different gaseous compounds which have adverse environmental effects. Like carbon dioxide and methane, one oxide of nitrogen, nitrous oxide, acts as a greenhouse gas contributing to global warming (Box 1.1). Nitrogen oxides can form acidic compounds which pollute the atmosphere at ground level, affecting plant growth as a result of acid deposition (Box 5.1) and, in conjunction with other pollutants in the presence of sunlight, causing photochemical smogs which directly affect human health (Box 6.2). Sulphur dioxide is also acidic, occurring as a pungent colourless gas which causes sensory and respiratory damage to humans and animals and, as the main contributor to acid deposition, corrodes buildings and affects the growth of plants.

These air pollutants – black smoke, oxides of nitrogen and sulphur dioxide – have great potential to affect physical life and the quality of the environment. It is, however, the release of greenhouse gases which has caused the greatest global concern in recent years. Energy production from fossil fuels accounts for 57 per cent of all greenhouse gases produced by human activity, and 26 per cent of this comes from home and commercial sources (Kelly and Granich 1995). Worldwide emissions of carbon dioxide have almost quadrupled since the 1950s (Hirschhorn and Oldenburg 1991), and there is growing evidence about the implications of this for global warming and subsequent climate change (Box 5.2).

Carbon dioxide is naturally emitted by the respiration of living organisms and is taken up by plants in photosynthesis. However, the burning of fossil fuels releases carbon dioxide which was fixed by plants many millions of years ago, increasing present concentrations in the atmosphere and currently accounting for about 60 per cent of the potential warming effect of man-made emissions (Box 1.1).

Different kinds of fossil fuel have different carbon and energy contents and release different amounts of carbon dioxide for each unit of heat produced. Lignite, or brown coal, produces particularly large quantities of greenhouse gases and other highly polluting emissions. The problem is exacerbated in parts of Central and Eastern Europe, where power plants tend to be largely fuelled by lignite, the fossil fuel which is most abundant in the area. Poland, for example, obtains three-quarters of its energy from this source. In Czechoslovakia, where two-thirds of energy is produced from brown coal, emissions of sulphur dioxide increased from 900,000 tonnes in 1950 to over three million tonnes in 1985 (Carter and Turnock 1993).

Box 5.1   Acid deposition

The deposition of acidic pollutants on land or water is often referred to as *acid rain*, but the term *acid deposition* is used to include the acid deposits which reach vegetation, soils and water from the atmosphere even in dry weather.

Acidity is measured using pH values. A pH value of 7 indicates neutrality, while values below this indicate acidity and values above, alkalinity. Rain is naturally slightly acidic, around pH 5 globally, and most natural waters fall into the range pH 5 to 8. The table below shows the pH values of some other common substances:

Substance	pH
Battery acid	< 1
Wine	4
Blood	7
Milk of magnesia	10
Oven cleaner	13

Sulphur dioxide and nitrogen oxides emitted during the burning of fossil fuels dissolve in water to produce acidic solutions. These are carried in the air, sometimes to great distances from their sources, before being absorbed by vegetation, soils and water surfaces or being deposited in rain, snow or mist droplets.

Increasing acidity can be damaging to plants, animals and buildings. 'It is now known that through acidification of soils in geologically sensitive areas, acid rain can inhibit plant nutrition and restrict the range of flora and fauna. Fresh waters in such areas can be made toxic to aquatic plants, invertebrates and fish. Through the effects on the food chain, this can lead to losses of other fauna such as natterjack toads, dippers and otters. Acid rain also damages building materials such as stone, concrete and metals' (Department of the Environment 1992a: 18).

Box 5.2   Global warming and climate change

Latest estimates suggest that by the year 2100 global mean surface temperatures will have risen by 1 to 3.5 °C, a rate of warming greater than anything seen in the last 10,000 years. Expected consequences include:

● more severe droughts and flooding in many places;
● land losses of around 6 per cent in the Netherlands, 17.5 per cent in Bangladesh and more than 80 per cent in some Pacific atolls;
● adverse effects on agriculture, particularly in developing countries;
● wide-ranging adverse impacts on health including significant loss of life;
● effects on growth and the regenerative capacity of forests in many regions.

Source: Bruce *et al.* 1996.

In 1995, coal, gas and oil still constituted almost 70 per cent of the energy sources used in power stations in the UK, but electricity can also be generated from non-fossil fuels. Nuclear energy, for example, provides about 28 per cent of the UK's electricity, and although renewable energy sources such as biomass, water, sun and wind currently provide only 2 per cent, there are plans to increase this to 5 per cent by the end of the century (HMSO 1994b). In 1995, 26 per cent of renewable energy for electricity generation came from the combustion of biomass from sewage sludge, municipal waste and landfill gas, but other renewable sources can be used, largely free from the pollutants that contribute to global warming and acid deposition. However, a well known saying among environmentalists is that there is no such thing as a free lunch, and even these sources have their impacts on the environment.

Nuclear power

Large amounts of energy are present in atoms, binding together sub-atomic particles. Nuclear power generation releases this atomic energy from certain radioactive fuels such as uranium, converting it to heat and then to electricity which can be transmitted in the usual national networks. The process produces none of the polluting gases resulting from fossil fuel combustion, so a switch from fossil fuels to nuclear power could be used to achieve a dramatic reduction in man-made emissions of greenhouse gases and consequently lower the possibility of an enhanced greenhouse effect leading to global warming and climate change. Yet, especially since 1986 when an accident occurred at the nuclear power plant at Chernobyl, there have been high levels of public concern about the environmental hazards of nuclear power production (Table 5.2).

By 1994, a further survey showed that 45 per cent of the British population perceived nuclear power stations to constitute an extremely or very serious risk to the environment (Witherspoon 1994). This concern is related less to any visually perceived environmental effects of nuclear power production than to the risks it carries of radioactive pollution (Box 5.3).

Table 5.2 British attitudes to the environmental hazards of nuclear power production

Statement	% agreeing
Waste from nuclear power stations has very or quite serious environmental effects	90
A serious accident at a British nuclear power station is very or quite likely in the next ten years	59
Nuclear power stations create very or quite serious risks for the future	74

Source: Young (1991).

Box 5.3   Radioactivity

Radioactive materials such as uranium are undergoing constant change or 'decay', during which they emit energy as forms of radiation which can cause biological damage. This radiation cannot be detected by any human senses, but it damages living cells in both plants and animals, disrupting the way in which they grow. In human beings it potentially causes degeneration and failure of bodily organs, or causes cancers such as leukaemia.

The extent of the damage caused depends on the exact type of radiation; different forms have differing capacities to penetrate living tissues, and different potentials for disrupting cell structures. It also depends on the amount of radiation which is received in a given time and on the total period of exposure. A short but intense exposure is dangerous, but damage can also be caused by less intense levels of radiation received over a longer time period. Any exposure carries some risk of damage, but the risk may range from being infinitesimally small to being extremely high.

Everyone is constantly exposed to low levels of natural background radiation which comes from both space and certain rocks in the earth. However, during the past century human activities have introduced new sources, such as X-rays used in medicine, nuclear weapons and nuclear reactors for power generation. These sources pose new risks, and opinions about their desirability depend on what is seen as an acceptable level of risk in the context of the benefits to be gained from nuclear technology.

The risks of radioactive contamination associated with nuclear power production mainly revolve around the possibility of accidents or breakdown at the power plant, but risks also arise during the processes of mining radioactive fuels, preparing fuel for reactors, operating reactors and dealing with waste and reprocessing. Even in the absence of accidents, the disposal of nuclear waste presents a very real problem. Some radioactive materials decay only very slowly, so wastes must be stored for hundreds or thousands of years before they are safe. High level wastes also produce large amounts of heat, so that they require constant cooling during storage and elaborate safety precautions must be taken.

There are clear differences of opinion about what constitutes an acceptable level of risk from nuclear power production. Even when all possible precautions are taken there still remains the possibility of accidents leading to radioactive emissions. Although this risk may be very small, the stakes are high and a nuclear accident could have devastating and long lasting effects on a global scale. On the other hand, continued use of fossil fuels as an energy source risks inducing the possible catastrophic and irreversible effects of global warming. These uncertainties give grounds for invoking the precautionary principle (Box 5.4) and, where possible, switching to energy sources which are capable of less environmental harm.

Box 5.4 The precautionary principle

The precautionary principle holds that whenever an activity poses a known risk of harm to environmental or human health, then we should err on the side of caution.

According to Principle 15 of the Rio Declaration, 'where there are threats of serious or irreversible damage, lack of full scientific certainty shall not be used as a reason for postponing cost-effective measures to prevent environmental degradation' (United Nations 1993: 10).

A stronger form of the precautionary principle omits the consideration of whether such measures are cost-effective on the grounds that environmental damage cannot be measured simply in financial terms.

Other renewable sources of energy

Tides and flowing water, wind, the sun and the earth's internal heat can all be used to provide energy for electricity generation without the environmental risks associated with fossil or nuclear fuels. Their environmental effects are mainly attributable to the physical structures of the power plants themselves. Large scale hydroelectric schemes are usually limited to mountainous areas and need big dams and reservoirs which change both the surrounding landscape and wildlife habitats. People living in the area, often poorer rural households, must move away to make way for dam construction.

These displaced persons often suffer psychological stress owing to the loss of lifetime occupations and relationships, the disruption of ordinary life, and the breakup of families. Other health problems are associated with the disruption of food supplies, and the lack of a healthy housing and living environment in the areas where the displaced people are resettled.

(WHO 1992: 158)

Smaller schemes utilize energy from naturally flowing rivers and waterfalls and consequently have less impact, but also have less storage capacity for supplying electricity as demand fluctuates. Tidal power schemes similarly have effects on the visual amenity of sites and can alter estuary ecosystems.

Wind powered electricity generation produces no waste products or greenhouse gases, but has met with different levels of success in different parts of the world, partly because of the availability of suitable sites but also because of concern about the visual intrusiveness of wind farms, local noise levels and possible effects on tourism. The Department of the Environment has estimated that 20 per cent of the UK's electricity could potentially be supplied by wind power given suitable investment and planning permissions (Whyte 1995). Much of the opposition to wind farms in the UK comes from local residents, but attitudes do appear to be changing. A survey carried out by the Department of Trade and Industry in 1990 and 1992, before and after a windfarm development in Cornwall, found that concerns raised by residents in 1990 were largely dispelled by the actual experience of the plant's operation (Taylor 1994).

Energy from the sun is used for power generation using two techniques. In the first, solar thermal systems collect sunlight through mirrors or lenses to heat fluids, which in turn heat water. The steam produced is used to drive turbines which are used to generate electricity. A second method uses sunlight directly by collecting it in photovoltaic cells.

In some parts of the world the heat produced naturally within the interior of the earth comes near enough to the surface to be utilized directly for power generation. In the early 1990s this geothermal energy was used to provide 10 per cent of the electricity generated in New Zealand, 20 per cent in the Philippines and 40 per cent in El Salvador.

Social implications

We have seen above how demands for energy can have serious consequences for the environment but the benefits from energy supplies are not equally distributed. 'People in industrial countries constitute a little more than a fifth of the world's population but consume nearly nine times more commercial energy per capita than people in developing countries' (United Nations Development Programme 1995: 17). A major source of energy to meet the high demands in the industrialized world at the present time is fossil fuel, and this means that most greenhouse gas emissions currently come from richer rather than poorer countries. 'A citizen in the USA typically generates five tonnes of carbon a year, compared with half a tonne produced by a Chinese citizen and a third of a tonne by a Brazilian' (Kelly and Granich 1995: 92). Variations in energy consumption with wealth and income are also reflected at national level. It has been estimated that in the UK, the poorest 30 per cent of households contribute only 24 per cent of domestic sector emissions of carbon dioxide (Boardman 1991). Wealthier people tend to do more environmental damage by heating bigger homes, purchasing and using more electrical goods and driving larger cars rather than using public transport. Although this chapter focuses on domestic energy use, it must be remembered that the huge contribution to greenhouse emissions made by large energy users in transport and industry also reflects social demands for particular lifestyles and production of consumer goods.

In some cases, however, this situation is reversed, and poverty can also be associated with high levels of atmospheric pollution from energy use. We have seen earlier that in poorer rural areas in developing countries agricultural and forestry residues are often the only fuels available. The low thermal efficiency of biomass means that it emits high levels of carbon dioxide and smoke per unit of energy produced. Similarly, in parts of Central and Eastern Europe we have seen how, because of the low price of fuel and the

Figure 5.1 Coal mining activities can have devastating impacts on local landscapes.

nature of housing construction and heating systems, high levels of energy consumption and atmospheric pollution are associated with low household incomes.

The adverse consequences of the world's increasing energy consumption are likely to fall most heavily on particular social groups. Patterns of increased morbidity and mortality at higher concentrations of pollution by suspended particulate matter are more marked among the very young and the elderly, especially for old people already suffering from chronic obstructive pulmonary diseases, heart diseases or pneumonia (International Bank for Reconstruction and Development 1992). Women are especially at risk from indoor pollution because of the time they spend in the kitchen. 'An estimated 700 million women in the world are likely to be affected by indoor air pollutants arising from the use of biomass fuel, making this the largest single "occupational health" problem for women' (WHO 1992: 161).

A survey of British social attitudes recently showed that 51 per cent of the population perceive 'a rise in the world's temperature caused by the green-house effect' to be an extremely or very serious threat to the environment (Witherspoon 1994: 120), but scientific uncertainties about levels of man-made emissions of greenhouse gases and the causal links between emissions and global warming have for some time resulted in controversy about the urgency of the need for action. By the end of 1995, however, the Inter-governmental Panel on Climate Change had concluded that 'the balance of evidence suggests that there is a discernible human influence on global climate' (Bruce *et al.* 1996). Rises in average global temperatures and changes in rainfall patterns are likely to affect agricultural productivity, and rapid changes in habitats will affect wildlife while sea level rises will inundate coastlines and result in changed distribution of water resources (Box 5.2).

Climate change will have its most direct effects on the world's poor, many of whom live in low lying areas such as the fertile flood plains of Bangladesh. They are likely to have little choice about migrating to safer areas or switching their means of obtaining a livelihood. People living in wealthier countries, however, are not immune and are likely to experience effects of climate change indirectly through the impacts of change on national economies and trade relations. The finite nature of fossil fuel supplies is one reason for using them sparingly, but it is the threat of climate change which has led national governments to take concerted action. At the Earth Summit in Rio de Janeiro in 1992, a Global Convention on Climate Change aiming to stabilize greenhouse gas concentrations in the atmosphere was signed by 168 countries, committing developed countries to take measures necessary to return their emissions of greenhouse gases to 1990 levels by the year 2000.

One way of reducing greenhouse gas emissions is to switch to less polluting forms of energy provision: for example, by increasing the contribution of renewable energy to the generation of electricity. A second way is to reduce demands for energy. In the domestic sector this could be achieved in principle by improving house design for maximum energy efficiency, as discussed in Chapter 4, by installing insulation and energy efficient heating appliances, by encouraging the purchase and use of energy efficient domestic appliances, by offering advice on energy efficient practices and by increasing energy prices. No one would argue against the desirability of such measures, but social factors must be taken into account and, as we shall see, each can have differential effects on different income groups.

Poorer sectors of society will be most vulnerable to changes in climate resulting from global warming caused by an enhanced greenhouse effect. In addition, they may suffer disproportionately from national and international measures taken to reduce energy consumption by increasing prices, yet the poor often have the least capacity either to lower their consumption or to change to more efficient systems of energy use.

Insulation and heating systems

There is little doubt that insulation of homes can achieve energy savings. In the UK, the number of homes with loft insulation increased from 42 per cent in 1974 to 89 per cent in 1989, while the number with cavity wall insulation rose from 2 to 20 per cent over the same period. It is estimated that domestic energy consumption in 1989 was 32 per cent lower than it would have been if insulation standards had remained at 1970 levels (Department of the Environment 1992a). However, the installation of insulation and efficient heating systems has capital financial costs which must be offset against lower consumption and running costs. The most cost-effective efficiency measures include improved control over heating systems, loft insulation, cavity wall insulation, draughtproofing and ventilation control. Secondary glazing, condensing boilers and heat pumps have longer pay-back periods (Elkin and McLaren 1991).

Home-owners are more likely to insulate their homes and improve their heating systems than are tenants (Brechling and Smith 1994). The latter are less likely to pay out the capital costs of improvement, knowing that much of the long-term value of their investment accrues to the landlord. Similarly, landlords may be reluctant to invest in energy efficient measures in their property when some of the benefit goes to tenants in the form of lower heating bills. Since lower-income households are those most likely to live in rented accommodation, it is once again the poorest sector of the population, least able to afford high fuel bills, who have the least likelihood of reducing energy consumption by improving their homes.

The UK government recognized this problem when it set up its Home Energy Efficiency Scheme (HEES) in 1991 to provide small grants for basic insulation and draughtproofing of the homes of low-income families, people with disabilities and householders over 60 years old. In 1995, however, the government announced 'changes to the Home Energy Efficiency Scheme, designed to target it more directly on those in greatest need, maintaining the level of help given to low income and disabled householders while saving £31 million in 1996–97' (HMSO 1996b: 19). These 'savings' amount to a cut in the scheme's budget of over 30 per cent, achieved by changing the rules governing the access to the scheme for people over 60 years old. Unless they are in receipt of certain qualifying social assistance benefits, elderly householders may now only receive a maximum of 25 per cent of the cost of the work carried out. The need to pay the remainder themselves may dissuade some of these people from taking effective action to improve the energy efficiency of their homes.

Energy efficient appliances

Consumption of electricity for domestic appliances and lighting is increasing by 3 per cent a year in the UK and the energy efficiency of new cookers, refrigerators, freezers, washing machines and dishwashers varies by a factor of two or more (Boardman 1995). However, it is not always easy to discover which are the most energy efficient appliances, or what the return is likely to be on replacing a central heating system. Information and advice play a crucial role. Over 60 utility companies in the United States have programmes to encourage the sales of electricity saving devices and, although energy efficiency labelling of domestic appliances is in its infancy in the UK, the government introduced a scheme called Wasting Energy Costs the Earth to provide advice and to promote the benefits of energy efficiency within households (Department of the Environment 1996a).

Everyone gains from the reduced levels of pollution associated with reduced use of fossil fuel energy, but in the face of high fuel prices the poorest stand to gain most financially from energy efficiency. In 1979, Americans with annual incomes of US$6000 were estimated to have implied discount rates of 89 per cent on energy efficient durable goods. For richer households with incomes of US$50,000, the comparable rate was only 5 per cent (Cairncross 1993). Where electricity costs are higher, more savings accrue to households using energy efficient appliances, and in Japan, where electricity is very expensive, energy saving compact fluorescent light bulbs make up 80 per cent of all bulbs used. However, limited incomes mean that poorer households must often purchase poor quality or second-hand electrical equipment which is cheaper to buy but costly and inefficient to run. Newer equipment may have lower running costs, but it is not so easy for low-income consumers to afford the capital outlay required. 'The better educated and more affluent might recognise that an investment in insulation or a more expensive water heater makes good sense and will save their money over the long run, but those with lower incomes do not have the extra money to make the initial investment' (Seitz 1995: 121).

Energy prices

It is frequently argued that energy prices do not reflect the costs of production and that subsequent underpricing leads to over-consumption of energy. This is especially true if the external environmental costs of electricity generation from fossil fuels are not included in market prices. The argument is that adjusting energy prices upward to reflect these costs would result in lowered consumption and greater efficiency of energy use. However, since poorer families spend proportionately more of their income on domestic energy than do better off households, this would have adverse distributional implications.

In countries with transitional economies, such as those in Central and Eastern Europe, housing and household energy subsidies act as social buffers, protecting households from the sudden exposure to market forces which is accompanying liberalization. Attempts to increase energy prices to reflect production costs would have sharp effects on the poor. 'Relative to other prices, for example, household electricity prices would have to rise roughly threefold in Bulgaria, the Czech Republic and Russia from levels of mid to late 1995' (International Bank for Reconstruction and Development 1996: 24). Unless compensatory payments could be made through social assistance schemes, energy price increases would result in severe hardship for many low-income families.

A similar situation applies in the UK, where, until 1994, VAT on domestic energy was zero-rated on the grounds of social policy objectives. When VAT on domestic fuel was introduced at 8 per cent (reduced by the new Labour government to 5 per cent) to increase tax revenue, government statements suggested that the move would have the environmental advantages of reducing the use of fossil fuels and encouraging investment in domestic energy efficient measures by making the costs of such measures cheaper relative to spending on fuel. In the light of the clearly regressive nature of the tax, revenue increases have been offset by the need to make additional social assistance benefit payments to vulnerable groups. Nor is there any evidence that environmental benefits have accrued from the imposition of the tax. In contrast to EU proposals for a carbon tax which reflects both the carbon and energy content of fuel, the UK tax is simply proportional to value and offers no incentive for consumers to switch from more polluting high carbon forms of fuel such as coal to less environmentally harmful fuels such as gas or renewables which have lower or no carbon content.

The tax certainly brings VAT on fuel closer to that on energy efficiency appliances, currently set at 17.5 per cent, but the effect on fuel prices makes it even harder for low-income families to afford to pay for such appliances. A more effective move might be to reduce VAT on the latter to 5 per cent to achieve the same end (Tindale 1996). At the time of writing, attempts are being made to pass an Energy Conservation Bill which would reduce VAT on energy saving materials to the same level as that on domestic fuel. It has been estimated that such a tax reduction would actually generate revenue by increasing sales, especially to low-income households, by 10 per cent, while at the same time resulting in reduced emissions of carbon dioxide and other harmful gases to the environment (letter from Alan Simpson MP 1996).

Issues for social policy

There are strong economic and political arguments for reductions in energy use, conserving non-renewable fuel in the face of inherent uncertainty about long-term availability and prices. Conservation helps to secure supplies, minimizing the chances of short-term supply disruptions and destabilizing price changes (Cheshire 1993). From an environmental point of view, energy conservation and a switch to cleaner renewable energy sources are essential in order to curb the deleterious effects of pollutants on the local, national and global environment. But changes such as these have far-reaching social impacts and social aspects of energy use are receiving increasing attention among social policy analysts. 'Since the energy crisis of 1973 social problems associated with fuel have emerged from being a marginal aspect of the wider problem of poverty to become a major social policy issue in their own right' (Bradshaw and Hutton 1983: 249). The efficient use of energy can increase standards of living by minimizing unnecessary consumer expenditure on energy, especially for those living on low incomes. Without increased efficiency, many households cannot use less fuel without risk to their health and well-being. Rising fuel prices underwrite and enhance existing social inequalities. However, tensions arise between the need to raise the living standards and well-being of the world's poor without concomitant costs to the environment of the waste and inefficiency associated with over-consumption of energy. Prices must be kept down to help the poor, but consumption must be reduced to help the environment. The problem occurs because lower prices tend to increase the use of energy with negative environmental impacts, but if prices are increased in efforts to reduce consumption it is the poor who suffer most while the better off can afford to use energy as usual. 'Indeed, the capacity to waste energy may be seen by some as a sign of status and affluence' (Bhatti 1996: 163).

'Fuel poverty' has been defined as 'the inability to afford adequate warmth because of the energy inefficiency of the home' (Boardman 1991: 4), and one answer might be to ensure wider access to information and the practical means to achieve greater efficiency in domestic energy use. However, an important issue in relation to energy efficiency is raised by Boardman (1995). She makes the point that even if huge improvements in energy efficiency were to be achieved, this would by no means guarantee a reduction in total energy consumption. It is possible that in some households the improved efficiency of appliances might lead to greater consumption of energy, through, for example, the use of more televisions, lights, washing machines and dish-washers. Lower-income households may benefit from access to sufficient energy at more affordable prices, but this in itself may increase their energy consumption in obtaining additional warmth. Without a greater understanding of human behaviour in relation to energy use it is impossible to predict whether efficiency gains are likely to be matched by energy saving.

Summary points

- Some people go without the energy they need for warmth and other domestic purposes because fuel is not available, others because they cannot afford to pay for it.
- Lack of domestic energy to provide sufficient warmth can lead to discomfort and exacerbate health problems, particularly for the elderly, sick or disabled and very young. Constraints may also be placed on the kinds of food which can be cooked and on access to hot water and lighting. Difficulties in finding money to pay for fuel often lead to anxiety and distress.
- The use of biomass and fossil fuels as energy sources has a wide range of detrimental effects on the environment. These include land disturbance from mining and drilling, as well as air pollution, acid deposition and the emission of greenhouse gases which contribute to global climate change. Nuclear power generation carries risks of radioactive contamination.
- There are other renewable sources of energy – water, wind and sunlight – which have very limited environmental impacts. These, however, are currently used to provide only a small fraction of the world's energy supplies.
- Wealthier groups of people consume far more energy than the poor. However, the latter are often constrained by cost and availability to use more polluting forms of fuel. They are also less likely to use energy

efficiently where the costs of buying energy efficient appliances or installing insulation and efficient heating systems in their homes are beyond their financial means.

● At both national and international levels the key problem is to find ways of reducing the negative environmental impacts of energy consumption while at the same time ensuring that all households have access to sufficient energy to maintain and improve their health and living standards.

MOBILITY AND TRAVEL

The ability to travel to a desired destination makes an important contribution to individual and social well-being. Most people can move about freely in their own homes, but it is important to remember that even this simple form of mobility can present difficulties for people with disabilities or health problems, difficulties which become harder to surmount when travelling outside of the home. With the development of mechanized forms of transport which speed up travel, there has been an expansion in the geographical space away from the home within which travel is seen as either necessary or desirable. The ability to travel ever further afield is now accepted as part of a contemporary social lifestyle, at least in industrialized countries, to the extent that 'not being able to get around, to be restricted to a particular place, to be dependent on other people for travel is often a characteristic of disability or imprisonment' (Cahill 1994: 78). This chapter explores some of the social inequalities which exist in relation to the ability to 'get around', inequalities related not only to personal fitness but also to income, gender and age. Growth in the use of mechanized forms of transport has taken place alongside social and demographic change, with patterns of travel and patterns of social development becoming mutually reinforcing. Ability to travel has, for example, allowed changes in the organization of work, so that employment is less dependent on the proximity of home and workplace. Labour mobility is more marked, and this in turn has helped to encourage recent trends towards self-employment and part-time work, sometimes in more than one job. Increases in female employment are associated with changes in patterns of childcare and transport of children to and from school, and the development of out-of-town shopping and leisure centres has been made possible by, and has in turn encouraged, increasing use of personal transport.

Passenger travel in the UK increased over threefold from 219 billion passenger kilometres in 1952 to 681 billion passenger kilometres in 1992 (HMSO
1994a). During that period, disposable incomes increased on average, and
although to some extent transport growth reflects a growth in people choosing
to spend more of their income on travel, choice is reduced for many people
on lower incomes. For some, the changing distribution of workplaces in relation to residential areas and the development of out-of-town facilities and
services means that the costs of travel place increasing demands on already
stretched household incomes. For others, inequalities in access to the means
of travel are associated with status, gender, age and health or disability.

Nevertheless, economic growth in general is accompanied by increasing
demands both for personal transport and for freight to move raw materials
and consumer goods. The provision of many goods and services increasingly
entails the use of transport in manufacture or distribution. The transport
industry in the UK accounts for around 4 per cent of GDP, employing over
900,000 workers directly, while a similar number are employed in transport-
related jobs (Department of the Environment 1992a).

Increased access to transport in the twentieth century has had major
impacts on both society and the environment. In the following section
we focus on social aspects of personal travel, looking at why, and by what
means, people move about in their daily lives and how access to transport
introduces new social inequalities and reinforces existing ones. We then
examine how the use of road transport in particular affects the environment, and finally we see how these effects are distributed across different
sectors of society.

Why and how people travel

Over the years 1992 to 1994, the average person in Britain spent 359 hours,
or 15 days, a year in travelling, covering an average distance of 10,400
kilometres (Central Statistical Office 1996). Women, however, travelled less
than two-thirds the distance of men. Among men aged 30 to 59 the average
distance travelled was 17,400 kilometres and about three-quarters of this
was covered by car. There are also gender differences in the purposes for
which people travel and the number of journeys made (Table 6.1).

In general, the reasons for travel by people of different ages and of different gender reflect their social roles and lifestyles. Commuting to and from
work accounts for nearly a fifth of the total distance travelled in Britain, but
whereas for men of working age commuting makes up around 30 per cent
of all trips, the figure is lower for women, closer to 20 per cent. Conversely,
women make more of their journeys to shop. Almost a quarter of the trips
made by women aged 30 to 59 were made for this purpose, reflecting perhaps the persisting role of women as homemakers and nurturers. Similarly,
women make proportionately more trips than men in escorting children to
school. Where journeys are made for social purposes, to visit friends or places
of entertainment or to take part in sports activities, for example, there is

Table 6.1   Purposes of journeys by age and gender in Great Britain, 1992–1994

Journey purpose	% of journeys				
	Aged 16 to 29		Aged 30 to 59		*All ages, all persons*
	Men	Women	Men	Women	
Commuting	30	23	29	21	19
Business	5	2	11	4	5
Education	6	5	0	1	5
Escort for education	0	2	2	5	2
Shopping	12	18	15	23	19
Other personal business	12	14	18	19	19
Social and entertainment	30	31	20	22	25
Holidays/other	4	4	5	5	6
Number of journeys for all purposes per person per year (100%)	892	826	988	865	742

Source: Central Statistical Office (1996).

Table 6.2   Mode of transport by purpose in Britain, 1992–1994

	Car/van	Rail	Local bus	Walking	Motorcycle	Bicycle	Other	All modes
Commuting	18	49	20	9	48	38	11	19
Business	6	7	1	1	4	3	4	5
Education	2	7	14	10	1	10	19	5
Shopping	19	9	33	23	12	11	10	20
Personal business	24	7	12	14	8	9	14	21
Leisure	31	21	20	44	27	29	41	31
All purposes	100	100	100	100	100	100	100	100

For each mode of transport the figures give the percentage of trips made for each purpose; journeys of under one mile are excluded.
Source: Central Statistical Office (1996).

little difference between men and women of working age. For journeys made by children under the age of 16 and people aged 60 or more, 75 and 91 per cent respectively are for shopping, personal or social purposes.

About half of all journeys made are for distances under two miles, and although longer trips of over 50 miles account for only 2 per cent of the total number, they make up 29 per cent of the total mileage travelled (HMSO 1994a). About a third of shorter journeys are made on foot or by bicycle, but a further third are made by car, mainly on local urban roads. Table 6.2 shows how different modes of travel are used for different purposes.

Over a half of all car journeys are for personal business or leisure purposes, and around one-third of bus journeys are made to shops or shopping centres. The highest percentage of rail journeys, which include those made on the London Underground, are commuting trips, and the majority of journeys by motorcycle and pedal cycle are also to and from work.

Travel choices

Sutton (1988: 57) categorizes mobility choice into three levels according to the extent to which demands for transport are met. The first level refers to situations where current mobility needs are satisfied by the means of transport available. His second level refers to the existence of 'latent demand', where mobility is depressed or limited either because of the lack of suitable means of transport or because of the costs of travel. Finally, he suggests that a third level of 'frustrated demands' can be identified when mobility is so suppressed that travel is not even considered as a possibility. These differences in mobility choice arise because access to travel options is conditioned by gender, age, disability, location and income. 'There is mobility deprivation as well as social deprivation' (Cahill 1994: 87).

The home responsibilities of women for childcare and shopping make them the main users of public transport. In 1989–91, women aged 16 to 29 made 133 bus trips a year on average, compared to 84 trips made by men. This pattern, however, is gradually changing. 'Women now increasingly have a car or access to a car, and the gap between women's and men's travel patterns is narrowing. The proportion of car mileage driven by women rose from 16% in 1975/76 to 25% in 1989/91' (Royal Commission on Environmental Pollution 1994: 16). In 1993–5, 56 per cent of women had a full car driving licence, compared to only 41 per cent in 1985–6, but this figure is still low compared to the number of men, 81 per cent, who hold a full licence.

Although increasing numbers of older people now have access to a car, elderly people often suffer from ill-health and many have never learned to drive. Because of this or because the costs of motoring prove prohibitive, older people frequently rely on walking or public transport to get around. In 1993–5, 27 per cent of the journeys made by women aged between 70 and 79 years were by local bus, compared to only 5 per cent of journeys made by those aged 30 to 59 years (Department of Transport 1996). In the UK, some local authorities have concessionary fare schemes for pensioners, but these vary considerably, so that regional inequalities pervade the travel options which are available.

For anyone who is disabled, even a short trip to the doctor or to local shops can be problematic, especially if a wheelchair is needed. Although the situation is gradually improving in the UK, only a very few buses and taxis allow wheelchair access, and taking a wheelchair by train often requires pre-booking and the assistance of railway staff. Journeys classed as essential may be possible using special transport services provided by local authorities,

Table 6.3   Household expenditure on transport by income group, 1994–1995

	% of total transport expenditure					
	Poorest quintile	Second quintile	Middle quintile	Forth quintile	Richest quintile	All households
Maintenance and running of motor vehicles	54.0	57.0	56.4	52.4	44.8	50.5
Net purchases of motor vehicles, accessories and spares	15.2	25.2	29.3	36.2	38.3	34.0
Bus and coach fares	13.4	6.8	3.7	2.4	1.6	3.1
Air fares	1.8	1.3	2.5	1.3	4.2	2.7
Rail fares	3.0	1.9	2.3	2.2	2.9	2.5
Other	12.5	7.8	5.7	5.5	8.2	7.1
Total transport expenditure (£ per week)	7.60	20.51	38.57	57.85	89.51	42.81

Source: adapted from Table 12.8, Central Statistical Office (1996).

hospitals or the voluntary sector, but in general travel options are severely limited unless people can drive themselves.

The transport options available to people living in rural areas are limited for everyone, regardless of gender, age and health. A decline in rural public transport provision has accompanied a growth in car ownership, but for people living on low incomes, running a car puts additional pressures on household budgets. Those who simply cannot afford a car must put up with poorer access to basic services, so that their poverty is exacerbated by further hardship and often a degree of social isolation (Boardman 1995). Richer people, on the other hand, can improve their quality of life by finding accommodation in more desirable or attractive rural residential areas, using cars for longer distance commuting between home and work, following a trend in what has been described as 'gentrification' (Findlay and Rogerson 1993: 38).

Public transport systems in Britain have their drawbacks. Travel by train or bus is often more time consuming than taking a car, and timetables may prove restrictive, even if buses and trains keep to them reliably. The routes offering the best services are usually those which are most profitable to the companies operating them, and for many people there simply is no accessible service available. Nevertheless, the costs of private motoring are high relative to public road transport, although the latter vary considerably with region. Table 6.3 shows UK household expenditure on transport for different income groups in 1994–5.

Since 1984 the percentage of expenditure on transport for all households has remained fairly constant at around 15 per cent, richer households spending more in absolute terms. When travel expenditure is broken down, however, it is clear that in the richest fifth of households expenditure on bus and coach fares is only 1.6 per cent of all travel expenditure, compared to 13.4 per cent in the poorest fifth. Motoring accounts for 83.1 per cent of all travel expenditure in the richest households and only 69.2 per cent in the poorest group, and in absolute terms the highest income group spends over 14 times more on motoring than the poorest. Although the percentage spent on running and maintaining vehicles is less variable, the percentage spent on purchasing vehicles and accessories increases markedly with income. Although car travel may occasionally be cheaper than public transport for larger families, one-third of households have no access to a car at all.

Modes of transport

Road transport accounts for 93 per cent of passenger travel in the UK, where the average daily flow of road traffic increased by just under 50 per cent from 2.2 thousand vehicles in 1981 to 3.2 thousand in 1994 (Central Statistical Office 1996). Other modes of transport are used less frequently but are discussed here briefly in relation to their implications for social policy.

Sea and air travel

Boats and ferries are mainly used for overseas travel in the UK, especially across the Channel to mainland Europe. In 1994, 6,330,000 passenger car journeys were made to and from UK ports, more than twice the number in 1981. The total number of international sea passengers increased by 6 per cent from 1993 to 37 million in 1994 but international air passenger travel increased even more, by 10 per cent to 96 million. Although business travel accounts for more than 40 per cent of air passenger traffic globally, tourist traffic is increasing more rapidly. The cost and accessibility of overseas holidays make them increasingly available to people on lower incomes, while richer families travel further afield (Chapter 7).

Walking and cycling

Walking and cycling account for only a tiny percentage of the distance travelled by people in the UK but, since trips by foot or bicycle usually cover only short distances, they make up 32 per cent of all journeys. Cycling in particular has declined since 1951, when 21 billion cycle kilometres were covered, accounting for a quarter of all traffic on public roads. By 1994, the total kilometres cycled had fallen to 4.4 billion and cycles represented only 1 per cent of all road traffic (Central Statistical Office 1996).

As public transport becomes increasingly marginalized, people from low-income groups often have no alternative but to walk or cycle, and their journey distances are therefore limited. Women with young children, pensioners and young people then become heavily reliant on local facilities and cannot take advantage of the often cheaper prices offered by large out-of-town shops and supermarkets. 'Walking as a means of transport is of central importance to women rather than men, to those on low incomes rather than to those on high incomes, and to the very young and very old rather than to those of working age' (National Consumer Council 1987: 3).

Walking and cycling are relegated to 'an inferior position in the transport hierarchy in spite of the fact that these modes are the ones that it is most in the public interest to promote owing to their low costs, environmental friendliness, the low risk of injury they pose to other road users, and so on' (Hillman 1992: 230). The health benefits of these modes of transport are well recognized. The regular physical activity entailed in walking and cycling can reduce mortality and morbidity from cardiovascular disease, while improving weight control, skeletal fitness, strength, mobility and mental health (Department of the Environment 1996a). The establishment of physical activity patterns in childhood is particularly important, as it has been shown to be a key to reducing adult cardiovascular diseases (Kuh and Cooper 1992). However, benefits are offset if the routes which must be travelled are unsafe or unattractive in terms of other traffic, poor street lighting and degraded urban environments. Wide pavements in good repair are particularly important for children, the elderly and people who are disabled or blind. Similarly, pedestrian crossings must provide sufficient time for everyone to cross in safety. In the UK, priority is increasingly given to motorists, although in other European countries, such as the Netherlands and Germany, the situation for walkers and cyclists is better.

Railways and buses

Although train and bus journeys each currently account for 6 per cent of the passenger distance travelled in the UK, the use of rail travel has remained at approximately the same level as in the 1950s, while the use of buses has declined progressively since 1952. Rail transport accounts for nearly a half of all journeys made for commuting purposes (Table 6.2) and is particularly important for people living in London where, during 1992–4, residents made 13 times more journeys by rail than people in the rest of Britain, excluding those in the South East (Central Statistical Office 1996). The cost of rail travel is high compared to bus fares, and until the mid-1980s many uneconomic bus routes were subsidized in the recognition that they met essential social needs. Public transport was seen as having the elements of a social service and some local governments, such as South Yorkshire County Council, maintained bus fares at their 1974 levels until they were obliged by central government to increase fares in 1984. Most of the benefits of such schemes were felt by people whose mobility was otherwise limited by age or low incomes.

Unemployed people appreciated the very low bus fares because they enabled them to keep up with activities which in other areas would have been impossible because of the high cost of fares – they could use the buses to travel to Sheffield city centre, to use the library and the shops. Elderly people appreciated the low fares for the same reasons and in addition they benefited from a travel pass which allowed free travel at off-peak times.

(Cahill 1994: 91)

Since the mid-1980s, however, there has been a growing divergence in the real price of public and private transport. 'It is notable that over the last decade the real price of both rail fares and bus fares has increased much faster than the index of all motor vehicle cost components and that the real price of private motoring has actually fallen' (Maddison *et al.* 1996: 3). In 1993 in Britain, only 0.5 and 0.7 thousand kilometres per head of population were travelled by rail and bus respectively, compared to 9.6 thousand kilometres per head of population travelled by car or taxi. Although car travel has extended enormously, this growth has not come about because people have switched from public to private transport. It reflects rather the fact that, for many people, rising incomes, changing consumption patterns and the relatively low cost of road use have led to changes in patterns of transport behaviour so that more and longer journeys are being made. 'It is clear that by far the largest change in patterns of travel has resulted from newly-generated travel by car' (Hillman 1992: 227).

Cars

Cars account for around 80 per cent of all road vehicles in the UK, and the number of cars on the road increased from 2.5 million in 1951 to 20 million in 1990 (Department of the Environment 1992a). Just under a third of British households have no regular use of a car or van, and the figure is lower in rural areas (22 per cent) than in cities (34 per cent). Car ownership also varies considerably with gender and socio-economic group. Gender differences are, however, gradually being eroded. In 1975–6 only 13 per cent of women owned a car, but this figure had increased almost threefold to 35 per cent by 1992–4, while car ownership by men increased by only a quarter during the same period. 'However, women are still far less likely than men to own a car, but are more likely to own a small car' (Central Statistical Office 1996: 207).

Households where the head of household is economically inactive or is in an unskilled or semi-skilled job are far less likely to own a car or van than households with a head in other socio-economic groups, while over half of those in professional or managerial jobs have two or more cars (Table 6.4).

Private car ownership offers individuals flexibility and freedom of choice to travel as and when they wish. It opens up options about where to live in relation to their work or their children's schools, and gives them access to

Table 6.4 British households with the regular use of a car or van by socio-economic group, 1994–1995

	% with no car	% with one car only	% with two or more cars
Professional	5	40	55
Employers and managers	4	40	55
Intermediate non-manual	15	56	29
Junior non-manual	28	54	18
Skilled manual and own account non-professional	14	54	32
Semi-skilled manual and personal service	33	53	14
Unskilled manual	45	47	8
Economically inactive	55	38	7
All groups	31	45	24

Source: Central Statistical Office (1996).

a wide range of social and leisure activity over a broad geographical area. Indeed, for some, driving is a form of recreation in its own right. A car may be regarded as 'essential' in order to maintain a preferred lifestyle and to take part in the normal activities of a certain social environment. A majority of people may feel they have no alternative to car ownership, especially if they live in a rural area where public transport is inadequate, expensive or non-existent (Maddison *et al.* 1996). Car travel also affords privacy and security, particularly important for women travelling alone at night or for transporting children safely to school.

For many people, cars have become symbols of identity, offering less tangible benefits to their owners. This is evident in the approach often taken by companies selling cars when they advertise them by emphasizing power, speed, performance, style and even sexual allure. Company cars are often given to staff as 'perks' which confer job status, while generous mileage payments can encourage car use rather than public transport for business purposes. In 1993–5, company cars were also used more intensively than private cars for non-business purposes (Department of Transport 1996).

In the light of these benefits it is no wonder that people without a car are seen as being disadvantaged or 'transport-poor' (Cahill 1994). Those least likely to own a car are elderly, infirm, unemployed or otherwise living on very low wages. Their carless status limits possibilities for finding jobs, visiting friends or relatives or reaching other places of entertainment. Their inability to benefit from the cheaper prices offered by out-of-town super-markets is exacerbated by the decline of smaller local shops. In 1980, 5 per cent of all retail sales were made from out-of-town locations, but by 1992 this figure had increased to 37 per cent (Royal Commission on Environ-mental Pollution 1994). For people living on low incomes in rural areas, the only alternative to car-dependency may be social isolation. Children are unable to visit friends, while the elderly may have difficulties in reaching post offices, shops and doctors' surgeries. It is estimated that around a quarter of rural households live in or on the margins of poverty, and 'the increasingly common assumption of countryside people as two-car-owning meritocracies (for whom the effort of making their own way to centralised services was a small price to pay for the environmental delights of rural living), can only serve to hide the plight of the non-mobile minority in gaining access to basic and necessary life-style opportunities' (Cloke *et al.* 1994: 144).

International comparisons

In the UK since the 1950s, growth in passenger travel has closely followed a growth in car ownership associated with economic growth, and the price of road fuel relative to household incomes has dropped by almost 40 per cent across most of the EU since 1980 (Environmental Data Services Report 260, September 1996: 6). More people than ever can afford to run a car, and car owners make more and longer journeys than others. The relationship between national wealth and car travel, however, varies with the development of attractive and efficient public transport systems. Table 6.5 shows, for instance, that although among developed industrialized countries Great Britain and the USA have particularly high levels of reliance on private cars for personal travel, the role of public transport is much greater in other countries, notably Japan.

Table 6.5 Modes of personal transport in developed countries, 1991

	% share of personal travel in 1991 (to nearest whole number)		
	Car	*Bus*	*Rail*
Belgium	82	11	7
Denmark	79	14	7
France	85	6	9
Germany	84	8	7
Great Britain	88	7	6
Italy	79	14	7
Japan	53	10	36
Netherlands	84	8	8
Portugal	81	13	7
Spain	73	19	8
Sweden	85	9	6
United States	98	2	1

Source: adapted from Royal Commission on Environmental Pollution (1994).

Table 6.6   Car ownership in selected countries

	Car ownership per 1000 persons			
	1985[a]	1988[b]	1991[c]	Projected 2025[a]
China	0.6			20
India	2.1			16
South Korea	11.2			210
Brazil	63.0			245
Mexico	64.0			250
Japan			240	
United Kingdom			320	
Italy			390	
France		400		
Canada		460		
West Germany		470		
United States			560	

Source: [a] Whyte (1995; after Mintzer 1992);   [b] OECD (1991);   [c] Blunden and Reddish (1991).

In Central and Eastern Europe, the public transport systems which played key roles under communism are now showing signs of serious deterioration as car ownership becomes a crucial symbol of a new freedom (Royal Commission on the Environment 1994), and in many developing countries, the increasing geographical size of cities and the growing numbers of employees travelling long distances to work are coupled with a lack of public transport facilities and weak or non-existent controls over private transport. Where buses are available they are often overcrowded and uncomfortable. Their poor state of repair makes travel slow, and although minibuses or collective taxis provide faster means of transport, they tend to be more expensive. In this context car ownership is increasingly more attractive, and vehicle densities are leading to severe problems of congestion in major cities in the developing world. In Mexico and Brazil, the numbers of road vehicles quadrupled between 1970 and 1980, while private car ownership in Bombay has virtually doubled over the past decade. As Table 6.6 shows, car ownership in developing countries is expected to show further dramatic increases by the year 2025.

Environmental effects of transport

Most mechanized transport relies on the combustion of petroleum products in petrol or diesel engines to produce energy for the propulsion of vehicles. In many ways this has similar effects to the burning of fossil fuels to produce energy for domestic heating (Chapter 5). In both cases the combustion of fuel in air produces carbon dioxide and water vapour, together with such

Table 6.7 The direct use of petroleum products in transport in the UK, 1994

	Petroleum products used (million tonnes)	% UK transport use
Road	35.76	79.8
Air	7.31	16.3
Water	1.16	2.6
Rail	0.60	1.3
Total	44.83	100.0

Source: Department of Transport (1995).

by-products as nitrogen oxides and sulphur dioxide. In motor engines using leaded petrol, these by-products include lead compounds. The extent to which fuel is completely burnt in vehicle engines varies, and products of incomplete combustion include carbon monoxide and volatile organic compounds (VOCs) and, especially in diesel engines, particulate matter. All these products and by-products are emitted from vehicles in exhaust gases, and the exact amounts and proportions released depend on a wide range of factors, including engine design and size, characteristics of the fuel, the conditions in which the vehicle is driven and the way it is driven, and the age and state of maintenance of the vehicle.

Table 6.7 shows the direct use of petroleum products in UK transport in 1994. Nearly 80 per cent of this use is by road transport, and road transport accounted for 83.3 per cent of all transport energy consumption in the EU in 1994. Global comparisons reveal that 'transport fuels account for more than 55 per cent of developing countries' total oil consumption, which has grown by 50 per cent since 1980, as against 10 per cent in the OECD economies' (International Bank for Reconstruction and Development 1992: 124).

Exhaust emissions from traffic include greenhouse gases which have major implications for global warming, but they also include other gases which affect air quality at both local and regional levels. The environmental effects of motor transport are not, however, confined to gaseous emissions. Vehicle noise and the impacts of road development on the landscape affect the quality of both urban and rural life, while risks of death or injury from traffic accidents pose an environmental hazard in their own right and, together with other factors, can lead to the disruption of social communities at a local level. Finally, the solid intractable wastes produced by broken down cars, used oil and old tyres pose severe problems of disposal and waste management.

Greenhouse gases

Although the production of greenhouse gases, mainly carbon dioxide, represents the only global environmental effect of road transport, it is a crucial one. Cars account for a fifth of global carbon dioxide emissions, and exhaust gases also contain small amounts of methane, both of which contribute to an enhanced greenhouse effect and so increase the risks of global warming (Boxes 1.1 and 5.2). In 1990, over a half of the UK's carbon dioxide emissions in the transport sector came from private cars, another 30 per cent from industrial and commercial road transport and the remainder from public transport (HMSO 1994b). Across the EU, vehicle emissions of carbon dioxide increased by 50 per cent between 1980 and 1994 (Environmental Data Services Report 260, September 1996: 7). Published figures make no reference to emissions from military transport and, although it is known that climbing and cruising aircraft make substantial contributions to carbon dioxide emissions, records for commercial aircraft only include those produced during ground movements, take-off and landing (Royal Commission on Environmental Pollution 1994). Concern about carbon dioxide from aircraft is, however, currently growing as emissions are forecast to treble by the year 2040 (Environmental Data Services Report 259, August 1996: 4).

Air quality

Road vehicles are the major source of the most significant air pollutants – carbon monoxide, nitrogen oxides, VOCs and black smoke – in towns and cities. The environmental effects of air pollution include damage to crops, materials and wildlife habitats, but traffic pollution also has a significant impact on human health. 'On the Department of Health's latest assessment, pollution causes several thousand advanced deaths each year, along with 10–20,000 hospital admissions and "many thousands" of cases of illness, reduced activity, distress and discomfort' (Environmental Data Services Report 257, June 1996: 15). The effects of transport-related air pollutants are complex and interrelated, as shown in Table 6.8.

Table 6.8 Summary of the main environmental effects of vehicle exhaust emissions

Environmental effect	Pollutant					
	Carbon dioxide	Methane	Carbon monoxide	Nitrogen oxides	VOCs	Ozone
Enhancement of the greenhouse effect	√	√	–	√	–	√
Damage to health	–	–	√	√	√	√
Acid deposition	–	–	–	√	–	–
Depletion of stratospheric ozone	–	–	–	√	–	–
Build-up of tropospheric ozone	–	–	√	√	√	√
Photochemical smog	–	–	√	√	√	√

Carbon monoxide. Carbon monoxide is a colourless, toxic gas which is a product of the incomplete combustion of vehicle fuels. Between 1982 and 1992, emissions from road vehicles in the UK increased by 31 per cent and, in 1994, road transport accounted for 89 per cent of all carbon monoxide emissions. However, the amount released for each vehicle-kilometre travelled has changed little since 1970, showing that increases in levels are owing to increased transport use.

The toxicity of carbon monoxide stems from its action in lowering the capacity of the blood to carry oxygen around the body. It can be lethal at high levels and even at low concentrations can cause headaches, drowsiness, impaired vision and slowed reflexes. In addition to its direct effects on human health, carbon monoxide indirectly enhances the greenhouse effect when, in the presence of sunlight, it takes part in photochemical reactions which increase levels of tropospheric ozone (Box 6.1).

Nitrogen oxides. Since 1970, it is estimated that the emissions of oxides of nitrogen from road transport in the UK have doubled, and motor vehicles

---

Box 6.1 Tropospheric ozone

Ozone is a highly toxic and irritant gas, but in the upper atmosphere, or stratosphere, it acts to protect life on the earth's surface from the damaging effects of solar radiation. There it is the depletion of ozone which causes environmental damage (Box 3.1). In contrast, in the lower atmosphere, the troposphere, increasing levels of ozone have a polluting effect.

High levels of tropospheric ozone can cause damage to growing plants and sensory and respiratory irritation in animals. It appears that some people are more sensitive than others to ozone, but it can cause breathing difficulties for some as well as increasing susceptibility to infections and impairing lung function (Royal Commission on the Environment 1994). In addition to its effects on health, ozone at lower levels in the atmosphere acts as a greenhouse gas, increasing risks of global warming and climate change.

Ozone does occur naturally at ground level at very low concentrations, but background levels have doubled over the past hundred years (HMSO 1994a). It is formed by the reaction of other chemicals, mainly nitrogen oxides and VOCs, in the presence of strong sunlight, and since its formation depends initially on other pollutants, it is known as a secondary pollutant.

Because ozone can persist for several days it can be transported long distances and ground level pollution tends to be a regional rather than a strictly local problem. Vehicle emissions on the coast of mainland Europe have been associated with pollution in southern England and vice versa, depending on wind directions.

Large-scale ozone pollution has mainly been recorded in Europe and the United States, especially in the summer. 'In California, it is estimated that ozone causes annual losses of up to 20 per cent of important crops like cotton and grapes' (OECD 1991: 48).

now contribute 70 per cent or more to nitrogen oxide levels in major urban areas (HMSO 1994a). Three oxides of nitrogen are implicated in fossil fuel combustion: nitric oxide (NO), nitrogen dioxide (NO$_2$) and nitrous oxide (N$_2$O). These gases have different properties owing to the different numbers of oxygen atoms attached to each nitrogen atom, but in the atmosphere they undergo complex transformations and are often referred to collectively as NO$_x$. All the oxides of nitrogen are involved in reactions producing nitrous and nitric acids and, like sulphur dioxide, are major contributors to acid deposition in the environment (Box 5.1). But the individual forms of NO$_x$ also have other environmentally damaging effects.

Nitrous oxide and nitric oxide are non-toxic, but the former is a potent greenhouse gas while the nitric oxide initially released on combustion is rapidly converted in the air to nitrogen dioxide, only small amounts of which are emitted directly from vehicles. Nitrogen dioxide is toxic in high concentrations and is associated with problems of respiratory irritation and infections through its action in reducing resistance to infection and in inflaming the cells lining bronchial tubes. In addition to these direct effects on health, nitrogen dioxide, together with volatile organic compounds from vehicle exhaust fumes, takes part in chemical and photochemical reactions in the air which lead to the formation of ground level ozone and photochemical smogs (Box 6.2).

Volatile organic compounds. The volatile organic compounds (VOCs) released in exhaust emissions include a whole variety of hydrocarbons and

---

Box 6.2   Photochemical smog

Ozone occurs naturally in small quantities at ground level, but concentrations are increased when certain chemical air pollutants produced by human activity take part in complex reactions in the presence of sunlight. These reactions involve both light and chemistry and are known as *photochemical* reactions. The main chemical air pollutants involved are the nitrogen oxides, volatile organic compounds (VOCs) and carbon monoxide, which are emitted from the burning of fossil fuels and from some industrial processes.

Motor vehicles are major emitters of VOCs, nitrogen oxides and suspended particulate matter in black smoke, and when these pollutants enter the air in sunny conditions photochemical reactions occur and a whole cocktail of new chemicals is produced. In extreme cases, the result is a *photochemical smog* containing ozone, oxides of nitrogen and carbon monoxide, in which visibility is reduced and eye irritation, smell and health problems can reach serious levels.

The key role played by weather conditions in influencing photochemical reactions means that photochemical smogs occur more often in some parts of the world than others, and the problem has recently been most pronounced in cities in Greece and in parts of the west coast of the United States, notably Los Angeles.

hydrocarbon derivatives from unburnt fuel and partially burnt fuel products. Their concentrations in the air are also increased by the evaporation of fuel. In the UK, road transport is responsible for 38 per cent of VOC emissions, and between 1982 and 1992 emissions from vehicles increased by 8 per cent.

Like nitrogen oxides, VOCs contribute to ground level ozone formation and photochemical smogs. Some, such as benzene, are known to cause cancer in humans, while others such as butadiene are suspected carcinogens. Many VOCs have other toxic properties and can cause drowsiness, eye irritation and coughing, while long-term exposure can cause lung damage. Like nitrogen oxides, these emissions are therefore air pollutants in their own right, as well as being precursors of ozone formation.

Black smoke. The term 'black smoke' is used to cover a range of fine suspended particulate air pollutants, including particles from dust and aerosols, particles formed in the atmosphere from sulphur dioxide and nitrogen oxides and carbon particles from exhaust gases emitted by vehicles and industrial processes. In the UK, it is road transport which is responsible for the largest share of emissions. In 1994, transport contributed 58 per cent (Table 5.1), a figure representing an increase of 147 per cent since 1970 (Department of Trade and Industry 1996). This huge increase is partly due to the increase in diesel vehicles which, although emitting less carbon dioxide, carbon monoxide, nitrogen oxides and VOCs than petrol engines, are responsible for more particulate pollution.

As discussed in Chapter 5 in relation to domestic use of fossil fuels, the environmental effects of black smoke include lowered visibility, soiling of buildings and damage to human respiratory systems. Emissions from vehicle exhausts, however, have an added danger, since the minute particles can carry carcinogenic VOCs on their surfaces.

Lead pollution

Airborne lead from vehicle exhausts enters the human body through the lungs or gut, and acts as a cumulative poison which is thought to cause subtle brain damage and learning problems in children. Lowered IQs, impaired attention capacity, speech and language defects and behaviour disorders leading to reductions in educational attainment, employability and the capacity to cope with stress have all been associated with increased blood lead concentrations.

The use of petrol containing lead compounds as additives has been declining in Western Europe under EU Directives introduced in 1981 and 1985. Unleaded petrol was introduced in the UK in 1986 and lead emissions from vehicle exhausts have fallen by 86 per cent from their 1975 level, despite a 36 per cent increase in petrol consumption (Department of Trade and Industry 1996). This is not the case, however, in Central and Eastern Europe, where lead pollution from transport and industrial sources remains a major problem.

In inner Budapest, for example, the concentration of airborne lead in high flow traffic areas is nearly 16 times higher than that in surrounding parkland. An EU Directive introduced in 1977 specified that no more than 50 per cent of any group in a population should have blood lead concentration levels above 20 micrograms per decilitre, the lowest level at which harmful effects have been adequately demonstrated in children. Over 57 per cent of inner-city children in Budapest have been found to have blood lead levels which exceed this figure, compared to fewer than 2 per cent of children living in the outskirts of the city (Hertzman 1995). In Mexico City, where 95 per cent of vehicle fuel still contains lead compounds, 29 per cent of all children are thought to have unhealthy blood lead levels (International Bank for Reconstruction and Development 1992).

Noise

Intrusive noise can cause disturbance to people's normal activities and can also affect sleep or rest, causing irritation and loss of concentration. The World Health Organization now recognizes noise as a health hazard and that, 'more than mere irritation, it signifies degradation in the quality of life' (WHO 1992: 213). A survey carried out in Great Britain in 1991 found that around three-quarters of respondents were disturbed at times by noise from aircraft and trains, and that over 80 per cent were disturbed by road traffic noise (Department of the Environment 1996b). That people are increasingly regarding transport noise as intrusive is indicated by the growing number of official complaints made. 'Since 1979, complaints to Environmental Health Officers in England and Wales about the noise from road traffic have grown by more than a quarter and complaints about aircraft noise have more than doubled' (Royal Commission on Environmental Pollution 1994: 47).

Landscape

The natural landscape is affected both by the quarrying of aggregates for use in road construction and by the increasing use of open land for building new roads or widening those that already exist. In the UK, 32 per cent of quarried aggregates are supplied to the road construction and maintenance industry. Although quarries can damage environmentally sensitive sites and natural habitats, relatively low costs discourage the use of alternative materials from industrial or demolition wastes which are increasingly used in other European countries, such as the Netherlands and Germany.

Roads and verges take up 3.3 per cent of land area in the UK, compared to only 0.2 per cent covered by railways. Between 1985 and 1990, around 14,000 hectares of land in Britain was used for new road construction, 9600 hectares of which was rural land. Certain areas of land are designated as National Parks, Areas of Outstanding Natural Beauty (AONBs) and Sites of Special Scientific Interest (SSSIs), and intended to be protected from road development whenever possible. The high conservation value of such land is often linked with low agricultural value and, where it cannot be used for housing or industrial development, it tends to command only a low market price. Paradoxically, it is this low price which makes it increasingly favoured for road construction, and in 1994 the Royal Commission on Environmental Pollution received evidence about the Department of Transport's new trunk road programme, which indicated that proposals for widening the M25 around London could affect ten SSSIs, 47 ancient woodlands and 24 other important wildlife sites. The development of good roads in itself encourages further developments which threaten the natural environment. As well as reducing unspoilt areas of peace and tranquillity, causing loss of hedgerows, species-rich verges and other wildlife habitats, road traffic has other repercussions on wild animals. 'The former Nature Conservancy Council estimated in its evidence that 47,000 badgers, 3000–5000 barn owls and 20–40% of breeding amphibians may be killed on the roads each year' (Royal Commission on Environmental Pollution 1994: 56).

Solid waste

Chemical wastes emanating from motor vehicles in use include oils, de-icing agents and leaked fuels, all of which can cause severe contamination of soils and groundwater. Used vehicles and parts can be even more of a problem environmentally. Some reusable parts, lead from batteries, ferrous metals and precious metals from the catalytic converters fitted to reduce harmful exhaust emissions can be recycled, but the remainder, around half a million tonnes a year in the UK alone, must be disposed of in landfill sites. Tyres pose particular difficulties. Of the 40 million tyres scrapped each year, two-thirds are put into landfill or dumped illegally, with resulting risks of fire, highly polluting run-off waters and air pollution.

Accidents

'Road accidents are the major cause of death and injury to children, accounting for a quarter of all deaths of school children and two thirds of all accidental deaths' (Cahill 1994: 91). In 1994, the road accident death rate for children in the UK was 2.5 per 100,000 population. Children themselves are aware of the dangers of road traffic. In a survey of four schools in Birmingham, 'an average 43 per cent of respondents in each of the schools reported that they "didn't feel safe" in their area, that "traffic is bad" and it was "dangerous crossing roads"' (Davis and Jones 1996a: 367). Between 1971 and 1993–4 adult road accident death rates fell in all EU countries except Portugal and Greece, 'the countries with the largest proportionate increase in the car ownership rate over the period' (Office for National Statistics 1997: 210). In the UK, the death rate fell from 16.5 to 7.4 per 100,000 population, but between 1986 and 1994 there was an increase in casualties for car drivers, around half of whom were between 22 and 39 years old.

Many road traffic accidents cause injury to non-driving road users. Over the period 1983 to 1993, for example, 68.8 pedestrians and 48.5 pedal cyclists were killed for each billion passenger kilometres travelled, compared to only 4.3 people killed in cars. 'In the past decade an average of 5 to 6 children are killed on the road each week as pedestrians and cyclists . . . child road traffic deaths are too frequent, and therefore too mundane, to be newsworthy. In that sense they have become an accepted feature of an increasingly motorised society' (Davis 1997: 12).

Social costs of transport-related environmental damage

We have seen above how the growth of more and faster means of transport confers benefits in the form of higher levels of mobility and freedom to travel, but that these benefits are not distributed evenly across different groups in society. Even within a single country such as the UK, differences in levels of private vehicle ownership reflect comparative levels of affluence; internationally, they reflect economic growth. While the rich increasingly travel by car, the poor are restricted to the use of public transport, particularly buses, or to walking or cycling. Women travel less than men and their journeys are more likely to be to shops or schools than to places of work. They travel more often as passengers in cars than as drivers, and use buses for more journeys than do men of the same age. Both the very young and the very old make most of their journeys by foot or by public transport, and even the latter presents considerable difficulties for people who are ill or disabled. They usually have to rely on their own means of transport or on family, friends or special services provided by the public or voluntary sectors.

Nevertheless, growing numbers of people do have access to private cars and road traffic is increasing rapidly throughout the world, with many important impacts on the environment. The emission of carbon dioxide and, to a lesser extent, methane from vehicle exhausts causes damage on a global scale by contributing to the greenhouse effect and so increasing the risks of global warming and climate change. Emissions of nitrogen oxides and sulphur dioxide add to problems of acid deposition damaging to plant growth, animal life and building structures. Air pollution is caused by emissions of carbon monoxide, nitrogen oxides, VOCs, ozone and smoke, and the environment also suffers from lead pollution, landscape degradation, waste production and accidents caused by traffic and transport infrastructures. Even effects which are regional or local 'can have substantial economic and social consequences, ranging from added costs of medical care and building restoration to reduced agricultural output, widespread forest damage, and a generally lower quality of life' (OECD 1991: 33).

Like the benefits of transport, its environmental costs are distributed unequally. Ironically, however, the sectors of society who pay the highest price are often those least likely to enjoy the benefits. Pollution from road vehicles is particularly serious in poorer developing countries, where vehicles are frequently in bad condition and lower quality fuels are used. Cities in

Figure 6.1 The benefits to health which cycling can bring are often offset by exposure to pollution in urban areas.
Photographer: © David Townend

low-income countries have levels of suspended particulate matter which are much higher than those in more developed countries. Vehicles tend to be concentrated in a few large cities, where many inhabitants spend a substantial proportion of their time in the open air and are thus exposed to exhaust fumes for long periods. Urban air pollution in low-income countries deteriorated between the late 1970s and the late 1980s, while the situation improved in middle- and high-income countries (International Bank for Reconstruction and Development 1992).

Rural or suburban households in higher-income countries cause disproportionate amounts of pollution because they tend to have more cars and to travel longer distances (Boardman 1995). They use cars not only for commuting but also for leisure trips to other parts of the countryside. However, the local effects of air pollution are most concentrated in central urban areas and not only drivers but also people who walk or cycle, often the poor, women, children and the elderly, are exposed. While the benefits of motorized transport are reaped by people in higher socio-economic groups, the costs are also borne by those in lower income groups. 'It is the lower income groups who are most likely to live alongside major arterial roads or in heavily trafficked streets. Noise and atmospheric pollution from motor vehicle exhausts are therefore disproportionately experienced by poorer households – those who are least likely contributors because they are not so likely to own a car' (Jones 1996: 257).

The health effects of atmospheric pollution from vehicle exhausts are complex and surrounded by scientific uncertainty. In the UK, for example, the prevalence of asthma is increasing, and although this coincides with large increases in motor vehicle emissions, it is difficult to establish any firm causal relationship. 'One of the basic difficulties in investigating the health effects of air pollution is that a number of pollutants are usually present together in the atmosphere' (Royal Commission on Environmental Pollution 1994: 29).

Poor air quality is more likely to have its worst effects on people who are already susceptible to respiratory problems or cardiovascular disease and on those whose age makes them particularly vulnerable. The latter group includes children, the elderly, pregnant women and their unborn children, the very people who in general are least likely to drive private cars and who thus contribute least towards pollution problems. Exhaust fumes are emitted relatively close to the ground, and kerbside pollution levels may be two or three times higher than the urban background level, so that children or babies in prams receive more exposure than adults. For the elderly, susceptibility because of age is often compounded by existing ill health. In the case of photochemical smogs, for example, 'when episodes occur in conjunction with heat waves and high humidity, as in Athens and other cities during recent summers, premature mortality occurs among the aged, especially those with respiratory problems' (WHO 1992: 157). Poverty exacerbates this situation. Poorer countries are less likely to be able to enforce regulations to reduce polluting emissions, let alone afford to carry out research and monitoring into air pollution. The rate at which toxic lead compounds, for example, are absorbed by the body is highest for children and for people who live on a poor diet. Richer countries such as those in the OECD are setting increasingly strict standards to reduce the use of lead additives in petrol, and average blood lead concentrations in the United States and Japan have fallen to only a third of their 1970 levels. Yet lead emissions are still a major source of concern in developing countries, especially in cities such as Bangkok and Mexico City. 'It is difficult, however, to assess the degree to which human health is being impaired by air pollution in cities around the world. Information on air quality levels is scarce, particularly in the poorer and less urbanized developing countries' (WHO 1992: 152).

People who live in areas with heavy traffic problems are most likely to be near the bottom of the income scale, and the lack of traffic restraint can make spatial social divisions even more marked. As well as effects on health, air pollution carries unpleasant smells and tastes, while traffic noise inhibits easy conversation in the street. If they have a choice, people are less likely to walk in such areas and conditions are created which are ideal for street crime, a problem which deters walking even more. Added to the danger of road accidents, all these effects can lead to a decline in the use of streets as living spaces, so that levels of social interaction are reduced and communities disrupted in a phenomenon which has been labelled 'community severance'. 'Severance of streets and communities by traffic and road building, bringing quantifiable accidents but also less detectable social isolation and mental health effects, are also most likely to affect lower income groups' (Jones 1996: 257).

It is ironic that one of the main effects of the increased mobility and freedom to travel which the private car offers to some sectors of society actually reduces the extent to which those same benefits are accessible to others. People who do not have cars are more dependent on social contacts within walking distance, yet the growth in roads and road traffic presents obstacles to the movements of mothers with young children, of the elderly and of the disabled, who are increasingly denied opportunities for wider social participation. Parents' fear of road accidents, or even fear of their children's abduction by car drivers, means that many children in the UK are no longer allowed to play or cycle in the streets. Their mobility is restricted to home, school or the parental car (Cahill 1994). Davis and Jones (1996b) review the impacts which limited independent mobility has on children's perceptions of their relationship with their environment and on the style and extent of their social participation. They argue that the current situation reflects a power relationship in which 'adults want to teach children to be careful and to be scared of cars, rather than attempting to limit the traffic' (Davis and Jones 1996b: 109). Low-income rural families are often dependent on cars for any form of social participation, but any increases in the costs of motoring, designed to curb the growth in road transport, would result in especial hardship for them. Similarly, suggested moves to reduce travel by encouraging the use of new technology for teleworking, video-conferencing or home shopping (HMSO 1994a) would be likely to result in even more social isolation.

The Royal Commission on the Environment (1994) warns that current transport trends have unsustainable environmental, social and economic impacts, and it would seem that social well-being could indeed be improved by a reduction in road transport (Maddison *et al.* 1996). 'The social and environmental costs of every journey by private transport exceed the equivalent costs of that journey being made by public transport' (Hillman 1992: 226). Although governments can affect attitudes through the use of price differentials, the potential for change ultimately depends on individual motoring behaviour. 'Cars are a key issue because, of all the major sources of pollution, they are probably the one most directly under the control of individuals' (Yearley 1991: 38). However, the problem is how to reconcile desires for a safer and healthier environment with individual desires to travel. On the one hand, we might see the increased access of women, the poor and the disabled to the freedoms of travel provided by private cars as an improvement in social well-being. On the other hand, this would only exacerbate the extent of environmental problems caused by car use. A survey of social attitudes in Britain found that a higher percentage of people without household access to a car were in favour of road improvements as opposed to improvements in public transport than those with access to a car. This could suggest that most non-car users are aspiring ones. 'In a culture which places a high value on mobility, the freedom to travel which the car confers appears to overcome the otherwise consistent concern for the quality of the environment' (Young 1991: 120). Such concern would, in principle, lead people to adjust their consumer behaviour to protect the environment, but the problem is that a 'minimalist approach to consumption is clearly at odds, not just with the expansionary dynamic of a market economy, but also with the common desire to improve the material well-being of everyday life' (Young 1991: 124). Another difficulty is that the immediate benefits of car use can appear more real than environmental costs which may be invisible, longer term or geographically distant, and which are not usually borne in full by the individual driver. 'Changing patterns of transport have shaped today's social and recreational lifestyles. But the impact of ever rising levels of transport on the environment is one of the most significant challenges for sustainable development' (HMSO 1994a: 169).

Summary points

● The use of motorized forms of transport for work, domestic and leisure purposes has increased dramatically over the past 50 years, in association with rising average incomes, changing patterns of employment and changing roles of women in society.

● Options about whether, where and how to travel are conditioned by gender, age, disability and location, as well as by income.

● Low-income groups are more likely to walk or cycle or to use public transport than those who are more wealthy, but car use is rapidly increasing as the relative costs of private motoring fall. Car ownership confers freedom and flexibility, and it is also seen as a symbol of social status in most parts of the world.

● Most motor engines burn petroleum products and release exhaust gases which contribute to global warming and reduce air quality on both a local and a regional scale, affecting human health and damaging the environment.

● Transport noise and congestion is a growing problem, especially in built-up areas and near busy arterial roads. Road building itself has both direct and indirect impacts on land and wildlife habitats, while chemical and solid wastes emanating from the use and disposal of motor vehicles pollute air, water and soils.

● Road traffic accident deaths and injuries are not confined to drivers and their passengers, but pose serious risks to walkers and cyclists, especially children.

● As more people enjoy the benefits of motor transport, its damaging effects on the environment are increasing. They are often felt severely by those who, being excluded from car ownership, reap few of the benefits. Nevertheless, the underlying ideals of market economics continue to foster the notion that material possessions and personal liberties lead to increased social well-being. Shifts away from lifestyles which depend on the intensive use of motor transport are likely to require radical changes in both attitudes and behaviour.

Chapter seven

RECREATION AND LEISURE

In recent years leisure has become a growth industry in most countries. In the UK, tourism alone contributes £37 billion a year to the national economy and employs around 1.5 million people (Department of the Environment 1996a). In addition, employment in the sports industry grew by some 22 per cent between 1985 and 1990 and in 1994 provided jobs for nearly 500,000 people (HMSO 1994a). Direct consumer spending on leisure between 1982 and 1988 increased by over 27 per cent in real terms (Cahill 1994), while the links between leisure and transport, energy use, urbanization and rural development give direct and indirect effects of leisure activities a major role in both national and many local economies.

Notions about what constitutes leisure are, however, really functions of social organization. Cahill (1994) gives a succinct historical account of the growth of leisure in the UK, and points out that 'the separation of work and leisure is a product of industrialisation' (Cahill, 1994: 152). Ideas about leisure are also associated with ideas about social development and well-being.

A society of free individuals is one where they have free time, as we have known since Aristotle. We need free time for civic life, to develop our autonomous activities. We need free time to consume what we have already bought: to listen to music, read books, indulge in sport or photography. We need free time above all for friendship and love.

(Lipietz 1995: 48)

The idea that people have needs for free time for rest and recreation outside of time spent in paid or unpaid work is fraught with philosophical difficulties. If work is seen as something which must be done, as opposed to a form of activity which need not be undertaken, then we have the paradoxical situation where we are suggesting that people have a need to do that which is, by definition, unnecessary! One way of dealing with this dilemma is to regard leisure simply as an indicator of the exercise of choice by individuals about how they spend their time. 'People seeking leisure want to experience feelings of freedom and to be given the scope to do their own thing as and when they wish' (Kinnersley 1994: 120). The element of need then becomes the need to experience feelings of autonomy and freedom. It allows us to dispense with rigid distinctions between work and leisure and to incorporate into discussion those aspects of work time which overlap with leisure time. These include, for example, the opportunities for social contact afforded by working outside the home. These can be especially important for lone parents who may otherwise be restricted by their childcare responsibilities in spending time in the company of other adults and forming friendships. Going out to work can in itself be a way of achieving feelings of freedom and autonomy.

Broad ideas about what constitutes leisure can also allow us to consider situations where two or more activities are undertaken at the same time. Cahill (1994) cites, for example, the case where a person may watch the television or listen to the radio while doing household work such as ironing. However, the notion of choice still remains problematic. Clarke and Critcher (1985) discuss the 'compulsory' leisure activities of mothers of young children, pointing out that many women spend most of their leisure time in activities centred on the home and family. Visits to parks or the seaside, for example, commonly regarded as leisure pursuits, may be done less to satisfy the needs of parents than to keep children happy.

It is clear that particular activities cannot be classified simply as 'work' or 'leisure'. In this chapter, therefore, we focus first on how people spend their time and on the differences between social groups in the amount of time which is not taken up primarily by the requirements of maintaining and reproducing the necessary functions of daily life. Although we cannot judge how far the use of this time is freely chosen, it is possible to examine what people do in their 'free' time and to identify some of the ways in which social factors fundamentally influence access to these loosely defined leisure activities. We then move on to discuss the impacts of such activities on the environment, and how these can both limit and enhance the potential for continuing use in the future.

Availability of free time

The amount of free time available to people in Great Britain is largely determined by the number of hours they work. Over the course of the twentieth century there has been a decline in the number of hours which people spend in paid employment. They have longer paid holidays and tend to retire earlier, all of which factors mean that people now have more free time. Table 7.1 shows that during the week retired men and women have almost twice as much free time as those in employment.

Table 7.1 Time use by employment status and gender in Great Britain, 1995

Weekly hours spent on	In full-time employment		In part-time employment		Retired		All adults
	Men	Women	Men	Women	Men	Women	
Sleep	57	58	62	60	67	66	61
Free time	34	31	48	32	59	52	40
Work, study and travel	53	48	28	26	3	4	32
Housework, cooking and shopping	7	15	12	26	15	26	16
Eating, personal hygiene and caring	13	13	13	21	15	17	15
Household maintenance and pet care	4	2	6	3	9	3	4
Free time per weekday	4	4	6	4	8	7	5
Free time per weekend day	8	6	8	6	10	8	8

Source: Central Statistical Office (1996).

Although retired women spend more of their time on housework, cooking and shopping than retired men, gender differences in time use are particularly marked among those who are employed. Women in full-time employment spend slightly fewer hours each week than men in work, study and travel, but spend more time doing work related to the home and caring. Consequently, gender differences in the average daily hours of free time are more pronounced at weekends than on weekdays. Among those in part-time jobs, women have substantially less free time than men. The fact that these women on average spend a third as much time again as men on eating, personal hygiene and caring probably reflects the status of many as mothers or informal carers who work part-time rather than full-time because of their home responsibilities. In addition, women in households where there are dependent children spend 70 per cent more time on housework, cooking and cleaning than women in households without dependent children (Central Statistical Office 1996).

Use of free time

People who have no paid employment potentially have plenty of time to pursue leisure activities, and many UK policies developed, for example, by the Sports Council, Arts Council and local authorities are aimed at encouraging their participation in certain forms of recreational activities. Explicit objectives of such policies are to enhance feelings of community identity and to create jobs, but the underlying implications are that organized use of

Table 7.2   Use of free time by age in Great Britain, 1995

Activity	Hours per week					
	16–24	*25–34*	*35–44*	*45–59*	*60 and over*	*All aged 16 or over*
Television or radio	14	15	13	17	26	19
Visiting friends	7	5	4	4	4	5
Reading	1	1	2	3	6	3
Talking, socializing and telephoning friends	3	3	3	4	4	3
Eating and drinking out	6	4	4	4	2	3
Hobbies, games and computing	2	2	1	3	3	2
Walks and other recreation	2	2	1	2	3	2
Doing nothing (may include illness)	1	1	1	2	2	2
Sports participation	3	1	1	1	1	1
Religious, political and other meetings	–	1	1	–	1	1
Attending concerts, theatres, cinemas and sports (as spectators)	1	1	–	–	–	–
Other	1	–	–	–	–	–
All free time	40	37	33	40	52	42

Source: Central Statistical Office (1996).

free time is somehow better than allowing individuals to do as they choose or to do nothing with their time. A lack of directed activity either in work or leisure among certain groups in society has been blamed for various phenomena indicative of social unrest, such as rioting, joyriding and general vandalism, in the UK in recent years (Cahill 1994).

Nevertheless, the use of free time in Great Britain is dominated by watching television or listening to the radio, especially among those aged 60 or over (Table 7.2). Together with visiting friends, reading, talking, socializing and telephoning friends, watching the television and listening to the radio are activities which are not formally organized and which incur little cost financially. Other activities can be more expensive, and income is a major determinant of people's use of free time. In a study of people living on low incomes, Huby and Dix (1992: 20) found that when respondents were talking about their needs, 'there was little discussion of leisure expenses – this was not an item at the top of most people's minds. Some went out for a drink, or to spend an evening with friends, but most said they did so rarely and saw it as a one-off "treat". Going out often required borrowing cash or relying on offers to buy drinks.' Spending money on the football pools or the lottery can become something more than a simple leisure activity since 'many people living on a low income could see no prospect of their situation improving "unless we win the pools"' (Kempson 1996: 22).

Spending time at home

People in the UK as a whole spend more than half of their leisure time in their own homes, especially when they are elderly or when they have young children. Kempson (1996) highlights the fact that for people living on low incomes many leisure activities are considered to be luxuries, and children in low-income families are less likely than others to participate in music, drama or dance classes or in sports activities which have to be paid for outside of school.

For many women, the home is both a work place and the place where they spend their free time. Restrictions on women's access to activities outside the home are sometimes related to their childcare roles but women may also find themselves limited because of potential problems of personal safety: for example, when going out after dark or when visiting predominantly male pubs or clubs. For some women, the freedom to spend time away from home is regulated by their husbands, either because of concern for the woman's welfare or as an expression of patriarchal control (Green *et al.* 1990).

Of course, not all time spent in leisure in the home is indicative of low income or gender or age inequalities. Reading is a popular pursuit across the population, and on average people aged 16 or over in Great Britain spend three hours a week reading. More than 27 million people read at least one national daily newspaper in 1994–5, and 40 per cent of the population made use of public libraries. The use of written material for leisure is, however, much more marked in industrialized countries where the average paper consumption per capita was 120 kilograms a year in 1991, compared to only eight kilograms in developing countries (OECD 1991).

Similarly, access to technology such as televisions, video recorders and home computers for leisure purposes is far more prevalent in richer countries, especially among more affluent households. 'Nowadays it is undoubtedly the case that the Englishman's home is his leisure centre' (Cahill 1994: 156). However, Cahill suggests that the growth of satellite and cable television, which offer the choice of more viewing channels but which also require the payment of monthly rental and purchase or connection charges, is creating a two-tier system for home entertainment in which the poorer sectors of the population are denied the choices and freedoms enjoyed by those who are better off. In contrast, 'public service broadcasting has provided a universal service for all age groups, catered for as many minorities as possible and done its best to educate and inform' (Cahill 1994: 68).

Going out

In the UK, people in better off households are more likely than those in poorer households to have help with childcare and domestic work and to

Table 7.3   Participation in leisure activities away from home by gender in Great Britain, 1994–1995

Activity	% of population aged 16 or over participating in each activity in the 3 months prior to interview		
	Men	*Women*	*All*
Visit a public house	70	68	64
Meal in a restaurant (not fast food)	60	64	62
Drive for pleasure	47	47	47
Meal in a fast food restaurant	45	40	42
Library	36	43	40
Cinema	35	32	34
Short break holiday	32	28	30
Disco or night club	29	22	25
Historic building	27	24	25
Spectator sports event	31	13	22
Theatre	19	22	21

Source: Central Statistical Office (1996).

have access to private transport (Chapter 6). Consequently, there are fewer constraints on how they spend their free time and they are more likely to take part in activities outside of the home. Going out usually costs money and, in general, people in the non-manual socio-economic groups spend more time going out than do those in manual jobs (Central Statistical Office 1996). The most popular way of doing this is to go out for a meal or for drinks, social activities for which the costs are highly variable and therefore within the reach of a wider sector of the population than some other activities (Table 7.3).

Driving for pleasure is a popular occupation for both men and women and going for a drive on a Sunday afternoon is often combined with having lunch in a public house or restaurant, shopping or visiting sports or leisure centres. The fact that people in low-income households, especially unemployed people, women with children or the elderly, are infrequent users of sports and leisure centres is probably because of the prohibitive costs of travel or car use as well as the need to buy or hire equipment. Access to facilities which are increasingly located on the outskirts of towns and cities where there is space for large car parks usually requires the use of a car, and 'it remains the case that the chief beneficiaries of leisure centres are white, male, mobile and mainly middle class' (Cahill 1994: 166).

Table 7.3 reveals little difference between men and women in most kinds of leisure activities, but watching sports events is a marked exception. Nearly three times as many men as women had been to such an event as spectators in 1994–5. Actually participating in certain kinds of sport, games and physical activities has been recognized as contributing to improvements in health and fitness and reducing problems of obesity, as well as conferring a sense of self-esteem and improving mental health. Nevertheless, Table 7.4 shows that the extent of participation varies widely with socio-economic group.

Walking, swimming, cycling and running or jogging are all widely acknowledged to be capable of conferring health benefits, reducing mortality and morbidity from cardiovascular disease and improving weight control and skeletal fitness. These activities are all possible at no or low cost, but they are nevertheless substantially more popular among the professional and managerial classes than among people in semi-skilled or unskilled socio-economic groups.

Other physical activities, such as golf, are also more common among professional and managerial classes, possibly because they involve the purchase or hire of relatively expensive equipment and the costs of club membership. Socio-economic differences in participation rates may reflect deeper social divisions based on perceptions of status. Playing soccer, darts, snooker, pool or billiards, on the other hand, is almost equally common across all socio-economic groups. Perhaps transport is again a critical determinant. Activities in the latter group are all more likely to be available to people in locations close to their homes, whereas most golf courses are located out of town and walking or running for leisure or exercise is unlikely to be popular in unpleasant environments, such as in areas of high urban pollution or where there may be potential risks to personal safety.

Use of the countryside

One aspect of leisure activities is that they should be enjoyable, increasing individuals' feelings of well-being and health. For town dwellers, 'getting away from it all' involves seeking a contrast to the urban and technological aspects of daily life, a contrast usually found in the countryside. Different aspects of the countryside are valued differently by different groups of people. Its amenity value may be found in its areas of undisturbed natural beauty, its peace and quiet, its wildlife interest or its villages and historic buildings. Even areas where the landscape has in the past been degraded by human activities such as quarrying or mining can become tourist attractions in themselves (Blunden and Reddish 1991). In addition to these sources of relatively intangible benefits, the countryside provides opportunities for a whole range of sporting activities, such as walking, climbing, fishing, cycling, riding, shooting, water sports, gliding, orienteering and running. Table 7.5 shows the results of a survey of the purposes of countryside recreation trips in England in 1990.

The use of the countryside for recreation and educational purposes helps people to develop an awareness and appreciation of the natural environment, while its increasing popularity produces pressures and incentives both for the provision of recreational facilities and for measures to protect and conserve wildlife habitats. Nearly 20 per cent of the land area of the UK consists of

Table 7.4 Participation in sports, games and physical activities by socio-economic group in Great Britain, 1993–1994

	Professional	Employers and managers	Intermediate and junior non-manual	Skilled manual and non-professional	Semi-skilled manual and personal service	Unskilled manual
% participating in the 4 weeks prior to interview						
Walking	57	46	42	39	36	31
Swimming	27	19	18	10	11	8
Snooker, pool, billiards	11	12	8	17	10	9
Keep fit, yoga	13	12	18	6	9	8
Cycling	14	9	9	10	8	9
Darts	6	5	4	8	6	6
Weight lifting, training	7	5	5	6	4	3
Golf	9	10	5	6	2	2
Running, jogging	11	6	4	3	2	2
Soccer	6	3	3	6	3	3

Source: Central Statistical Office (1996).

Table 7.5 Countryside recreation trips in England, 1990

Relative popularity of activities	%
Drives, outings, picnics	19
Long walks (more than two miles)	14
Visiting friends or relatives	13
Visiting the sea coast	10
Informal sport	10
Organized sport	9
Visiting historic buildings	6
Visiting country parks	4
Watching sport	4
Pick your own	2
Others	9

Source: Countryside Commission (1991).

National Parks, Areas of Outstanding Natural Beauty (AONBs) in England, Wales and Northern Ireland, or National Scenic Areas in Scotland. In addition, 33 per cent of the coastline of England and Wales is assigned the status of Heritage Coastline. The legal status of these areas is designed to protect the finest areas of landscape and, especially in the case of National Parks, to provide opportunities for public recreation. The responsibilities of National Parks explicitly recognize the relationships between the natural and social environments, in that they are 'to protect and enhance the natural beauty of the Parks and to promote their quiet enjoyment by the public while having due regard for the social and economic well-being of the local community' (North York Moors National Park 1995: Education Topic Leaflet 1). However, should conflicts arise between these objectives, conservation of the environment must take precedence.

Other areas of the UK are designated as having scientific and environmental value and are protected by statutory measures as shown in Table 7.6. Although most of these measures are based on national legislation, Special Protection areas, Biosphere Reserves and Wetland Sites for wildfowl, designated in accordance with the Convention signed at Ramsar in Iran in 1971, are protected under international nature conservation obligations.

The Forestry Commission, which owns or manages nearly 40 per cent of forests and woodlands in Great Britain, is the largest single provider of countryside recreational facilities, and has designed forest parks and woodland parks that are open to the public for the enjoyment and recreation of local people. However, as Table 7.7 shows, its parks are also designed to attract tourists from further afield by providing accommodation, picnic sites and visitor centres, as well as forest walks and drives.

Leisure has become a major industry in the countryside. The North York Moors National Park alone was estimated to have received 12.6 million visitors in 1993, and tourism supports over 7000 jobs in the summer season.

Table 7.6　Statutory protected areas in the UK, 1991

Status[a]	Number	Area (thousand hectares)
National Nature Reserves	286	172.5
Local Nature Reserves[b]	241	17.1
Sites of Special Scientific Interest	5671	17.1
Areas of Scientific Interest[c]	46	63.4
Areas of Special Scientific Interest[c]	26	6.9
Environmentally Sensitive Areas	19	785.6
Special Protection Areas	40	134.4
Biosphere Reserves	13	44.3
'Ramsar' Wetland Sites	44	133.7

[a] Some areas may be included in more than one category; [b] Great Britain only; [c] Northern Ireland only.
Source: Department of the Environment (1992a).

Table 7.7　Numbers of Forestry Commission public recreational facilities in Great Britain, 1992

	England	Wales	Scotland	Total
Camping and caravan sites	22	1	9	32
Picnic places	357	94	193	644
Forest walks and nature trails	296	77	274	647
Visitor centres	10	5	9	24
Arboreta and forest gardens	13	6	3	22
Forest drives	6	1	3	10
Forest cabins and holiday homes	107	0	67	174

Source: Department of the Environment (1992a).

Table 7.8　Visitor spending in the countryside in England, 1990

Category	Average spent per trip (£)	Total spent per year (£ million)	%
Food and drink	3.05	5002	40
Petrol	1.37	2247	18
Entrance fees	1.05	1722	14
Impulse purchases	0.77	1263	10
Craft and souvenirs	0.39	640	5
Fares	0.17	279	2
Parking	0.10	164	1
Information	0.06	98	1
Other	0.62	1017	9
Total	7.58	12,432	100

Source: Countryside Commission (1991).

Visitor centres provide information but also usually have shops and cafes. Added to the fact that, in 1994, 70 per cent of day trips to the Park were made by car, it is apparent that countryside leisure can cost money. The resources which visitors provide are often important for local economies and can aid efforts to protect and conserve the environment. Table 7.8 shows the amount of spending by visitors in England in 1990.

However, the costs incurred by visitors imply that access to the countryside is not equally available to all sectors of the population. In the North York Moors National Park, for example, surveys suggest that a large proportion of visitors are from high-income social groups (North York Moors National Park, 1995).

Holidays and tourism

At the beginning of this chapter, leisure was said to be a function of social organization, and Krippendorf (1991) discusses the ways in which socio-cultural, economic, environmental and political sub-systems shape and influence the relationship between time spent at work, at home and in pursuing leisure and travel opportunities. The idea of leisure is associated with rising incomes and more paid free time for people in the workforce, and this is particularly the case when we consider extended periods of leisure spent as holidays away from home. Holidays have been described as opportunities for the 'reclamation of self in communion with nature' (Clarke and Critcher 1985: 172), but these opportunities are denied to many sectors of the population. Kempson (1996) found that holidays are rarely taken by people living on low incomes in the UK, although day trips are an alternative form of activity for families with children. In the summer of 1992, 1.3 billion day trips were made for leisure purposes and 60 per cent of the UK population made at least one leisure trip in any given two-week period (HMSO 1994a). People in ethnic minority groups also tend to take fewer holidays than others. Urry (1990) remarks that non-white people are rarely portrayed as holiday-makers in promotional literature and brochures in the UK. Instead, 'they are likely to be employed in those enterprises concerned with servicing visitors, especially in the major cities' (Urry 1990: 143).

The growth in holiday-making stems not from more people taking holidays but from some people taking more frequent holidays. The percentage of British adults who take at least one holiday a year has remained almost constant at around 60 per cent for the past 20 years. However, since 1961, the percentage who take two or more holidays has more than quadrupled, to 26 per cent in 1994, and within this overall average figure are substantial differences between socio-economic groups. While 45 per cent of people in the professional and managerial groups took more than one holiday, only 15 per cent of people in manual groups did so (Central Statistical Office 1996).

Not only are better-off people taking more frequent holidays but they are travelling further afield. The growth in car ownership has resulted in greater mobility in spending holiday time and, in 1994, around three-quarters of the 32 million holidays taken by Britons in the UK involved travel by car. During the past 25 years, the development of air travel and of relatively cheap package holidays has made trips overseas more accessible for many people. Britons took a total of nearly 58 million holidays in 1994, and over half of these were abroad, especially to mainland Europe. This compares to only 18 per cent of foreign holidays taken in the early 1970s.

The association of leisure, and especially holiday-making, with higher incomes perhaps helps to explain the dearth of literature about the leisure activities of people in developing countries or in the previously centrally planned countries of Eastern and Central Europe. However, foreign tourism has major impacts on developing regions of the world and revenues provided by tourists from richer countries can play a major role in the economies of less affluent nations (Lea 1988).

Tourism accounts for around 26 per cent of total export services in OECD countries, and employs up to 14 per cent of the workforce in some service sectors. Employment in industries related to tourism increased by 16 per cent in Great Britain between 1987 and 1992 (British Tourist Authority 1992). In marginal rural areas, tourism can exert a significant influence on local economies and employment. It accounts for 7.8 per cent of GDP in Austria, 6.4 per cent in Switzerland, 5.5 per cent in Portugal and 4.9 per cent in Spain (OECD 1991). In many Central and Eastern European countries, foreign tourism is a 'growth export industry' and is treated as an economic development priority. Rates of development, however, are variable. Hungary, for example, already receives 20 million foreign visitors a year, a number which is nearly double the population of the country. Other countries are still seeking to promote tourism on the basis of the attractions of their natural countryside. Albania, for example, has developed legislation which covers protected areas, including National Parks which have a dual role of protecting the landscape while providing public access for recreational and educational purposes (Hall 1993).

Environmental impacts of leisure activities

Consumption

The notion of leisure as a form of consumption is not new in the social policy literature. Cahill (1994), for example, examines in some detail the commodification of the leisure market in the UK. He points out that 'television, alcohol, tobacco, sex and gambling are the five most popular ways of spending our leisure time' (Cahill 1994: 157), but that even sex is not necessarily free if it is taken to include the enjoyment of magazines, films and books or the use of sex shops or prostitution. Consumer spending on sports-related items in the UK in 1990 reached nearly £10 billion, and visits to museums and art galleries now usually have to be paid for, so that even 'heritage is something that can be packaged and marketed and sold' (Cahill

1994: 159). Cahill suggests that what he terms 'lifestyle shopping' typifies leisure as a consumption activity. This kind of shopping is distinct from shopping to purchase goods purely for their use value. It refers instead to the purchase of, or desire for, goods which are perceived to confer a particular status on the individual or to endow him or her with a certain style or identity. 'The touchstone for many people has become the criterion of self-fulfilment, or self-realization, and with this new standard for judgement on life advertisers can then appeal to people with claims that a particular product would enhance their identity' (Cahill 1994: 119).

The commodification of leisure has obvious implications for the differential access to different activities available to people with different levels of income. But because it highlights actual physical consumption it also has major implications for the environment. All forms of leisure and recreation have the potential to affect the environment, either by consuming natural resources, including land and space, or by generating waste materials with polluting properties. It is in richer countries such as those of the OECD and among better off sectors of national populations that the consumption of resources associated with affluent lifestyles has the most impact.

The growth in the popularity of theme parks, electronic games and shopping for leisure can clearly be seen to involve consumption of manufactured goods and raw materials, but even activities as apparently innocuous as visiting the countryside to enjoy its peace and tranquillity involve the consumption of energy for travel and of materials used in the development of transport systems and vehicles. Ironically, many of the aggregates used in road building are extracted from upland areas in the UK, and quarries are frequently established in Areas of Outstanding Natural Beauty (Stokes *et al.* 1992). Reading books or newspapers necessitates the consumption of paper, the manufacture of which requires the felling of trees. Although trees used for paper making are usually softwoods from managed forests, these forests themselves use up large tracts of the natural landscape, changing wildlife habitats and sometimes reducing the amenity value of the area.

Waste

Consumption and the generation of waste are intricately linked processes. Some consumer products, such as pre-cooked meals, paper towels or disposable nappies, generate enormous quantities of waste but are used in order to save time. This time is then spent in chosen leisure pursuits which involve their own consumption patterns and generate even more waste. Watching television is a form of leisure not usually associated with environmental problems, but in the United States nearly eight million television sets are thrown away each year, adding to problems of waste disposal (Hirschhorn and Oldenburg 1991). Television advertising at the same time promotes ever higher levels of consumption. 'Every hour on British commercial television there are seven minutes' advertising devoted to extolling the merits of a range of products' (Cahill 1994: 63). Advertising, in turn, generates its own waste, especially paper. One-half to three-quarters of the volume of American daily newspapers is made up of advertisements, most of which are disposed of in municipal waste together with the millions of items of unsolicited advertising mail arriving in homes each year (Hirschhorn and Oldenburg 1991).

The disposal of household or municipal waste in uncontrolled tips or in the countryside can be hazardous to human health and safety, as well as spoiling the visual landscape. In the UK, household waste is classed, together with commercial waste and some sewage sludge, demolition, construction and industrial waste, as 'controlled waste', while 'special waste' refers to materials, usually produced by complex industrial processes, which are harmful to living organisms. In the UK, 70 per cent of special waste and 85 per cent of controlled waste is disposed of in specially licensed landfill sites. Although controlled by regulations governing, for example, their physical construction and containment features, these sites still pose environmental problems. In some cases polluting materials become dissolved in water and leach out from the site, contaminating surface or groundwaters. The breakdown of certain wastes by the biological action of bacteria and other organisms can lead to the production of landfill gas, which contributes to the greenhouse effect and also poses local risks of fire (Box 7.1).

Incineration is increasingly being used as an alternative method of waste disposal in most European countries. It has the advantage of reducing the total volume and weight of waste material and the energy produced by waste combustion can be harnessed for power generation. In Luxembourg, Switzerland and Japan, for example, around 65 per cent of municipal waste is incinerated and 100, 80 and 27 per cent respectively of that waste is used for the generation of energy (Middleton 1995). The UK government has set a target to recover 40 per cent of municipal waste as energy by the year 2005, but the number of incinerators has actually gone down since 1991. This is because of the introduction of increasingly strict emission limits contained in EC Directives (Department of the Environment 1996a). The main disadvantage of incineration is that the gases emitted can be highly polluting in the atmosphere. A further disadvantage is that any hazardous or toxic substances contained in the original waste, or produced by incineration and not emitted as gases, become concentrated in ash deposits which must then be disposed of in landfill sites.

It is not possible to make direct estimates of the contribution to waste made specifically by leisure-related consumption, but this is likely to increase as non-durable items, such as disposable cameras which are thrown away after a single use, become increasingly common. Where longer lasting items are available, their higher cost can place them beyond the reach of low-income consumers. It is important to note that waste is generated in the manufacture as well as in the disposal of consumer products. The printing of newspapers, magazines and books, for example, can involve the emission of volatile organic compounds (VOCs) when these are used as solvents in cleaners and inks. In the UK, print works were responsible for 10 per cent of the 379,000 tonnes of VOCs emitted from industrial sources in 1995 (Environmental

---

Box 7.1   Landfill gas

About 60 per cent of domestic waste is made up of organic material such as food, paper and cloth. When waste is disposed of at landfill sites it is tipped into large pits in layers, and each layer is covered by earth or some similar material. As time goes by, the complex organic components of the waste are broken down by bacteria into much simpler chemical compounds, a process which can take 15 to 50 years, or even longer.

In the early stages of decomposition, the most active bacteria are species which use the organic waste together with oxygen and water to obtain the energy they need for their own growth and reproduction. Because of their dependence on free oxygen they are known as *aerobic* bacteria. Eventually, however, the oxygen available in the buried waste is used up, and other species of bacteria take over the decomposition process. These latter obtain their energy without using oxygen, and in the process they release methane gas and carbon dioxide. They are known as *anaerobic* bacteria.

The different gases released during the anaerobic stages of decomposition are collectively known as *landfill gas*. The greenhouse gas carbon dioxide typically makes up about a third of the volume of landfill gas produced, but around 30 to 60 per cent consists of methane. Methane (CH_4) is an even more powerful greenhouse gas than carbon dioxide and, in 1990, 39 per cent of the five million tonnes of methane emitted by human activity in the UK came from landfill waste.

Landfill gas therefore has harmful effects on the environment when it is released into the atmosphere. But methane is highly combustible and at some sites landfill gas is collected, extracted and used as fuel to provide energy. Where this is not possible for practical or economic reasons, systems must be used to vent the gas from the tip into the air, since it may otherwise build up and cause explosions such as the one which occurred in Loscoe in Derbyshire in 1986.

Data Services Report 259, August 1996). The use of the plastic PVC (for example, to make records and toys) poses particular problems. PVC production releases dioxins, chemicals which are toxic in even minute concentrations and which are linked to certain cancers and damage to human immune systems. To make some PVC plastics more flexible, phthalates are added, some of which are known to have hormone disrupting effects. Although largely safe in use, waste PVC products are difficult to dispose of safely, since whether they are incinerated, recycled or put into landfill they can release dioxins or other toxins as they are broken down.

Wildlife and habitat disruption

Not only does the countryside provide physical space for leisure, but spending time away from towns and cities can enrich the quality of life in its own right. The natural environment and its flora and fauna are often an integral part of the pleasure and aesthetic enjoyment derived from recreational activities, and can contribute to the character of local areas, imbuing local communities with a sense of place.

> Biodiversity is strongly linked to cultural diversity and identity. Human cultures are shaped to a large degree by the natural environment. Historically, biological resources have played an important part in local folklore and traditions. Plants form an integral part of many customs and rituals, and may be the source of superstitions. They have been celebrated in literature and in song, and are used frequently as a source of decoration for arts and crafts.
>
> (HMSO 1994c: 109)

Creatures such as birds, butterflies and badgers are often the subject of species watching activities which are leisure pursuits in themselves, while other species in their natural environments offer opportunities for hobbies such as painting and wildlife photography.

Although in many countries certain natural areas have been designated as having conservation value for reasons of their beauty or scientific interest, measures such as these do not guarantee environmental protection. In Great Britain in 1990–1, for example, recreational activities caused short-term damage to 38 Sites of Special Scientific Interest. A further five sites suffered long-term damage and one was damaged to the extent that it lost the features which had formed the basis for its special status (Department of the Environment 1992a).

The countryside as a place for recreation has become a victim of its own success. When its peace, tranquillity and remoteness attract visitors in large numbers, those qualities are destroyed by the very people who have come to enjoy them. The noise and disturbance caused by high concentrations of people affect wildlife, while vegetation suffers from wear and tear, trampling often causing serious problems of plant loss and soil erosion on popular walking routes. In some cases visitor pressures have led to inappropriate developments, such as extended car parks and enlarged facilities for eating, drinking and shopping, which change the character of the local area. The imposition of an alien city-based culture on rural areas can often damage or destroy the indigenous 'sense of place'. Even away from these central areas, careless visitor behaviour can cause damage by littering the countryside or by the start of uncontrolled fires caused by cigarette ends, matches, camping stoves or discarded bottles. Not only the natural environment, but also agricultural crops and livestock, can be harmed.

Some forms of leisure activity in themselves have deleterious effects on the environment. Off-road motor cycling and the increasingly popular four-wheel off-road driving, for example, can cause rapid erosion, especially in fragile upland or coastal ecosystems, while vehicle noise may disturb wildlife, walkers and local residents alike. Field sports such as hunting, shooting and some kinds of angling have a direct impact on wildlife species but can also have secondary effects on others. Deaths of target species are an obvious effect, but other species may suffer from habitat disruption. Lead shot and lead fishing weights can cause direct damage because of their toxic nature, and food chains may be affected by the deaths of species which form the main food of, or which prey upon, others. Where fisheries or other natural populations are increased by artificially introduced stocks, native species may be displaced. There is evidence in some areas, for example, that high stocking levels of rainbow trout for fishermen are displacing native brown trout, which are becoming increasingly rare (HMSO 1994c).

Country field sports do play an important role in maintaining rural employment and population levels and are not always bad for the environment. Their impact depends largely on the way that sporting estates and target populations are managed. However, this is only true of legitimate and legal sports. Some field sports, such as badger baiting, are now illegal in the UK, but there is evidence that they still go on. Between 1985 and 1988, it is estimated, 10.5 per cent of the main breeding setts of badgers had been dug out during the previous 12 months (Department of the Environment 1992a).

The scope for using rivers, lakes and reservoirs for sporting activities has increased with greater personal mobility for parts of the population. Sailing and boating, however, can cause visual intrusion to the landscape and noise from outboard motors or jet skis can be a source of annoyance. Intensive use of bodies of water for recreation tends to exacerbate problems of water pollution and, where waters receive high levels of organic waste and sewage, eutrophication (Box 2.1) can lead to the enhanced growth of certain toxic species of blue-green algae. In the UK, these have been associated with illnesses affecting the users of lakes and reservoirs for sport when they have swallowed or swum through algal scum. Sewage deposits can also contain pathogenic organisms harmful to human health, and the environmental quality of UK bathing waters and beaches is regularly monitored to measure compliance with EU standards. Although, in 1991, the overall compliance rate was 76 per cent, there was substantial regional variation, Northern Ireland having 100 per cent compliance while in north-west England the rate was only 30 per cent. One surfer in the south-west of England summed up the problem: 'You learn not to open your mouth when you fall in' (*The Guardian* 29 July 1996).

We have seen how the environment can suffer harm from visitor pressure, but not all effects are negative. Conscientious visitors to the countryside can often alert the appropriate authorities to the existence of problems or damage; their ecological observations, from bird-watching, for example, can contribute to the growing body of information which assists in developing conservation measures; increasing use of the countryside is often accompanied by increasing respect for wildlife; and the financial income from tourism can be used to conserve the environment as well as benefiting local communities.

In general, most of the damage caused to the countryside environment by leisure activities results simply from the congregation of too many people in the same area at the same time. Tourist resorts must usually cope with fluctuating demands on resources. During peak periods, for example, adequate and safe supplies of drinking water are required, and means are needed to dispose of increased volumes of liquid and solid waste without environmental harm. The problem is exacerbated where the areas which attract tourists are those with fragile ecosystems, such as Alpine mountain regions, wilderness areas or coastal zones in the Mediterranean, which attract over 40 per cent of all tourist arrivals in Europe each year.

> The impact of tourism on physical resources and the environment is sub-stantial and is expected to increase. But since a high-quality environ-ment is an essential prerequisite for tourism, there is a growing concern with the sustainable development of the tourism industry. This issue is of crucial importance for all countries and in particular for Southern Europe.
>
> (OECD 1991: 249)

Traffic

The growing popularity of the countryside as a location for leisure activities has gone hand in hand with the growth of car use, which enables many town and city dwellers to travel further from home for day trips or holidays. 'Most of the traffic in the countryside is produced by urban travellers rather than rural ones' (Stokes *et al.* 1992: 4). Some of the increase in rural traffic in recent years is accounted for by passenger and freight travel from city to city and some by journeys made to work, shops and other facilities in peripheral urban locations. However, in 1988–9, 44 per cent of all rural mileage travelled was for social purposes, entertainment and leisure. This figure is expected to increase, partly because increasing mobility is leading to the geographical separation of many people from their friends and families and partly because the attractions of the countryside present a more welcome contrast to urban life. 'More travel is likely to be for leisure purposes, with people valuing greater access to the countryside' (Stokes *et al.* 1992: 4).

The environmental effects of traffic have been discussed in detail in Chapter 6, and include greenhouse gas production, air and lead pollution, noise, accidents and waste generation. In the countryside these effects are tending to reproduce the same form of environmental degradation that visitors are attempting to escape by travelling out of urban areas for recreation. The problem of visual intrusion caused by heavy traffic on small rural roads is compounded by congestion, which not only frustrates the visitor but can cause serious disruption to the lives of people who live and work in the area. Journeys to remote mountain areas in Europe for skiing trips, for example, usually require travel by road for at least part of the way, and it is estimated that 'each weekend on the Swiss St Gotthard Pass, automotive traffic deposits 30 tons of nitrogen, 25 tons of hydrocarbons, and 75 kilo-grams of lead often creating layers of black soot on the snow' (Denniston 1995: 47).

Figure 7.1 The most popular parts of the countryside suffer increasingly from traffic congestion during peak holiday periods.
Photographer: © Martin Bond

Conflicts of interest

Tourism and industry

In heavily industrialized regions of the world, such as parts of Eastern Europe, the growth of industry has usually preceded the growth of environmental awareness and large-scale use and enjoyment of the countryside for leisure purposes. The economic interests of industry frequently conflict with conservation and recreational interests, and this problem is particularly marked where pollution crosses national borders in air or water. 'Legal protection afforded to sensitive areas is no defence against the ravages of pollution which may originate hundreds of kilometres away, perhaps in another country' (Carter and Turnock 1993: 204).

Wastes, spillages and discharges from industry and transport are causing severe marine pollution along coastal areas of the Black Sea, the Baltic and the Adriatic, with consequent impacts on local tourist resorts. Effects such as these are compounded by pollution generated by tourism itself: the littering of the coastline with rubbish, car parking, transport-related pollution and vandalism, causing damage to buildings or even forest fires.

Conflicting forms of recreation

The use of the natural environment for leisure purposes can bring different kinds of user into conflict. Water use provides a good example. We have seen how the increasing use of water space for recreation can cause problems of litter and waste pollution, and it is clear that there are limits to the extent to which increasing numbers of people can make use of the water environment without causing congestion. Kinnersley (1994) divides the pleasures provided by natural bodies of water into three categories: 'the necessarily organised (in clubs or competitive activities such as canoe racing), the individually active or participatory, and the mostly contemplative' (Kinnersley 1994: 144). Although many activities cut across these boundaries, it is easy to see how essentially active forms of leisure may be at odds with quieter pursuits. Water skiing and the use of motorized pleasure boats, for example, use up water space, make a noise and disturb the water and wildlife, causing annoyance to bird watchers and anglers. It is interesting to note here that, from the point of view of social inequalities, it is the better off recreationists who often cause the most habitat disturbance, since most of the activities concerned cost money.

Recreation and conservation

Despite the rising popularity of motor sports such as off-road driving, many forms of leisure activity still depend on the existence of a clean and healthy natural environment. It would appear that the interests of both nature conservationists and visitors to the countryside should be similar. Conflicts between the two, however, are far from rare. A vivid illustration of the irony of this situation is provided by Kinnersley (1994), who describes a period in England in 1991 when conservationists wanted to have the Basingstoke Canal declared as a Site of Special Scientific Interest on the grounds of its high species diversity. Their proposals were strenuously opposed by other people who enjoyed using the canal for boating, an activity which would be severely restricted if the plan went ahead. One of the arguments of the conservation lobby concerned the Greywell Tunnel at the start of the canal, which attracts over two thousand bats as winter residents.

> The boaters countered this with the observation that the canal and especially the tunnel were clearly items of man-made infrastructure, not part of the natural scene. The plants and bats had colonized them; but why should this be accepted as limiting the very activity for which the canal was built?
>
> (Kinnersley 1994: 117)

Blunden and Curry (1996) give a more detailed discussion of this kind of conflict using the example of the Broads in eastern England. The low-lying Broads landscape with its water bodies linked by an intricate network of rivers and drainage channels is almost entirely a construct of human activity.

Peat digging, the major industry in the area in medieval times, left hollow areas which filled with water and which, over later centuries, have been harvested for reeds and drained for grazing and agriculture. More recently, agricultural activity in the region has intensified, the population has increased and the Broads waterways are now used almost exclusively for leisure. More than a million tourists each year are attracted by the availability of hire boat holidays, local accommodation, day trips and areas ideal for fishing, shooting and nature study, and tourism brings £20–30 million a year into the local economy. The rich diversity of Broadland habitats and species of wetland plants, insects and birds has been recognized internationally, and it also forms the key attraction of the area for tourists. 'The landscape of Broadland, with its vast skies, open water, vivid colours and rich wildlife, provides a unique sense of place – a place of peace, remoteness and contact with nature' (Blunden and Curry 1996: 42).

But the development of wildlife and wildlife habitats is now being threatened by the development of social and economic activities, activities which have historically been intimately linked with the environment itself. Leisure activity is not the sole cause of environmental damage to the Broads, but it contributes to other damage stemming from agricultural and industrial sources. Bankside fishing, the use of unofficial moorings and the wash from boats all add to problems of erosion along the waterways, maintenance of which requires construction work, which lowers both amenity and conservation value of the areas affected. Lead pollution from fishing and shooting and waste and fuel pollution from boats have harmful effects on all forms of wildlife, again lowering the inherent value of the area. Managing and regulating authorities are faced with the problem of protecting the natural beauty and biodiversity of the Broads, while maintaining their amenity value for the tourists on whom the local economy has come to depend.

Local economic sectors

The management of National Parks of England and Wales explicitly recognizes the importance of tourism to local rural economies, as visitors bring both money and employment into remote areas.

> Some spending is direct, such as when a visitor buys a meal in a cafe or buys a souvenir from a gift shop. But there is also the indirect route. For instance, the owner of a holiday cottage will use some of the money paid by visitors to improve the property. Thus the local plumbers or electricians may find themselves paid, indirectly, by the tourist. In a similar way, a local hotelier may buy local produce and in this way income generated by tourism will go to the local butcher or egg producer.
> (North York Moors National Park Education Topic Leaflet 9)

Tourism can increase the economic prosperity of rural areas, stimulating the establishment of new businesses and sustaining existing ones. At the same time, however, prosperous retirement households are attracted to migrate into the countryside and, as we have seen in Chapter 4, in many areas their impact on the housing market has led to a shortage of affordable housing for local low income families (Department of the Environment 1994). Increasing prosperity is also associated with more private car ownership, so that richer people can travel more easily to schools and shops in nearby towns. This can often leave the poorer families in a worse position than before; while local businesses increasingly cater for tourists, shops and facilities for everyday essential requirements may decline.

In Europe '40 million annual visitors spend a total of 250 million days in the Alpine region, eroding footpaths, littering the countryside and forming mile-long queues for the ski-lifts' (Wood and House 1991: 36). Again, incoming visitors tend to be more affluent than many local people, and tourist developments benefit larger companies rather than small business concerns. The building of luxury hotels, golf courses and airport terminals uses up local land but also causes further disruption as water, sanitation and energy supply systems are installed in remote areas (Wood and House 1991).

The leisure pursuits of the wealthier sectors of society have impacts not only upon natural environments but also upon the social and cultural environments of local populations. 'In industrial countries, mass tourism and recreation are now fast overtaking the extractive economy as the largest threat to mountain communities and environments' (Denniston 1995: 47). Mountain areas in the tropics are similarly threatened. 'Each year, for example, more than 100,000 people visit Machu Pichu, the fifteenth-century stronghold of the Incas, leaving behind garbage, vandalized stonework, and polluted streams' (Denniston 1995: 47). Although much is made of the positive importance of tourism and recreation to local economies, there are negative impacts as well, and where increasing numbers of visitors are encouraged in order to bring money into a region, the negative environmental, social and cultural costs can be devastating.

The development of sustainable tourism

The rich diversity of the natural world brings pleasure to the lives of many people, as demonstrated by the popularity of protected areas as well as zoos and botanical gardens as places in which to spend leisure time. Nevertheless, we have seen how conflicts can arise between the need to conserve and protect the environment and the encouragement of people to visit and enjoy its beauty. Many governments and the tourism industry itself increasingly favour the term 'sustainable tourism development', which encompasses economic, environmental, social and cultural sustainability. The idea of ecotourism, for example, reflects recent attempts to aid local economies and improve levels of local infrastructure, while at the same time stimulating the development of environmental protection of the physical environment and landscape, wildlife and natural habitats and historic sites of interest. It is promoted as ecologically and socially responsible tourism, but in reality it serves as a vivid example of the difficulties in marrying environmental conservation with social and economic development.

Many developing countries have resources such as rain forests, coral reefs or mountain ranges which can be exploited as commodities and sold as tourist amenities. Sunday newspapers in the UK increasingly carry advertisements for expensive 'nature' holidays in unspoiled remote destinations: for example, to visit coral reefs in Belize, to follow Darwin's trail in the Galapagos or to see animals in the wild in the game parks of East Africa. Governments of such countries are often eager to promote tourism as an earner of foreign currency and to reduce dependency on agriculture, which is more vulnerable to fluctuations in world trade. The idea is to make natural resources 'pay their way' by generating income to help with their maintenance and conservation. The destruction of tropical rain forests, for example, leads to loss of biodiversity, flooding and massive soil erosion problems and is a contributory factor in climate change. To answer the economic imperative, often voiced most forcefully by developers and commercial loggers, some other way must be found to gain income from the forest itself. If local people can earn more by keeping forests intact than by cutting them down, the arguments for conservation are considerably strengthened.

Ecotourism, however, is in danger of replicating the social, economic and environmental problems associated with conventional tourism. The setting aside of land for nature conservation often overlooks the subsistence needs of local people: for example, those rainforest dwellers who rely on slash and burn forms of agriculture for their livelihood. Instead, in many cases land is sold to overseas companies for the development of ecotourism, so that those who benefit most tend to be travel agencies, tour operators, transport companies and hotel and resort developers, rather than the indigenous population. The protection of environmental areas benefits the international community and a few rich tourists, while local people may lose their rights over or access to the resources they need for production (Stocking *et al.* 1995).

There have been a few local community-based initiatives designed to promote ecotourism, but if they become successful there is the danger that ever increasing tourist numbers will have increasingly adverse impacts on the environment. Conflicts between the needs of local populations, the protection of the environment and the demands of tourists still persist, and ecotourism, like many of the other forms of leisure discussed in this chapter, may ultimately threaten the very resources on which it depends.

Summary points

- The activities which people pursue for recreation and leisure depend on the time and resources they have available. These in turn are influenced by their patterns of work, where they live, their family responsibilities and their age and gender.

- The extent to which leisure time is spent going out or taking holidays may be constrained by income but is also influenced by the social and cultural context of people's lives.
- Many leisure pursuits involve forms of consumption. People pay, for example, for meals in restaurants, for sports goods and facilities, for travel on day trips or holidays and even for books and televisions for home 'consumption'. Those with lower incomes have fewer options open to them.
- All consumption ultimately generates waste, and whether this is disposed of in landfill or is incinerated its effects on the environment are substantial.
- Even apparently non-consumptive forms of leisure have environmental impacts, but the extent of damage largely depends on the concentration of people involved. Intensive use of particular areas of the countryside by visitors, for example, can result in disturbance to wildlife habitats and erosion of vegetation.
- The use of motor vehicles as a leisure pursuit in itself or as a means to reach particular locations carries its own environmental costs (Chapter 6).
- Conflicts between recreation and conservation can arise when different groups of people, such as bird watchers and jet skiers, have different priorities for land or water use. In popular tourist areas there may also be tensions between visitors and local residents, and between different local interest groups. Meeting the demands of tourists may bring economic gains for some but be detrimental to the local environment and culture.
- Overseas holidays are often expensive and wealthy tourists sometimes have demands which are difficult to reconcile with the needs of poor local communities and environmental protection. Although an attempt has recently been made to encourage forms of 'sustainable tourism' in some parts of the developing world, success is likely to depend on placing strict limits on visitor numbers, a move which, while protecting the environment, would also reduce any economic benefits to local people.

Chapter eight
SUMMARY AND DISCUSSION

Environmental impacts of human activity

Each chapter in this book has focused on a particular kind of need which people experience and examined how the ways in which the need is met affect the environment. Here we summarize these effects by focusing on different forms of environmental damage and the kinds of human activity with which each is associated. Table 8.1 presents a typology of environmental impacts, based on whether they result from the use of natural resources or from the associated generation of wastes.

The environmental impacts of natural resource use

The provision of water for human use can cause changes to the landscape either as a result of over-abstraction leading to a drying out of wetlands and reduction of river flows, or when dams and reservoirs are constructed for water storage. Increasing demands, exacerbating these problems, come not only from the domestic sector but also from the electricity generating industries, food processing plants and industries manufacturing packaging, building materials, motor vehicles and other kinds of consumer goods.

Increases in the use of motor transport are both driven by and encourage a growth in the area of land used for road building, while increasing use of the countryside for recreation and leisure may be accompanied by problems of inappropriate development and the dumping of litter.

Quarrying, mining and drilling operations are necessary for obtaining the raw materials for fertilizers used in food production, mineral ores, stone and cement for building purposes, fossil fuels to produce energy, aggregates for

Table 8.1   A typology of the environmental problems caused by human activity

Problems caused by use of natural resources	Problems caused by the generation of wastes
Physical degradation of the landscape	Water pollution
Land subsidence	Land pollution
Flooding	Air pollution
Soil deterioration	Enhanced greenhouse effect
	Acid deposition
	Depletion of the ozone layer
	Radioactivity
Habitat disruption and loss of biodiversity	

road construction and maintenance, ores for metal production and coal and oil for the manufacture of plastics and other complex compounds. These activities not only leave gaping scars on natural landscapes but may also leave heaps of unsightly, and sometimes toxic, spoil or mine 'tailings'. Mining activities themselves can result in land subsidence and instability and, in some places, over-abstraction of water from underground aquifers also results in the subsidence of land in surrounding areas, making it unsafe for building on and causing problems of drainage.

The excessive use of water for irrigation in agricultural food production can result in flooding of rural areas, while urban areas may be affected by the flooding of sewerage systems caused by increased groundwater levels. Excessive irrigation together with the use of heavy machinery for agricultural production can cause soil compaction and waterlogging. Soil erosion often follows the clearing of trees and hedgerows to make larger, more easily accessible fields or the clearing of new areas for agricultural production or livestock grazing.

The environmental impacts of waste generation

Water, land and air pollution are all intimately related, since many pollutants produced as waste from human activities move from one medium to another by natural processes. Sulphur dioxide, for example, initially pollutes the air when it is emitted from power station chimneys and vehicle exhausts. Later, however, it is deposited in rain, snow or mist on to the earth's surface where it pollutes soils and water and damages plant growth.

Natural water sources can be polluted by direct discharges of domestic waste water from sewerage systems and by organic wastes from agricultural and livestock production. In extreme cases this causes eutrophication, leading to deaths of fish and other aquatic life. Chemical effluents from manufacturing, mining and the agro-chemical industry may also run off into water sources causing problems of toxicity. In addition, leachates from landfill sites or contaminated land and some air pollutants are deposited in water. The extraction, processing and transport of oil for fuel and manufacturing purposes all carry risks of accidental spillages and discharges, which have the potential to cause serious pollution of marine, freshwater and terrestrial environments. The pesticides used to produce higher quality food at lower prices are toxic to living organisms and can cause severe contamination of water courses and land. Industries producing pesticides or manufacturing and processing materials such as copper piping, PVC and paints used in the building of houses generate numerous toxic air pollutants.

In addition to waste pollution stemming from the production and use of goods to meet the demands of society, further problems arise in disposing of solid waste after use. The food industry generates both organic and chemical waste from food processing, and waste emanating from food packaging and domestic waste also includes discarded items such as paper, household appliances and leisure goods. The use of transport causes air pollution and leaves a legacy of chemical wastes, used vehicles and tyres, all of which must be disposed of in some way. Whether solid wastes are tipped in landfill sites or burned in incinerators, they inevitably put pressures on the environment in the form of land degradation or pollution of water and air.

There are few societies today in which provision to meet people's needs for water, food, housing, warmth, transport and leisure does not involve the use of fossil fuels for energy supply; and all activities which involve the combustion of fossil fuels to produce energy release polluting exhaust products such as black smoke, nitrogen oxides and sulphur dioxide into the air. The food industry, for example, is highly energy intensive, particularly where farming is mechanized, and the processing and packaging of food for transport and distribution and the refrigeration necessary for storing some types of food all consume large amounts of energy. The use of transport for freight, work or leisure purposes is responsible for atmospheric pollution by VOCs, and tropospheric ozone and toxic lead compounds are emitted unless lead-free fuels are used.

Two major components of emissions to the air when fossil fuels are burned in vehicle engines or to produce energy for domestic or industrial use are greenhouse gases and acidic sulphur dioxide, both of which cause particular environmental problems. Greenhouse gases such as carbon dioxide and methane occur naturally in the atmosphere, but the additional contribution made by human activities enhances the greenhouse effect, potentially leading to global warming and associated climate change. On a smaller geographical scale, sulphur dioxide is responsible for acid deposition or acid rain. The generation of energy from nuclear power stations avoids these emissions, but it carries its own risks and presents the serious problem of disposal of radioactive wastes. Alternative sources of energy, such as solar, hydroelectric, wind and geothermal power, put far less pressure on the environment but are not currently used globally on any significant scale.

Damage to the ozone layer, which protects the earth from the harmful effects of certain wavelengths of ultraviolet light from the sun, is caused by a number of manufactured chemical substances. Although the production and use of some of the most powerful ozone depleting chemicals is being phased out by international agreement, some are still being produced and used to meet demands for refrigerants, air conditioning, dry cleaning fluids, fire extinguishers, solvents, pesticides and pharmaceuticals.

Finally, as shown in Table 8.1, the environmental problems of wildlife habitat disruption and loss of biodiversity can be caused by all aspects of resource use and pollution. Rapid changes to water, land and air environments do not allow sufficient time for species to adapt, so that the composition of natural ecosystem communities alters as species move away or die out.

Social costs of environmental damage

There is continuing philosophical debate about the value of human beings in relation to the rest of the natural world, and one ideological view is that any human activities which harm the environment are wrong, since the whole of nature has an intrinsic value in itself. Proponents of this 'deep green' or ecocentric view argue that the interests of the natural world should be paramount, even where furthering those interests means curtailing human activities. Unsustainable exploitation of the environment is unacceptable even if human beings stand to gain immediate benefits from it. In contrast is the 'light green' or anthropocentric position. According to this view, only human beings have intrinsic value and should be at the centre of our environmental concerns. The rest of the natural world merits protection only by dint of its extrinsic value to humans (Dobson 1990; Martell 1994; Garner 1996).

Even if 'deep green' arguments are rejected, there is good reason for preventing environmental damage simply on the grounds of its negative impact on human societies.

> Human society remains dependent on the natural productivity of both land and water ecosystems for most basic needs, including most staple foods and many other products such as biomass fuels, timber, resins, spices and medicinal products. The ways in which soil and water resources are used in farming, forestry, and fishing within any country or region have important implications for its economy, the distribution of income, and the extent of poverty and malnutrition. They also have important implications for the environment and for the possibility of sustaining production in the future.
>
> (WHO 1992: 61)

The social costs of environmental damage include risks to health, the decline of human and natural resource productivity, the loss of amenity and quality of life and, in extreme cases, threats to social stability at local or international levels.

Risks to health

Environmental problems can lead to ill-health and premature mortality in a host of different ways. Direct exposure to toxic pollutants in contaminated air or water has clear implications for human health, although incontrovertible causal links may be difficult to establish, and it is not easy to assess the effects of long-term exposure to low levels of pollutants. In the case of road transport, for example, the correlation between increasing levels of exhaust pollution and incidence of respiratory illnesses is complicated by the number of chemical substances involved and their own interactions to form new substances in the atmosphere. It is rarely possible to isolate a particular air contaminant as the sole cause of a particular disease. Relationships between health problems associated with contaminated water supplies or food can also prove problematic to unravel, but are easier to identify when an individual pathogenic organism, such as a bacterium or parasite, is the cause. Human health is affected indirectly by environmental degradation: for example, when the pollution of land or water affects food production and results in inadequate levels of nutrition in locally dependent populations. On a wider scale, atmospheric pollution by ozone depleting chemicals results in the exposure of people in affected areas to harmful wavelengths of ultra-violet sunlight, causing cancers and cataracts.

The achievement and maintenance of good health depends upon having access to the resources to meet basic needs in a safe and unpolluted environment, and improvements to health do not depend solely upon access to health services. 'Many inequalities of health within and between nations are attributable to differences in incomes and environments (both within and outside the home)' (Hill 1996: 116). Whereas the environment-related health risks in developing countries consist largely of the undernutrition and communicable diseases caused by inadequate or contaminated supplies of food and water, more affluent countries with relatively equitable income distributions and more stable populations are affected by environmental health risks which stem directly from increasing prosperity and economic stability. These include exposure to harmful chemicals released in industrial and traffic pollution and dietary problems resulting from too much food of the wrong type.

Health ultimately depends on the ability to manage successfully the interaction between the physical, spiritual, biological and economic/social environment. Sound development is not possible without a healthy population; yet most developmental activities affect the environment to some degree, which in turn causes or exacerbates many health problems. Conversely, it is the very lack of development that adversely affects the health of many people, which can be alleviated only through development.

(United Nations Development Programme 1993: 42)

In all countries and among rich and poor alike, both physical health and mental health in the sense of well-being and security depend on the extent to which the environment is damaged by the proliferation of pathogenic agents, naturally occurring physical or chemical polluting agents or other noxious agents added by human activities.

Decline in productivity

Reduced levels of physical and mental health caused by environmental deterioration can lower human productivity and consequently economic productivity at household and national levels. Polluting activities in particular societies incur clean-up costs which are often borne by municipal or community institutions rather than by the polluters themselves. Further declines in human activity are the result of lowered resource production. In China, for example, crop yields have been reduced by high levels of water, air and land pollution. Construction activities and erosion have led to the loss of valuable farm land, while erosion and deforestation have resulted in soil nutrient loss and flooding. Smil (1988) has estimated that environmental damage is responsible for losses in productivity equivalent to 15 per cent of China's gross domestic product, and the average annual global costs of environmental damage are currently thought to be between 1 and 15 per cent of gross national product (Brown 1995). In Europe, 60 per cent of commercial forests suffer from acid deposition, damage which causes economic losses of US$35 billion each year. Air pollution also affects agricultural productivity, and annual losses have been estimated at US$1.5 billion in Sweden, US$1.8 billion in Italy, US$2.7 billion in Poland and US$4.7 billion in Germany (United Nations Development Programme 1996).

Some forms of environmental damage have immediate effects on productivity and the economy. When fisheries collapse or water becomes scarce, the impacts on employment may prove to be unsustainable in the long run. Other kinds of damage are indicative of future potential problems. Declines in the numbers of some species of birds, for example, may reflect processes such as deforestation, wetland drainage, urban encroachment, air or water pollution or acid deposition, processes which, if continued, may ultimately result in more marked socially and economically damaging outcomes. 'A crucial test of the "health" of a local environment is reflected in the wildlife community appropriate to the area or habitat. If the rate of change or loss is markedly greater than ordinary evolutionary processes would imply, this could indicate a systematic problem to which we should pay serious attention' (HMSO 1994c: 10).

Loss of amenity

Land dereliction, unpleasant smells, discoloration of water in streams, rivers and lakes and the loss of natural vegetation and wildlife all represent a loss in the amenity of an area. Landscapes, wildlife and habitats are often valued for their own sakes. Even for people who do not use the area directly, the idea that peaceful, clean and beautiful environments exist and that future generations will be able to enjoy them has a value in itself.

Political conflict

Political problems are often pronounced where environmental pollution crosses national boundaries. They also arise in conflicts surrounding the export of hazardous and radioactive wastes and in the trade in endangered species. The over-consumption of natural resources, either through direct use of water, forests, soils, fossil fuels and mineral ores or through the indirect use of air, land and water as sinks for waste, leads to levels of environmental degradation which have been linked to the precipitation of civil and international strife. Although a whole series of political, social and economic factors are involved in initiating social conflict and unrest, resource scarcity, especially in the context of growing population size and unequal resource distribution, can also make an important contribution.

A recent large-scale study in the United States has assembled evidence suggesting that 'there are significant causal links between scarcities of renewable resources and violence' (Homer-Dixon *et al*. 1993: 45). In the Philippines, for example, the 1980s saw a massive growth in rural unemployment and erosion of wage levels. In order to survive, landless labourers were forced to move into areas of the least productive, marginally fertile land, which was ecologically highly vulnerable. Forest clearance for subsistence agriculture led to environmental damage in the form of landslides, erosion and changes in hydrology. This in turn resulted in even more deprivation for the farmers and, according to Homer-Dixon *et al*., helped to produce the resulting social climate for revolutionary action. On the other hand, rural poverty stemming from resource scarcity can increase rates of migration to urban areas where the development of impoverished squatter settlements places massive demands on state provision and aggravates population grievances. The authors also point out the contribution which water shortages make to political discord in the Middle East. Israel, for example, has an annual fresh water deficit which is currently met by over-pumping aquifers. However, nearly 40 per cent of the aquifer groundwater used by Israel originates in occupied territory, and the Arabs living there have had limits placed on the number of wells they are allowed to drill, the amount of water they are allowed to abstract and the periods during which they can draw water for irrigation. 'The entire Middle East faces increasingly grave and tangled problems of water scarcity and many experts believe these will affect the region's stability' (Homer-Dixon *et al*. 1993: 45).

Social responsibility for the environment

We have seen above how the impacts of human activity on the environment have repercussions on people's personal, economic and social living

Table 8.2   Future environmental concerns in England and Wales, 1993

Environmental concern	% of respondents
Traffic, including congestion, fumes and noise	36
Level of air pollution	29
Global warming and climate change	27
Level of pollution in lakes, rivers and sea	24
Depletion of the ozone layer	20
Radioactive waste	15
Loss of tropical rain forest	15
Toxic waste	13
Population growth	12
Using up the world's natural resources	11
Loss of countryside to urban development	10
Loss of rare species	8
Disposal of household waste	8
Acid rain	5
Decay of inner cities	5
Too many roads and motorways	4

Source: Central Statistical Office (1996).

conditions. Since the 1970s, concern for the environment has been demonstrated by the results of opinion polls in several OECD countries (OECD 1991). In the UK, a 1993 survey which asked people what environmental issues or trends they felt would cause them the most concern in about 20 years time revealed a wide range of unprompted answers (Table 8.2).

One indicator of the extent to which such concerns are expressed as action to protect the environment is the percentage of the population recycling waste paper, glass and steel and aluminium cans. The percentage of the UK population recycling each of these products increased between 1990 and 1993. Some people act on their concerns for the environment by joining voluntary groups which work for environmental protection and conservation. UK membership of Greenpeace and Friends of the Earth, for example, increased from 30,000 to 300,000 and from 18,000 to 112,000 respectively between 1981 and 1994 (Central Statistical Office 1996).

The environment is also high on the political agenda, and the UK government has frequently declared its commitment to environmental protection and to policies for sustainable development. In the private sector, companies are increasingly aware of the effects of their activities on the environment and many are taking positive steps either to clean up their production processes, or at least to convey an image of environmental responsibility.

Yet despite this growth in environmental awareness, the UK, like most other countries in the world, appears to be progressing only slowly in addressing the problems. Issues of responsibility for causing, repairing and preventing environmental damage can be difficult to resolve for a number of reasons. Some of these are connected with the unequal distribution of benefits accruing from the pursuit of activities which cause the damage and of the costs which that damage incurs.

Externalities

One explanation for the unequal distribution of costs and benefits is the existence of externalities. Economists use the term 'externalities' to refer to the impacts of market activity which are not fully accounted for in the price of commodities or in the processes of production. Externalities may be either positive or negative but in the case of environmental impacts are usually the latter. Negative environmental externalities arise when the costs of environmental damage resulting from a particular activity do not fall solely upon those carrying out the activity but on a broader sector of society. The manufacture of a product, for example, carries private costs to the manufacturing company which are reflected in the price of the product to the consumer. But if the production process releases air pollutants which damage public health and amenity these social costs are not paid by the company but by other people. These include both those living in the polluted area and taxpayers in general who provide the resources for state healthcare provision. Similarly, we have seen in Chapter 7 how people using the countryside for leisure and recreation can have impacts upon the environment but do not pay the full price of the environmental change caused by their activities.

These wider social costs represent externalities which are not always easy to identify or quantify. External social costs of environmental damage often become invisible to the perpetrators when they are transferred elsewhere. The installation of tall chimneys at power stations, for example, allows local residents access to clean air but shifts the environmental and social costs of sulphur dioxide pollution further afield. The import of minerals, timber and manufacturing materials to produce goods which improve the quality of life for people in one country leaves a legacy of environmental degradation in another, and the export of hazardous wastes from richer to poorer countries actually exports externalities through trade relations.

The environmental damage caused in poorer countries tends to result largely from over-exploitation of soils, land and forests, and the costs are borne by the people living in those countries. 'Poorer groups generally bear the immediate cost and suffer the direct consequences of the environmental degradation' (WHO 1992: 14). Wealthy countries, on the other hand, damage the environment mainly through the consumption of non-renewable resources such as fossil fuels, emitting greenhouse gases and generating industrial and hazardous wastes. OECD countries account for only 15 per cent of the world's population, but are responsible for 77 per cent of hazardous wastes (WHO 1992). The generation of greenhouse gases, ozone depleting chemicals and other wastes results from activities which confer benefits to some sectors of society, producing goods and services to improve their standards of living. The costs which they incur may be invisible to those who feel the immediate benefits, but they fall heavily on people in other sectors of society and on future generations.

The tragedy of the commons

There is an argument which claims that the public interest is best served when each individual person acts in rational way to increase his or her own utility. However, in many cases and particularly in relation to the environment, it is by no means obvious that 'decisions reached individually will, in fact, be the best decisions for an entire society' (Hardin 1968: 1244). Hardin supports his argument by reference to the 'tragedy of the commons', using the example of a common pasture, a finite area of land on which local people put their cattle to graze. It is to the advantage of any individual herdsman to put as many cattle as possible on to the pasture even when the vegetation and soil begin to deteriorate because of overgrazing. This is because the herdsman receives all of the profit made by selling each extra animal reared. The negative effects of overgrazing, however, are shared by all the herdsmen using the pasture so that the individual bears only a fraction of the cost. 'Each man is locked into a system that compels him to increase his herd without limit – in a world which is limited. Ruin is the destination toward which all men rush, each pursuing his own best interest in a society that believes in the freedom of the commons. Freedom in a commons brings ruin to all' (Hardin 1968: 1244).

Just as grazing land is a natural resource used for rearing animals for food, so water used for drinking and other purposes, fossil fuels for domestic energy and transport, and marine fish stocks are natural resources which, if used freely by individuals, provide other examples of the tragedy of the commons. In each case it may be to the benefit of an individual person, firm or nation to use as much of the resource as possible, even though the overall end effect of such use is the loss of the resource for everyone. The depletion of fish stocks in the North Sea, for example, is leading to destruction of wildlife as well as unemployment and its associated problems in many fishing communities. Nevertheless, immediate short-term benefits still accrue to individual fishermen who must continue to catch as many fish as they can to maintain their livelihoods.

This idea of the tragedy of the commons is not restricted to the use of common resource 'pools', but can also refer to the use of common 'sinks' such as water, air and land for the absorption of wastes. Private transport by car, for example, confers a number of immediate personal benefits to the individual car user (Chapter 6). However, the combined effect of many car users reduces air quality and contributes to global warming, costs which are shared by everyone.

Hardin argues that, by its very nature, the tragedy of the commons is unlikely to be averted by simple appeals to individuals, firms or nations to behave differently of their own volition. Instead, forms of social arrangement are required which coerce people into taking responsibility for the environment, arrangements such as environmental regulations and taxes to control social use of common resource pools and sinks. Such arrangements, of course, challenge individual rights and freedoms and raise issues of social justice and equity. They also involve questions about who should be responsible for making the arrangements.

Responsibility and power

Some environmental problems, such as global warming, ozone depletion and the loss of global biodiversity, pose risks which are unpredictable but inescapable. Their indiscriminate nature means that they affect everyone, but no individual can act alone to dispel the risk, and consequently it is possible for everyone to evade responsibility. The action of any single individual will have a negligible impact on the environment. 'One can do something and continue doing it without having to take personal responsibility' (Beck 1992: 33).

Even if individuals are able to appreciate the combined effects likely to stem from the behaviour of all individuals, they still may not be in a position to take action to improve the environment. The availability of clean air, water, soil and green space in cities, for example, is not directly under the control of individual urban residents. Changes in the methods of energy production and moves towards supply systems which open up possibilities for more efficient domestic use of energy are to a large extent in the hands of fuel industries, planners, architects and governments so that it may be difficult for individuals to initiate change. Lack of money can also inhibit action for environmental protection. In Chapter 4, for example, we saw how the problems of energy inefficiency in Eastern Europe are due to the form of housing construction, but insulating dwellings and transforming heating systems would incur massive costs which are beyond the capacity of individuals, and even governments, in those countries to meet. Even taking environmentally responsible action by buying products such as organically grown vegetables, free-range eggs, phosphate-free detergents and catalytic converters is similarly not an option open to people who cannot afford them.

Ideas about who should be responsible for action to protect the environment vary widely and the role of the state is often seen as being to pick up the bill for the social costs incurred by the environmentally damaging activities of a few. 'It is not cities that are responsible for most resource use, waste, pollution and greenhouse gas emissions but particular industries and commercial enterprises and middle and upper income groups who indulge in high consumption lifestyles' (Satterthwaite 1994: 20). Satterthwaite argues that because many of these enterprises and consumers are concentrated in cities, 'good governance' is essential to ensure the well-being of all citizens. This idea of the state in a protective role is not new to social policy. 'People need to come to terms with the fact that state social policy – broadly defined – offers in many cases the best way of socialising costs that will otherwise fall heavily, unpredictably and inequitably on individuals and families' (Hill 1996: 318).

Polluting industries often target economically poorer areas where unemployment is high. Companies are therefore in a powerful position to recruit a workforce willing to live and work in environmentally poor conditions with high risks of pollution incidents. This phenomenon of 'jobs blackmail' again reflects the fact that the poor tend to be less politically powerful than the wealthy and are less able to militate against environmentally damaging activities. 'There has tended to be an assumption that once the public are informed about the seriousness of environmental problems they will eventually come round to accepting the need to act. Such an assumption is naive, not least because it fails to recognize the power relations central to an understanding of decision-making' (Garner 1996: 181).

Sustainability revisited

We have examined the effects that human activity has on the environment and the kinds of social costs which these effects incur. It is clear that current trends in resource use cannot be sustained without risking irreversible damage to both the environment and social structures. In Chapter 1 we discussed the idea of sustainable development as a unifying theme for both environmental issues and social policy, and we return to that theme here in the light of the issues raised in later chapters.

Sustainable development means reconciling two basic aspirations of society:

- to achieve economic development to secure rising standards of living both now and for future generations;
- to protect and enhance the environment now and for the future.

(Department of the Environment 1996c: 1)

The difficulty of understanding what sustainable development might look like stems from the potential tensions between these two objectives. Economic development to raise living standards implies economic growth but, according to one school of thought, the natural limits of the environment in providing resources and absorbing waste place limits on the capacity for growth in both production and consumption. Therefore, continued economic growth is incompatible with environmental objectives and one must be traded off against the other.

This idea has been challenged by proponents of the concept of 'ecological modernization', who deny that any such trade-off is necessary. They hold that environmentally sustainable economic growth is possible using a switch from non-renewable to renewable resource use and by limiting potentially negative impacts on the environment through regulation and control. Regulation can be used to internalize the environmental and social costs of the use of public goods such as air and water so that the costs are borne by polluters. Far from hindering growth, environmental protection can even stimulate it through the growth of the pollution and waste control sector and the promotion of demand for new clean technologies to produce goods which are the least damaging to the environment (Weale 1992; Pearce 1993; Garner 1996).

On the one hand, then, is the argument that economic growth and higher levels of GDP lead to increased pollution and depletion of natural resources. On the other is the idea that increasing GDP not only increases demands for higher environmental standards but also provides the financial resources needed to meet these demands.

In many industrialized countries today, however, it is the economic imperative that holds most sway, regardless of environmental concerns. 'The achievement of high levels of consumption and the maintenance of those levels (with their consequent benefits for employment) have been seen as of higher priority than curbing the growth of environmental problems' (Hill 1996: 290). Between 1970 and 1988, final consumption expenditure in OECD countries increased on average by nearly 80 per cent but, as we have seen, higher levels of consumption often act against the protection and enhancement of the environment. More prosperous consumers make greater use of water for 'luxury' uses such as car washing and watering gardens, and contribute to demands for more intensive food production, particularly for meat and dairy products. They tend to live in bigger houses and consume more energy for heating, and to operate electrical household appliances such as dishwashers, computers and music systems. Over 60 per cent of households in OECD countries own at least one private car and more affluent car owners make longer and more frequent journeys. Rising prosperity brings more opportunities for leisure, more trips to the countryside and more overseas holidays as well as placing increasing demands on industry for the production of leisure goods.

In addition to the environmental problems caused by high levels of consumption of resources in the form of water, food, energy and raw materials, more affluent sectors of society are also responsible for the production of polluting waste. This includes the atmospheric pollution and greenhouse gases emitted from the use of energy for domestic purposes, transport and industry. Although industrialized countries account for only a fifth of the world's population, they are responsible for more than three-quarters of global atmospheric emissions (United Nations Development Programme 1996). Massive amounts of solid waste are generated from packaging and used consumer goods. The daily output of solid municipal waste in Paris is nine million kilograms, in New York 14 million kilograms and in Tokyo more than 30 million kilograms (OECD 1991).

'The average person in the developed world consumes natural resources at a rate which is at least 10–20 times as high as the corresponding figure for the poorest countries' (OECD 1991: 242). But it is not only the rich who are responsible for environmental damage. In poorer parts of the world many people have no choice but to make maximum use of the natural resources of water, land and forests, for agriculture and fuel collection, which are available to them. Their immediate livelihoods depend on these resources, but at the same time growing poverty, population density and pressures on land mean that overuse results in environmental degradation. Developing countries are facing increasing problems of water scarcity, deforestation, desertification and pollution. Water supplies per capita are only a third of what they were in 1970; forests are being cleared at a rate of eight to ten million acres a year; in Sub-Saharan Africa 65 million hectares of productive land have been lost through desertification over the past 50 years; and around 700 million people are thought to be affected by indoor smoke pollution from burning biomass fuels in chimneyless kitchens (United Nations Development Programme 1996).

Earlier chapters in the book have shown that the activities of poorer people in more affluent countries have negative effects on the environment. The demand for cheap food puts pressure on agricultural intensification and on the provision of frozen and pre-packaged foods which are wasteful in terms of energy use and packaging. People living on low incomes are less likely to live in well insulated homes and more likely to use resources inefficiently since they often cannot afford to buy energy and water efficient appliances. They are similarly less able to afford to buy 'green' products because these are usually more expensive than other brands.

On both local and global scales, however, there is a huge difference in the way in which rich and poor groups of people experience environmental damage. The rich can usually afford to move away from problem areas while 'poorer groups generally bear the immediate cost and suffer the direct consequences of environmental degradation' (WHO 1992: 14). They not only bear the brunt of the damage to which they have contributed themselves, but are also often victims of the polluting activities of the rich. Sites for chemical plants, toxic waste incinerators, radioactive waste repositories, nuclear power stations, major roads, railways, airports and even wind farms are often in socially and economically marginalized areas with high unemployment and low income levels where the possibility of local objections to the proposed development is minimized. At a global level, 'it is important to recognise most global sinks are located in the less developed countries where the "costs" of disposal – including the value of the poor's labour – are much lower!' (Redclift 1996: 123). The impacts of global warming, climate change and sea level rises are likely to be most severe in poorer countries. Bangladesh, for example, is responsible for only 0.3 per cent of total greenhouse gas emissions, but could lose 17 per cent of its land area if the sea level rises by one metre.

There are even disparities between rich and poor when efforts are made to protect the environment, for example, by setting aside areas for nature conservation. 'In general, while there is growing recognition that many of the benefits from conserving biodiversity go to the world as a whole, in many cases the costs are borne at national and local levels. The heaviest burden tends to be borne by poorer countries, and especially by impoverished people

living in remote rural areas of these poor countries in the proximity of protected areas' (Wells 1992: 237).

'To begin to achieve sustainable development we need to address issues
of poverty and equity within a global perspective' (Redclift 1996: 123) but
income inequalities across the world have increased over the past 30 years.
During that time, the share of global income going to the richest 20 per
cent of the population rose from 70 to 85 per cent, while the share going
to the poorest 20 per cent fell from 2.3 to 1.4 per cent. The gap in average per capita income between the industrialized and the developing world
almost tripled, from US$5700 in 1960 to US$15,400 in 1993 (United Nations
Development Programme 1996). In relation to the environment poverty is
a double-edged sword. It makes people victims of the very environmental
degradation that it pushes them into causing. 'Economic and political forces
have produced global imbalances in the way human society interacts with
the environment, not just between city and countryside, but between groups
within society with different levels of power and influence' (Middleton 1995:
20). The relationship between economic power and political power leads to
further marginalization of the poor. They often lack the ability to mobilize
effectively for environmental protection but instead find themselves in 'a
culture in which acceptance, cynicism and defensiveness against external
influence are mixed, thereby reinforcing the situation of isolation and powerlessness' (Blowers and Leroy 1996: 267).

The role of social policy

'Given that there have to be changes in the form and nature of the economy
and society in order to incorporate environmental considerations the imple-
mentation of green measures is still fraught with difficulties, especially along
the Social Policy dimension' (Cahill 1994: 181). Social policies in different
parts of the world or even within the same country have widely varying
effects, sometimes intended, sometimes not. The study of social policy concerns itself, among other things, with examining the ways in which policies
have the potential to affect the inequalities which exist between complex
social strata based on income, class, gender, age, ethnicity and disability. Some
policies can be implemented to reduce inequalities, others may enhance or
reproduce them, while yet others may have no effect on inequalities at all
but merely reflect their existence. This book has shown that social divisions have important implications for the relationships and interactions which
occur between societies and the environment. Consequently, in the study of
social policy, and indeed in the whole process of public policy development,
it argued that it is essential to take into account the wider environmental
implications of changing social structures and relations. Social policies influence the distribution of elements of welfare between groups and individuals
through their impacts on consumption levels and patterns but they also
influence public attitudes, preferences and behaviour and ideas about power

and responsibility. They both reflect and determine prevailing sets of values and shape ideas about the standards of living which are desirable and attainable in particular societies.

In Western industrialized countries increased levels of material well-being have been accompanied by rising awareness of and interest in the environment. Surveys in the UK, for example, have revealed public support for government programmes to protect the environment. People do not, however, always act upon their declared preferences. Sometimes this is because of a belief that individual actions can have little effect; in some cases the environment is seen as a free resource and the environmental costs of certain activities are not recognized. In many cases conflicts and tensions arise between a commitment to social and environmental goals and a desire to increase individual utility. Private car use provides a good example here. Even though an individual may be fully aware of the environmental damage caused by cars – local noise, pollution, congestion and global damage through greenhouse gas emissions – the immediate benefits of freedom of movement and independence offered by car travel usually override environmental concern, especially if alternative transport is not available. It is in cases such as this that government policies can come into play, the state acting through legislation, regulation and fiscal measures to protect the environment. State measures to encourage environmental protection, however, may have important distributional consequences, and the costs of such measures often fall disproportionately on the poor, with concomitant implications for social assistance policies.

The natural environment supplies the resources used to meet human needs and wants and acts as a repository for waste products, emissions and effluents. We have seen above that threats to the environment arise as a result of both resource use and waste generation and that these threats depend on the demands placed on resources as either pools or sinks. Demands on resources increase with increasing prosperity, for example, demands for energy, transport and leisure goods and facilities. But they also increase with population size, for example, demands for water, food and housing. In addition, some demands, such as those for housing and shelter, energy and warmth, vary with geographical location and climate. It is through its effects on these factors, levels of income and wealth, population size, structure and distribution, and population migration and urbanization that social policies influence the impacts of human beings on the environment.

Policies on employment, prices, wages and social assistance have effects on both levels of income and its distribution across different social groups, consequently determining patterns and levels of resource consumption and waste generation. Trends towards private car ownership in the UK, for example, are intimately linked with rising income levels, changing patterns of employment and the erosion of gender differentials (Chapter 6).

The size and structure of populations is influenced by these policies, but also by policies on health, housing and education. Improved levels of nutrition, safe, sufficient supplies of water and adequate sanitation act through their effects on longevity, birth rates and mortality to determine population patterns and hence demands on resources. Demographic change and social trends underlie changing patterns of family structure and household formation. In the UK, for example, increases in life expectancy, rising divorce rates and community care policies are leading to the formation of more small households (Chapter 4). This not only puts pressure on housing provision, but leads to a growth in demand for durable household goods and supplies of domestic energy (Chapter 5). As the percentage of retired people in the population grows, so does the number of people with more time to spend on leisure activities (Chapter 7).

The geographical distribution of human populations, both nationally and globally, is a major determinant of demands placed on natural resources and patterns of migration and urbanization change with employment patterns, housing and service provision, industrial and agricultural development and transport networks. Once again, this relationship is vitally dependent on income distribution and employment policies.

Well-being and the quality of life

A study of migration patterns in Britain shows that 'for many of those who are able to migrate, the search for a higher quality of life is critical in determining their choice of local destination' (Findlay and Rogerson 1993: 48). Some variables which contribute to decisions about where to live are clearly economic and related to employment options and living costs. However, the study shows that social and environmental dimensions are equally, if not more, important. Housing and health provision and the degree of dereliction and pollution in local areas play a key role. It is likely that economic factors are more likely to be important to poorer families, but they are the ones who are least likely to have moved home to a destination of their choice.

The quality of life is an elusive concept, incorporating social, environmental and economic elements. It is highly culture specific and dependent on personal attitudes and preferences. It is impossible to compare, for example, the relative quality of the lives of people living on low incomes in a beautiful environment with others living on high incomes in a degraded environment. Affluence may enable the latter group, at least temporarily, to insulate themselves from the direct effects of their immediate surroundings. Nevertheless, Redclift (1996) argues that above a certain threshold improvements in standards of living, accompanied by increased negative environmental effects of consumption and the generation of wastes and pollution, can actually contribute to a fall in the quality of life. Surveys in OECD countries have shown that growing feelings of insecurity and dissatisfaction are accompanying increasing per capita incomes. 'The purpose of growth should be to enrich people's lives. But far too often it does not' (United Nations Development Programme 1996: 1).

The goals of both social and environmental policies are often seen as subordinate to economic goals. Social arguments against continued economic growth are based on the belief that the growth imperative encourages people to act as passive consumers pursuing material comforts, rather than as active citizens obtaining fulfilment and satisfaction from their emotional, intellectual and spiritual lives (Garner 1996). Unequal distribution of the benefits of economic growth can, for some people, result in loss of job security and increased feelings of dependency on social welfare benefits, leading to personal uncertainty and lack of confidence. 'Traditional forms of coping with anxiety and insecurity in socio-moral milieus, families, marriage and male-female roles are failing. To the same degree, coping with anxiety and insecurity is demanded of individuals themselves' (Beck 1992: 153).

In this context, and especially for the poor, local, immediate and short-term interests and concerns understandably tend to take precedence over concern for the environment and for the sustainability of environmental and social well-being for future generations. Poverty and environmental degradation perpetuate each other, and intimate links exist between rising inequalities at local and international level, environmental damage and a decline in social well-being and the quality of life. Social policy plays a key role in understanding poverty, not only in terms of income level but also taking into account health, life expectancy, literacy, access to public goods and common property resources, security against crime and physical violence and participation in economic, cultural and political activities of the community. We have seen throughout this book that both poverty and wealth, with their associated qualitative patterns and quantitative levels of consumption, crucially influence the state of the environment, which is central to well-being and the quality of life.

GLOSSARY OF SCIENTIFIC AND TECHNICAL TERMS

Abstraction: the removal of water from natural sources on the surface or in the ground for domestic, commercial or industrial use.

Acid deposition: the deposition of acidic pollutants in rain, snow, mist or dry air on to vegetation, soils or water surfaces.

Aerobic bacteria: *bacteria* which require free oxygen in order to grow and reproduce.

Algae: non-flowering plants which grow in damp places on land and in fresh and sea water. Many are microscopic single cell plants which occur in large numbers.

Algal blooms: the rapid growth of *algae* in the surface waters of ponds, lakes or seas.

Anaerobic bacteria: *bacteria* which survive, grow and reproduce in the absence of free oxygen.

Anthropogenic: resulting from human intervention or activity.

Aquifer: a porous underground rock formation holding significant quantities of water.

Area of Outstanding Natural Beauty: a region of England or Wales which is considered sufficiently attractive to be preserved from over-development.

Bacteria: microscopic living organisms, each bacterium usually consisting of a single cell.

Benzene: C_6H_6, a *carcinogenic organic* compound found in petrol and motor vehicle exhausts.

Biodiversity: a term referring to the number, variety and variability of living organisms, but often used to mean the total variety of life on earth.

Biomass: mass of living or dead *organic matter*.

Biosphere: all living things on the earth.

Carbon monoxide: CO, a toxic colourless gas produced by the incomplete burning of fossil fuels.

Carbon dioxide: CO_2, a colourless non-toxic gas naturally present in the air and produced by the *respiration* of living organisms. It is also produced by the burning of fossil fuels and is an important *greenhouse gas*.

Carcinogen: a substance which has the potential to cause cancer.

Catalytic converter: a device fitted to motor vehicle exhausts to reduce emissions of *carbon monoxide, nitric oxide* and *VOCs*.

CFCs: chlorofluorocarbons manufactured for use as refrigerants, insulating material and other purposes. They are potent *greenhouse gases* and also damage the *ozone layer*.

Dioxins: powerful poisons released during the manufacture and incineration of a number of man-made chemicals.

Ecology: the study of the relationships between living organisms and their environments.

Ecosystem: a community of interdependent living organisms and the environment they inhabit and interact with.

Eutrophication: the enrichment of water by plant nutrients.

Food chain: the flow of energy in the form of food between living organisms.

Global warming: an increase in the mean surface temperature of the earth.

Greenhouse effect: the warming effect which certain gases, *greenhouse gases*, in the atmosphere have on the earth's surface. This effect occurs naturally but is enhanced by additional emissions of greenhouse gases as a result of human activity.

Greenhouse gases: gases which 'trap' some of the heat radiated from the earth's surface causing surface temperatures to increase. These include naturally occurring gases such as *carbon dioxide, nitrous oxide, methane* and *ozone*, as well as manufactured gases such as *CFCs*.

Hydrocarbons: compounds made up of hydrogen and carbon atoms. They are the main components of fossil fuels.

Hydrological cycle: the continual movement of water between the atmosphere, living organisms, the surface of the earth and underlying rocks.

Leaching: the removal of dissolved substances from soil or other solid material.

Methane: CH_4, a simple hydrocarbon gas produced by the breakdown of *organic matter*. It is the main constituent of most natural gas and is a potent *greenhouse gas*.

Monoculture: the repeated cultivation of a single crop species on the same area of land.

National Park: in England and Wales, an area designated for the purpose of preserving and enhancing its natural beauty while affording access for open-air recreation.

Nitrate: a compound of *nitrogen* and *oxygen* which is highly soluble and taken up by plants where it provides the nitrogen essential for growth. Its high solubility, however, means it is easily leached from soils.

Nitric oxide: NO, a non-toxic gas released by the burning of fossil fuels. In the air it is rapidly converted to *nitrogen dioxide*.

Nitrogen: N_2, a naturally occurring gas which makes up about 80 per cent of the earth's atmosphere.

Nitrogen dioxide: NO_2, a compound of *nitrogen* and *oxygen* which is toxic in high concentrations. It contributes to the formation of *ozone* and to *acid deposition*.

Nitrogen oxides: a range of compounds formed from *nitrogen* and *oxygen*, including *nitrogen dioxide, nitric oxide* and *nitrous oxide*.

Nitrous oxide: N_2O, a relatively inert oxide of *nitrogen* but a potent *greenhouse gas*.

Organic matter: plants, animals and their constituent parts, living or dead, which contain carbon compounds.

Oxygen: O_2, a gas essential for the *respiration* of most living organisms, and making up nearly 20 per cent of the earth's atmosphere.

Ozone: O_3, a pungent, irritant gas occurring naturally throughout the atmosphere. It is a toxic pollutant in the lower atmosphere or *troposphere* but at higher levels in the *stratosphere* it protects the earth from harmful ultraviolet radiation.

Ozone layer: *ozone* surrounding the earth in the upper atmosphere or *stratosphere*.

Particulates: fine solid or liquid particles suspended in the air and in emissions such as dust, smoke or smog.

Pathogenic: disease causing.

pH: the measure of acidity or alkalinity of a substance. A neutral substance has a pH of 7.

Photochemical reactions: chemical reactions requiring the energy from sunlight.

Photosynthesis: the conversion by plants, in the presence of sunlight, of *carbon dioxide* and water to simple sugars and *oxygen*.

Plankton: tiny animals (*zooplankton*) and plants (*phytoplankton*) that float or swim in fresh or salt water, usually near the surface.

Phytoplankton: tiny plants, usually *algae*, which grow and float in surface waters.

Principle of energy conservation: the total amount of energy in a physical system is constant and energy cannot be either created or destroyed.

Radioactivity: the spontaneous emission of biologically damaging forms of radiation.

Respiration: the chemical reactions which take place in living organisms to produce energy. In most plants and animals respiration entails taking in *oxygen* and releasing *carbon dioxide*.

Site of Special Scientific Interest: area of land in Great Britain notified as being of special nature conservation interest.

Stratosphere: the layer of the atmosphere approximately 15 to 50 kilometres above the surface of the earth.

Sulphur dioxide: SO_2, a compound of sulphur and *oxygen* which occurs as an acidic gas, toxic at high concentrations.

Troposphere: the layer of the atmosphere between ground level and about 15 kilometres above the ground.

Ultraviolet radiation: radiation within a particular wavelength range, shorter than visible light but longer than X-rays.

VOCs: volatile organic compounds which evaporate readily in the air.

Water table: the level below which soil or rocks are permanently saturated with water.

Zooplankton: microscopic animal organisms, such as small crustaceans and larvae, which live in surface waters.

REFERENCES

Adams, J. (1995) *Risk*. London: UCL Press.

All-Party Parliamentary Water Group (1996) Minutes of Annual General Meeting: Environmental Aspects of Water, 11 June.

Anthony, K. (1996) Water poverty and direct payments, unpublished MA thesis, University of York.

Bakker, G. (1993) Energy conservation – the Dutch experience, conference paper, Neighbourhood Energy Action, 'Towards an Energy Efficient Europe', Birmingham, 20–1 January.

Barde, J. P. and Potier, M. (1996) A 'green' impact on jobs?, *OECD Observer*, No. 198, 17–21.

Beck, U. (1992) *Risk Society: towards a New Modernity*. London: Sage Publications.

Beckerman, W. (1986) How large is the public sector?, *Oxford Review of Economic Policy*, 2, 2.

Bhatti, M. (1996) Housing and environmental policy in the UK, *Policy and Politics*, 24, 159–70.

Blowers, A. and Glasbergen, P. (1995) The search for sustainable development, in P. Glasbergen and A. Blowers (eds) *Perspectives on Environmental Problems*. London: Arnold.

Blowers, A. and Leroy, P. (1996) Environment and society: shaping the future?, in A. Blowers and P. Glasbergen (eds) *Prospects for Environmental Change*. London: Arnold.

Blunden, B. and Curry, N. (1996) Analysing amenity and scientific problems: the Broadlands, England, in P. B. Sloep and A. Blowers (eds) *Environmental Problems as Conflicts of Interest*. London: Arnold.

Blunden, J. and Reddish, A. (eds) (1991) *Energy, Resources and Environment*. London: Hodder and Stoughton.

BMA (1994) *Water: a Vital Resource*. London: British Medical Association.

Boardman, B. (1991) Ten years cold: lessons from a decade of fuel poverty, policy discussion paper, Neighbourhood Energy Action, Newcastle upon Tyne.

Boardman, B. (1993) Energy inefficient Europe: the scale of the problem, conference paper, Neighbourhood Energy Action, 'Towards an Energy Efficient Europe', Birmingham, 20–21 January.

Boardman, B. (1995) *Energy and Environment Programme. Environmental Change Unit Annual Report 1994–95*. Oxford: University of Oxford.

Bolsius, E. and Frouws, J. (1996) Agricultural intensification: livestock farming in the Netherlands, in P. B. Sloep and A. Blowers (eds) *Environmental Problems as Conflicts of Interest*. London: Arnold.

Bradley, P. (ed.) (1991) *Woodfuel, Women and Woodlots. Volume 1: The Foundations of a Woodfuel Development Strategy for East Africa*. London: Macmillan.

Bradley, P. and Huby, M. (eds) (1993) *Woodfuel, Women and Woodlots. Volume 2: The Kenya Woodfuel Development Programme*. London: Macmillan.

Bradshaw, J. and Hutton, S. (1983) Social policy options and fuel poverty, *Journal of Economic Psychology*, 3, 249–66.

Brechling, V. and Smith, S. (1994) Household energy efficiency in the UK, *Fiscal Studies*, 15, 44–56.

British Tourist Authority (1992) *Digest of Tourist Statistics No. 16*. London: British Tourist Authority.

Brown, I. (1993) The problems of energy inefficiency in Hungary, conference paper, Neighbourhood Energy Action, 'Towards an Energy Efficient Europe', Birmingham, 20–21 January.

Brown, L. R. (1993) A new era unfolds, in L. R. Brown *et al.* (eds) *State of the World – 1993*. New York: W. W. Norton.

Brown, L. R. (1995) Nature's limits, in L. R. Brown *et al.* (eds) *State of the World – 1995*. New York: W. W. Norton.

Bruce, J. P., Lee, H. and Haites, E. F. (eds) (1996) *Climate Change 1995: Economic and Social Dimensions of Climate Change*. Cambridge: Cambridge University Press.

Brundtland, G. H. (1987) *Our Common Future* (The World Commission on Environment and Development). Oxford: Oxford University Press.

Burrows, R. (1997) Virtual culture, urban social polarisation and social science fiction, in B. Loader (ed.) *The Governance of Cyberspace*. London: Routledge.

Byatt, I. (1990) The Office of Water Services: structure and policy, *Utilities Law Review*, Summer, 85–90.

Cahill, M. (1994) *The New Social Policy*. Oxford: Blackwell.

Cairncross, F. (1993) *Costing the Earth*. Boston: Harvard Business School Press.

Carley, M. and Christie, I. (1992) *Managing Sustainable Development*. London: Earthscan.

Carter, F. W. and Turnock, D. (eds) (1993) *Environmental Problems in Eastern Europe*. London: Routledge.

Central Statistical Office (1994) *Economic Trends 1994*. London: HMSO.

Central Statistical Office (1996) *Social Trends 26, 1996*. London: HMSO.

Cerni, J. (1993) Urban environmental pollution and child health in Houston, USA: the links to economic growth, in J. Holder, P. Lane, S. Eden, R. Reeve, U. Collier and K. Anderson (eds) *Perspectives on the Environment*. Aldershot: Avebury.

Chavangi, N. (1993) Towards an extension strategy, in P. Bradley and M. Huby (eds) *Woodfuel, Women and Woodlots. Volume 2: The Kenya Woodfuel Development Programme*. London: Macmillan.

Cheshire, J. (1993) The economics of energy efficiency: achieving an effective policy, conference paper, Neighbourhood Energy Action, 'Towards an Energy Efficient Europe', Birmingham, 20–21 January.

Choi, P. (1993) Creating a decent environment for the poor: housing for low-income groups, in C. Chan and P. Hills (eds) *Limited Gains: Grassroots Mobilization and the Environment in Hong Kong*. Hong Kong: Centre of Urban Planning and Environmental Management, The University of Hong Kong.

Clarke, J. and Critcher, C. (1985) *The Devil Makes Work: Leisure in Capitalist Britain*. London: Macmillan.

Cloke, P., Milbourne, P. and Thomas, C. (1994) *Lifestyles in Rural England*. Rural Development Commission. London: HMSO.

Countryside Commission (1991) *National Survey of Countryside Recreation 1985–1991*. Cheltenham: Countryside Commission.

Cuninghame, C., Griffin, J. and Laws, S. (1996) *Water Tight: the Impact of Water Metering on Low Income Families*. London: Save the Children.

Davis, A. (1997) The public health impact of motor transport in the UK, Health and Transport Research Group, School of Health and Social Welfare, Open University, Milton Keynes.

Davis, A. and Jones, L. J. (1996a) Environmental constraints on health: listening to children's views, *Health Education Journal*, 55, 363–74.

Davis, A. and Jones, L. J. (1996b) Children in the urban environment: an issue for the new public health agenda, *Health & Place*, 2, 107–13.

Denniston, D. (1995) Sustaining mountain peoples and environments, in L. R. Brown et al. (eds) *State of the World 1995*. London: Earthscan.

Department of Employment (1995) *New Earnings Survey 1995*. London: HMSO.

Department of the Environment (1991) *Digest of Environmental Protection and Water Statistics, 14*. London: HMSO.

Department of the Environment (1992a) *The UK Environment*. London: HMSO.

Department of the Environment (1992b) Using water wisely, a consultation paper from the Department of the Environment and the Welsh Office, July.

Department of the Environment (1993) *English House Condition Survey 1991*. London: HMSO.

Department of the Environment (1994) *Action for the Countryside*. London: Central Office of Information.

Department of the Environment (1996a) *United Kingdom National Environmental Health Action Plan*, Cm 3323. London: HMSO.

Department of the Environment (1996b) *Digest of Environmental Statistics, 18*. London: HMSO.

Department of the Environment (1996c) *Indicators of Sustainable Development for the United Kingdom*. London: HMSO.

Department of Trade and Industry and Office for National Statistics (1996) *Digest of United Kingdom Energy Statistics 1996*. London: HMSO.

Department of Transport (1995) *Transport Statistics Great Britain 1995*. London: HMSO.

Department of Transport (1996) *National Travel Survey, 1993/95*. London: HMSO.

Dixon, J. A., James, D. E. and Sherman, P. B. (1989) *The Economics of Dryland Management*. London: Earthscan.

Dobson, A. (1990) *Green Political Thought*. London: Unwin Hyman.

Dobson, A. (ed.) (1991) *The Green Reader*. London: Andre Deutsch.

Dobson, B., Beardsworth, A., Keil, T. and Walker, R. (1994) *Diet, Choice and Poverty: Social, Cultural and Nutritional Aspects of Food Consumption among Low-income Families*. London: Family Policy Studies Centre.

Dobson, B., Trinder, P., Ashworth, K., Stafford, B., Walker, R. and Walker, D. (1996) *Income Deprivation in the City*. York: York Publishing Services.

Doyal, L. and Gough, I. (1991) *A Theory of Human Need*. London: Macmillan.

Economic and Social Research Council (1995) *Thematic Priorities*. Swindon: ESRC.

Elkin, T. and McLaren, D. (1991) *Reviving the City*. London: Friends of the Earth.

Elson, D. and Cleaver, F. (1994) Gender and water resource management: integrating or marginalising women?, conference paper, OECD/DAC Expert Group on Gender and Water Resource Management, Stockholm, 1–3 December.

Ernst, J. (1994) *Whose Utility? The Social Impact of Public Utility Privatization and Regulation in Britain*. Buckingham: Open University Press.

Fai, N. Y. (1993) The environment and grassroots participation in squatter areas, in C. Chan and P. Hills (eds) *Limited Gains: Grassroots Mobilization and the Environment in Hong Kong*. Hong Kong: Centre of Urban Planning and Environmental Management, The University of Hong Kong.

Findlay, A. and Rogerson, R. (1993) Migration, places and quality of life, in T. Champion (ed.) *Population Matters: the Local Dimension*. London: Paul Chapman.

The Food Commission (1996) Lindane residues found in milk, *The Food Magazine*, 34, 1.

Ford, J. (1997) Mortgage arrears, mortgage possessions and homelessness, in R. Burrows, N. Pleace and D. Quilgars (eds) *Homelessness and Social Policy*. London: Routledge.

Ford, J., Quilgars, D., Burrows, R. and Pleace, N. (1996) *Young People and Housing*. Salisbury: Rural Development Commission.

French, H. F. (1991) Restoring the East European and Soviet environments, in L. R. Brown *et al.* (eds) *State of the World 1991*. New York: W. W. Norton.

French, H. F. (1995) Forging a new global partnership, in L. R. Brown *et al.* (eds) *State of the World 1995*. London: Earthscan.

Garner, R. (1996) *Environmental Politics*. London: Prentice Hall, Harvester Wheatsheaf.

George, V. and Wilding, P. (1994) *Welfare and Ideology*. Hemel Hempstead: Harvester Wheatsheaf.

Gilbert, A. (1991) Urban problems in the third world, in P. Sarre (ed.) *Environment, Population and Development*. London: Hodder and Stoughton.

Glasbergen, P. and Blowers, A. (eds) (1995) *Perspectives on Environmental Problems*. London: Arnold.

Glendinning, C. and Millar, J. (1992) *Women and Poverty in Britain: the 1990s*. Hemel Hempstead: Harvester Wheatsheaf.

Green, A. (1994) *The Geography of Poverty and Wealth*. Warwick: Institute for Employment Research, University of Warwick.

Green, E., Hebron, S. and Woodward, D. (1990) *Women's Leisure, What Leisure?* London: Macmillan.

Greenpeace (1996) Precautionary principle at work: Unilever and Sainsbury's ban fish oils, *Greenpeace Business*, 31, 4.

Hall, D. R. (1993) Albania, in F. W. Carter and D. Turnock (eds) *Environmental Problems in Eastern Europe*. London: Routledge.

Hardin, G. (1968) The tragedy of the commons, *Science*, 162, 1243–8.

Herbert, A. and Kempson, E. (1995) *Water Debt and Disconnection*. London: Policy Studies Institute.

Hertzman, C. (1995) *Environment and Health in Central and Eastern Europe*. Washington, DC: The World Bank.

Hill, M. (1993) *Understanding Social Policy*. Oxford: Blackwell.

Hill M. (1996) *Social Policy: a Comparative Analysis*. Hemel Hempstead: Prentice Hall, Harvester Wheatsheaf.

Hillman, M. (1992) Reconciling transport and environmental policy, *Public Administration*, 70, 225–34.

Hills, J. (1995) *Inquiry into Income and Wealth. Volume 2: a Summary of the Evidence.* York: Joseph Rowntree Foundation.

Hinrichsen, D. (1990) *Our Common Seas.* London: Earthscan.

Hirschhorn, J. S. and Oldenburg, K. U. (1991) *Prosperity without Pollution.* New York: Van Nostrand Reinhold.

HMSO (1990) *This Common Inheritance*, Cm 1200. London: HMSO.

HMSO (1994a) *Sustainable Development: the UK Strategy*, Cm 2426. London: HMSO.

HMSO (1994b) *Climate Change: the UK Programme*, Cm 2427. London: HMSO.

HMSO (1994c) *Biodiversity: the UK Action Plan*, Cm 2428. London: HMSO.

HMSO (1996a) *Health Survey for England, 1994.* London: HMSO.

HMSO (1996b) *This Common Inheritance: 1996 UK Annual Report*, Cm 3188. London: HMSO.

Homer-Dixon, T. F., Boutwell, J. H. and Rathjens, G. W. (1993) Environmental change and violent conflict, *Scientific American*, February, 38–45.

Huby, M. (1990) *Where You Can't See the Wood for the Trees.* Stockholm: Beijer Institute/Stockholm Environment Institute.

Huby, M. and Dix, G. (1992) *Evaluating the Social Fund*, Department of Social Security Research Report No. 9. London: HMSO.

International Bank for Reconstruction and Development (1992) *World Development Report 1992: Development and the Environment*. Washington, DC: Oxford University Press.

International Bank for Reconstruction and Development (1996) *World Development Report 1996: From Plan to Market*. Washington, DC: Oxford University Press.

IUCN/UNEP/WWF (1980) *World Conservation Strategy: Living Resource Conservation for Sustainable Development*. Gland, Switzerland: International Union for Conservation of Nature and Natural Resources, United Nations Environment Programme and the World Wildlife Fund.

Jackson, C. (1995) Environmental reproduction and gender in the Third World, in S. Morse and M. Stocking (eds) *People and Environment*. London: UCL Press.

Joffe, M. (1991) Food as a social policy issue, in N. Manning (ed.) *Social Policy Review 1990–91*. Harlow: Longman.

Jones, L. J. (1996) Shifting the boundaries of social policy: the case for putting transport on the social policy agenda, in M. May, E. Brunsdon and G. Craig (eds) *Social Policy Review 8*. London: Social Policy Association.

Jowell, R., Brook, L. and Taylor, B. (eds) (1991) *British Social Attitudes: the 8th Report*. Aldershot: Dartmouth.

Jowell, R., Curtice, J., Park, A., Brook, L. and Ahrendt, D. (eds) (1994) *British Social Attitudes: the 11th Report*. Aldershot: SCPR.

Jowell, R., Curtice, J., Park, A., Brook, L. and Ahrendt, D. (eds) (1995) *British Social Attitudes: the 12th Report*. Aldershot: SCPR.

Keeble, D. E. (1990) Small firms, new firms and uneven regional development in the United Kingdom, *Area*, 22, 234–45.

Kelly, M. and Granich, S. (1995) Global warming and development, in S. Morse and M. Stocking (eds) *People and Environment*. London: UCL Press.

Kempson, E. (1996) *Life on a Low Income*. York: Joseph Rowntree Foundation.

Kinnersley, D. (1994) *Coming Clean*. Harmondsworth: Penguin Books.

Krippendorf, J. (1991) *The Holiday Makers*. Oxford: Heinemann.

Kuh, D. J. L. and Cooper, C. (1992) Physical activity at 36 years: patterns and childhood predictors in a logitudinal study, *Journal of Epidemiology*, 46, 114–19.

Lang, T. (1995) Local sustainability in a sea of globalisation? The case of food policy, conference paper, Political Economy Research Centre, University of Sheffield, 'Planning Sustainability', 8–10 September.

Lang, T. (1996) Food security: does it conflict with globalization?, *Development*, 4, 45–50.

Lang, T. (1997a) *Food Policy for the 21st Century: Can It Be Both Radical and Reasonable?* Discussion Paper 4, Centre for Food Policy. London: Thames Valley University.

Lang, T. (1997b) Dividing up the cake: food as social exclusion, in A. Walker and C. Walker (eds) *Britain Divided: the Growth of Social Exclusion in the 1980s and 1990s*. London: Child Poverty Action Group.

Lang, T., Caraher, M., Dixon, P. and Carr-Hill, R. (1996) Class, income and gender in cooking: results from an English survey, in J. S. A. Edwards (ed.) *Culinary Arts and Sciences*. Southampton: Computational Mechanics Publications.

Lea, J. (1988) *Tourism and Development in the Third World*. London: Routledge.

Lenssen, N. and Roodman, D. M. (1995) Making better buildings, in L. R. Brown *et al.* (eds) *State of the World 1995*. London: Earthscan.

Liberatore, A. (1995) The social construction of environmental problems, in P. Glasbergen and A. Blowers (eds) *Perspectives on Environmental Problems*. London: Arnold.

Lipietz, A. (1995) *Green Hopes: the Future of Political Ecology*. London: Polity.

Maddison, D., Pearce, D., Johansson, O., Calthrop, E., Litman, T. and Verhoef, E. (1996) *Blueprint 5: the True Costs of Road Transport*. London: Earthscan.

Manning, N. (ed.) (1991) *Social Policy Review 1990–91*. Harlow: Longman.

Martell, L. (1994) *Ecology and Society*. Cambridge: Polity Press.

Middleton, N. (1995) *The Global Casino*. London: Edward Arnold.

Mintzer, I. M. (ed.) (1992) *Confronting Climate Change*. Cambridge: Cambridge University Press.

Morse, S. and Stocking, M. (eds) (1995) *People and Environment*. London: UCL Press.

Musgrave, R. A. and Musgrave, P. B. (1984) *Public Finance in Theory and Practice*. New York: McGraw-Hill.

National Consumer Council (1987) *What's Wrong with Walking? A Consumer Review of the Pedestrian Environment*. London: HMSO.

National Consumer Council (1994) *Water Price Controls: Key Consumer Concerns*. London: National Consumer Council.

Neighbourhood Energy Action (1996) *Fuel Poverty Factsheet – Heating and Insulation*. Newcastle upon Tyne: Neighbourhood Energy Action.

North York Moors National Park (1995) *Student Fact File*. Danby: North York Moors National Park Education Service.

OECD (1989) *Agricultural and Environmental Policies: Opportunities for Integration*. Paris: OECD.

OECD (1991) *The State of the Environment*. Paris: OECD.

Office for National Statistics (1996) *Family Spending 1995–96*. London: HMSO.

Office for National Statistics (1997) *Social Trends 27*. London: HMSO.

OFWAT (1993) *Why Water Bills Are Rising and How They Are Controlled*, Information Note No. 3. Birmingham: OFWAT.

OFWAT (1995) *Annual Report of the Director General of Water Services 1995*. London: HMSO.

OFWAT (1996a) *Report on Recent Patterns of Demand for Water in England and Wales.* Birmingham: OFWAT.

OFWAT (1996b) *Annual Report of the OFWAT National Customer Council 1995–96.* Birmingham: OFWAT.

Oliver, D., Elliott, D. and Reddish, A. (1991) Sustainable energy futures, in J. Blunden and A. Reddish (eds) *Energy, Resources and Environment.* London: Hodder and Stoughton.

Oppenheim, C. and Harker, L. (1996) *Poverty: the Facts.* London: Child Poverty Action Group.

Pearce, D. (1993) *Blueprint 3: Measuring Sustainable Development.* London: Earthscan.

Pleace, N., Quilgars, D. and Burrows, R. (1997) Homelessness in contemporary Britain: conceptualisation and measurement, in R. Burrows, N. Pleace and D. Quilgars (eds) *Homelessness and Social Policy.* London: Routledge.

Power, A. (1994) *Area-based Poverty, Social Problems and Resident Empowerment,* STICERD Discussion Paper 107. London: London School of Economics.

PUAF (1990) Payment direct for water, electricity and gas, a discussion paper produced by the Public Utilities Access Forum, May.

Raven, H. and Lang, T. (1995) *Off Our Trolleys? Food Retailing and the Hypermarket Economy.* London: IPPR.

Redclift, M. (1993) Sustainable development: needs, values, rights, *Environmental Values,* 2(1), 3–20.

Redclift, M. (1996) *Wasted: Counting the Cost of Global Consumption.* London: Earthscan.

Reid, D. (1995) *Sustainable Development: an Introductory Guide.* London: Earthscan.

Royal Commission on Environmental Pollution (1994) *Eighteenth Report: Transport and the Environment,* Cm 2674. London: HMSO.

Royal Society for the Protection of Birds (1996) Crisis point for UK birds, *Birds,* 16, 17–21.

Ryan, M. and Flavin, C. (1995) Facing China's limits, in L. R. Brown *et al.* (eds) *State of the World – 1995.* New York: W. W. Norton.

Sarre, P. (1991) *Environment, Population and Development.* London: Hodder and Stoughton.

Satterthwaite, D. (1994) Sustainable cities, *Resurgence,* 167, 20–2.

Seitz, J. L. (1995) *Global Issues.* Oxford: Blackwell.

Sen, A. (1995) Food, economics and entitlements, in J. Dreze, A. Sen and A. Hussain (eds) *The Political Economy of Hunger.* Oxford: Clarendon Press.

Sloep, P. B. and Blowers, A. (eds) (1996) *Environmental Problems as Conflicts of Interest.* London: Arnold.

Smil, V. (1988) *Energy in China's Modernization: Advances and Limitations.* New York: M. E. Sharpe.

Social Security Advisory Committee (1995) *The Review of Social Security – Paper 3, Housing Benefit.* Leeds: BA Publishing Services.

Spicker, P. (1995) *Social Policy – Themes and Approaches.* Hemel Hempstead: Prentice Hall/Harvester Wheatsheaf.

Statham, D. (1991) *North York Moors National Park: Second Review.* Helmsley: North York Moors National Park.

Stilwell, E. J., Canty, R. C., Kopf, P. W. and Montrone, A. M. (1991) *Packaging for the Environment.* New York: AMACOM.

Stocking, M., Perkin, S. and Brown, K. (1995) Coexisting with nature in a developing world, in S. Morse and M. Stocking (eds) *People and Environment.* London: UCL Press.

Stokes, G., Goodwin, P. and Kenny, F. (1992) *Trends in Transport and the Countryside – the Countryside Commission and Transport Policy in England*. Manchester: Countryside Commission Publications.

Sutton, J. (1988) *Transport Coordination and Social Policy*. Aldershot: Avebury.

Taylor, A. (1994) A question of attitude, *Review*, Issue 22. London: Department of Trade and Industry.

Taylor, M. (1996) Public health and water quality, in C. Hewitt, C. Hogg, M. Leicester and H. Rosenthal (eds) *Health and the Environment*. London: Socialist Health Association and Socialist Environment and Resources Association.

Taylor-Gooby, P. (1995) Comfortable, marginal and excluded: who should pay higher taxes for a better welfare state?, in R. Jowell, J. Curtice, A. Park, L. Brook and D. Ahrendt (eds) *British Social Attitudes: the 12th Report*. Aldershot: SCPR.

Tellegen, E. (1996) Environmental conflicts in transforming economies: Central and Eastern Europe, in P. B. Sloep and A. Blowers (eds) *Environmental Problems as Conflicts of Interest*. London: Arnold.

Thomas, D. S. G. and Middleton, N. J. (1994) *Desertification: Exploding the Myth*. Chichester: Wiley.

Tilly, L. A. and Scott, J. W. (1987) *Women, Work and Family*. London: Methuen.

Tindale, S. (1996) *Jobs and the Environment*. London: Socialist Environment and Resources Association.

Turnock, D. (1993) Romania, in F. W. Carter and D. Turnock (eds) *Environmental Problems in Eastern Europe*. London: Routledge.

United Nations (1993) *Earth Summit Agenda 21: the United Nations Programme of Action from Rio*. New York: United Nations Department of Public Information.

United Nations Development Programme (1993) *Human Development Report 1993*. New York: Oxford University Press.

United Nations Development Programme (1995) *Human Development Report 1995*. New York: Oxford University Press.

United Nations Development Programme (1996) *Human Development Report 1996*. New York: Oxford University Press.

Urry, J. (1990) *The Tourist Gaze: Leisure and Travel in Contemporary Societies*. London: Sage.

Walker, R. and Parker, G. (1988) *Money Matters: Income, Wealth and Financial Welfare*. London: Sage.

Water Services Association (1991) *Water Facts*. London: Water Services Association.

Weale, A. (1992) *The New Politics of Pollution*. Manchester: Manchester University Press.

Wells, M. (1992) Biodiversity conservation, affluence and poverty: mis-matched costs and benefits and efforts to remedy them, *Ambio*, 21, 237–43.

Wetherly, P. (1996) Basic needs and social policies, *Critical Social Policy*, 16, 45–65.

Whyte, I. D. (1995) *Climatic Change and Human Society*. London: Arnold.

Wilcox, S. (1996) *Housing Review 1996/97*. York: Joseph Rowntree Foundation.

Williams, F. (1989) *Social Policy: a Critical Introduction*. Cambridge: Polity Press.

Witherspoon, S. (1994) The greening of Britain: romance and rationality, in R. Jowell, J. Curtice, L. Brook and D. Ahrendt (eds) *British Social Attitudes: the 11th Report*. Aldershot: Dartmouth.

Wood, K. and House, S. (1991) *The Good Tourist*. London: Mandarin.

World Health Organization (1992) *Our Planet, Our Health*. Report of the WHO Commission on Health and Environment. London: HMSO.

Yearley, S. (1991) *The Green Case: a Sociology of Environmental Issues, Arguments and Politics*. London: Routledge.
Yearley, S. (1996) *Sociology, Environmentalism, Globalization*. London: Sage.
Young, K. (1991) Shades of green, in R. Jowell, L. Brook, and B. Taylor (eds) *British Social Attitudes: the 8th Report*. Aldershot: Dartmouth.

INDEX